Arms and Judgment

Arms and Judgment

Law, Morality, and the Conduct of War in the Twentieth Century

Sheldon M. Cohen
University of Tennessee

Westview Press
Boulder, San Francisco, & London

Published in 1989 in the United States of America by Westview Press, Inc., 5500 Central Avenue, Boulder, Colorado 80301, and in the United Kingdom by Westview Press, Inc., 13 Brunswick Centre, London WC1N 1AF, England

Library of Congress Cataloging-in-Publication Data
Cohen, Sheldon M.
Arms and judgment: law, morality, and the conduct of war in the 20th century / by Sheldon M. Cohen.
p. cm.
Bibliography: p.
Includes index.
ISBN 0-8133-0702-3. ISBN 0-8133-0703-1 (pbk.)
1. War (International law). 2. War—Moral and ethical aspects.
I. Title.
JX4511.C64 1989
341.6—dc19

88-20670
CIP

Printed and bound in the United States of America

The paper used in this publication meets the requirements of the American National Standard for Permanence of Paper for Printed Library Materials Z39.48-1984.

10 9 8 7 6 5 4 3 2 1

To

Lillian Klein

and

Nettie Ziskind

Contents

Preface

In April 1986 the Cable News Network was getting the reactions of passersby to the U.S. air strike against Libya. A young California woman expressed her concern: "I feel that negative acts only lead to more negative acts."

It sounded like such a wholesome thought. But would she have thought it on the beach at Normandy on D day? Looking down at the great armada of ships disgorging tens of thousands of British, Canadian, and American troops for the final assault on Hitler's bastion—for most, their first time under fire, for many their last—watching as the big naval guns thundered at the coastal bunkers, would she have disapproved? As hundreds of planes roared overhead and the earth shook beneath her feet, as sleek destroyers darted in to silence the artillery firing at the landing craft, would she feel that these negative acts would only lead to more negative acts? Or was all this horror and sacrifice somehow for the good?

On the one hand we have the undeniable horrors of war and the repugnance they rightly evoke in decent people. War is not a good. It is a great, vivid evil.

But we also live in a world in which the weak are accustomed to being at the mercy of the strong and in which nations go unarmed only if they have powerful protectors. So it is important to inquire calmly into how the use of force can be morally justified, the circumstances in which it is warranted, and the degree of force they warrant. This book is an examination of those justifications and their limits. It is, then, a moral inquiry. But it adopts an interdisciplinary approach.

My first attempt to teach a course on war and morality proved to be nothing more than a review of basic themes in moral philosophy. War provided at most a context, at worst a pretext, for discussing points I would have covered in any introductory ethics course—an excuse for selling those goods under another label. That was unfair to the topic.

Modern warfare raises many complex issues that the ready-made, all-purpose distinctions with which philosophers instinctively approach moral questions cannot gain a purchase on. I decided to treat those issues anyway. I would cover the moral issues that really arise in the practice of war. If they reflected normal topics in ethical theory, fine; if not, they would have to be addressed on their own terms. The course would be a moral inquiry into twentieth-century military practice, not a general ethics course illustrated with examples from military history.

This pedagogical decision was, on another level, theoretical as well. Instead of coming to the discussion with my distinctions neatly lined up in the box, I wanted them to percolate out of the subject matter. I wanted the subject matter to generate them. An examination of the laws and customs of war provided the means for doing this. They are a product of attention to detail by soldiers and statesmen. Their nuances grew out of the details; their haggling is informed.

The laws and customs of war reflect the imperfect but subtle mesh between ideals and reality in the harsh terrain where nations clash. The principles that grow there are not principles a utopian world would accept. But then utopian principles count only as Mark Twain counted the coal dealer's prayer for warm weather: as so much wind, useful to the angels only to drive the ships of the faithful.

The law of war provided the road map for the discussion, so this book examines that law. But legality and morality are different, and though the law may serve as a useful guide to morality, their two paths frequently diverge. Sometimes that divergence is academic; sometimes it is a question of life and death. This divergence, and its significance, is one of the underlying themes of this book. If a corporate officer engages in an immoral yet legal practice to boost his company's profits, we are inclined to grumble and shrug our shoulders. What should our response be when a legal but immoral military practice destroys a city? Do we want military commanders to do what is most effective so long as it is perfectly legal? Or do we want them to do what is morally right no matter what the cost?

This book is also laced with historical accounts. We cannot judge the morality of policies or practices without a reasonable acquaintance with the circumstances in which they arose. We cannot even understand what these policies and practices *are* without understanding some of the details. The real questions—the ones that do not begin with "all other things being equal"—cannot be answered with patent assertions about casualties or rights, civilian or military. They begin with an understanding of what the campaigns that raised these questions were like. Does "military necessity" justify the bombardment of inhabited towns? Did it justify the bombardment of St. Lô? The Allied breakout from Normandy, the bomber campaign against Germany, the ground war in Vietnam—we have to understand these things before we can address the moral questions they raised. These historical accounts are the basis for everything in this book, but each historical account introduces a wider theme. For example, the historical account in Chapter 3 covers the efforts to restrict war in the 1920s and 1930s; its thematic concern is the justification of war. The historical content of Chapter 4 is the strategic air war in World War II, which leads us to another thematic concern: civilian immunity. The chapters are arranged historically according to the issues that became paramount in different decades. As a result, some of the questions philosophers typically ask are missing. Would it be morally justifiable to torture an innocent child to prevent a world war? That is an interesting question, but not the sort of question I address. My excuse is that no one is likely ever to be in that position. The questions I am interested in have confronted hundreds of thousands of people in the twentieth century. Some of these questions have not until now had much of a literature: Why is it permissible to camouflage a tank to look like a hot dog stand, but not to disguise its crew to look like hot dog vendors? Why is it permissible to destroy a city's center with aerial bombs, but not with car bombs? Why do the legal restraints on naval and ground forces differ? All of these questions should be of interest to anyone who wants to review our century from a moral point of view.

Sheldon M. Cohen

Acknowledgments

I thank two people at Westview Press: Spencer Carr, for his support and encouragement, and Marian Safran, for her keen eye, good ear, and gentle humor.

S.M.C.

1

Morality and International Law

> *The existing body of moral convictions of the best people is the cumulative product of the moral reflection of many generations, which has developed an extremely delicate power of appreciation of moral distinctions; and this the theorist cannot afford to treat with anything other than the greatest respect.*[1]

Origins of the Modern Law of War

In 1859 the Austro-Hungarian Emperor Franz Josef led his army to battle at Solferino, where he fought the Piedmontese and Napoleon III's French army. The Austrian center collapsed after a grueling daylong struggle; only the enemy's own exhaustion and a gallant delaying action of the Austrian cavalry saved the bulk of Franz Josef's forces from annihilation. As a consequence of this defeat, the nation of Italy would be founded two years later.

When Franz Josef was born, Goethe was still alive; and on the U.S. frontier in Illinois, settlers armed with muzzle loaders were fighting Indians. When Franz Josef died, fighter planes, coughing oily smoke, were dogfighting in the skies over France, and in England the 56,000-pound Mark I tank was in mass production. In the emperor's lifetime, the ancient art of war developed into something new and different. And because a Swiss businessman, Henri Dunant, was waiting in Solferino to meet with Napoleon III on the day of the devastating battle, something else new and different developed as well. But I must begin three hundred years earlier.

In 1559 the Duke of Savoy, with holdings in what would become the modern states of France, Switzerland, and Italy, had lost Geneva and the surrounding lands to the new and militant Swiss Confederation, whose pikemen, ignoring medieval rules of chivalry, fought with uncommon ferocity and barbarity: "The *Kriegsordnung* [War Instructions] of Lucerne in 1499 stipulated that no prisoners were to be taken; all the enemy should be put to death. That of Zurich in 1444 thought it necessary to prohibit combatants from tearing out the hearts of their dead enemies and cutting up their bodies."[2] With the loss of Geneva, the center of the duchy shifted southeast to Turin in the Piedmont highlands; the duke held Turin as a legacy of the eleventh-century marriage of Humbert the Whitehanded, the first recorded head of the House of Savoy. Italian, not French, was the language of Turin, but like all Italian cities, it had its attractions. The duke decided to move his capital there.

By 1859 the House of Savoy spoke Italian as its native tongue and had added Sardinia, Genoa, and Liguria to Savoy and Piedmont. The house had also acquired a reputation as a troublemaker. "Keep an eye on the Piedmont—it is a hotbed of unwholesome tendencies," wrote Franz Josef to his viceroy in Lombardy. In Turin, Victor Emmanuel II and his prime minister, Count Camillo Cavour, were encouraging, even leading, the risorgimento, the Italian movement for unification and independence. Austria, which ruled Lombardy and Venetia, had the most to lose in the rising tide of Italian nationalism.

Franz Josef decided to solve the problem. He issued an ultimatum to the Piedmontese: Disband your army. But Cavour had bought insurance by having made a secret alliance against Austria with Napoleon III. The French would help the Piedmontese take Lombardy from the Austrians, and the Piedmontese in return would cede Savoy to France. The ancestral French province from which the House of Savoy derived its name was now negotiable: The house's future was tied to Italy. Cavour rejected the Austrian ultimatum.

The Franco-Piedmontese and Austrian armies clashed at Magenta, where the Austrians were defeated. Franz Josef relieved his commander, took personal charge of the army, and led it to battle at Solferino, with the result we have seen. The Piedmontese gained Lombardy and, in 1866, Venetia. Franz Josef's elderly, ailing uncle and imperial predecessor, Ferdinand, hearing of the loss of Venetia, protested: "Is this what they made me abdicate for? I could have lost those provinces myself." Two months before Cavour's death in 1861 the nation of Italy was founded under the House of Savoy.

But the losses had been appalling. At Solferino the two armies, numbering about 120,000 each, had suffered 30,000 dead and wounded. At Solferino and Magenta the Piedmontese lost a fourth of their army. French losses disheartened Napoleon so much that, abandoning his ally, he hastened to Villafranca to sign a truce with Franz Josef.

Dunant, a citizen of Savoy's former prize, Geneva, was disheartened too, but by the misery of the wounded left unattended in the field after the battle. He organized aid for them and did what he could. Later he could not drive the scene from his mind. In 1862 he published a book about that day, *Le Souvenir de Solferino* (The memory of Solferino), which became a best-seller.

Across the Atlantic the U.S. Civil War raged, with even heavier casualties: The losses at Solferino were approximated or exceeded at Seven Days, Second Bull Run, Antietam, Gettysburg, Chancellorsville, and Chickamauga. Between 1861 and 1865 the United States suffered as many casualties as it would in World Wars I and II, Korea, and Vietnam, together.

Meanwhile a German immigrant to the United States, Francis Lieber, worked on a military law code. Lieber, who had arrived in his new country at the age of twenty-seven, in his sixties was a distinguished law professor at Columbia. His code, at President Abraham Lincoln's request, was revised by a panel of military officers and issued, in 1863, as General Order No. 100 (*Instructions for the Government of Armies of the United States in the Field*), the first modern code of law for military operations published by any nation. That same year, back in Geneva, Dunant founded the International Red Cross.

The next year, under the sponsorship of the Red Cross, the first Geneva convention was signed, "for the Amelioration of the Condition of the Sick and Wounded of Armies in the Field." The convention was opposed by the military, who feared it would clutter camps and battlefields with noncombatants, but it was supported, according to the March 1875 issue of *Macmillan's Magazine,* by "all the crowned heads of the Continent, whatever might be the attitude of ministers and generals." Many of those crowned heads had read *Le Souvenir.* Dunant, who was not a crowned head, had devoted all his energies since Solferino to improving the care of the wounded. His neglected business floundered, and soon he was bankrupt. In 1867, at the age of thirty-nine, he left Geneva and disappeared. Twenty-eight years later a journalist discovered the old man living in poverty in the tiny village of Heiden, and Dunant became an overnight celebrity. He was awarded the Nobel Peace Prize in 1901.

A historian has said that the Victorians thought they knew the answer to most questions, and the answer was usually no.[3] In the 1860s and 1870s the Victorians said no to some of the excesses of war. They did not think that war could be made proper—it would never belong in the parlor—but they did think that, like other activities that might arouse passion, it could and should be restrained. The article in *Macmillan's* said: "War can no more be made agreeable than can the small-pox. It may, like the small-pox, be deprived of some of the virulence formerly attendant upon it, but not to such an extent as to render it agreeable."[4] General Order No. 100 and the Geneva convention had started a movement. Before the 1860s ended, Alexander II, czar of all the Russias, convened an international conference in St. Petersburg. The 1868 Declaration of St. Petersburg, signed by most of the European powers, outlawed the newly invented exploding bullet; it was the first treaty in modern times restricting weapons and hence the ancestor of today's Strategic Arms Limitation Talks (SALT) and antiballistic missile (ABM) treaties.[5] The broad humanitarian grounds the declaration invoked in banning the exploding bullet could be applied to wider areas:

- the only legitimate object which states should endeavor to accomplish during war is to weaken the military force of the enemy;
- for this purpose it is sufficient to disable the greatest possible number of men;
- this object would be exceeded by the employment of arms which uselessly aggravate the sufferings of men, or render their death inevitable;
- the employment of such arms would, therefore, be contrary to the laws of humanity.

Six years later, in 1874, Alexander II proposed another international conference to formulate a whole body of rules of war. Brussels played host, and delegates came from all over Europe to a meeting that was the culmination of a twelve-year effort dating from the publication of Dunant's book. They found themselves at an awkward gathering. Almost every nation represented there had within recent memory fought one of the others present. England had attacked Denmark and fought the battle of Copenhagen. Denmark and Prussia had gone to war with each other twice in fourteen years. Sweden had fought Napoleon Bonaparte and had turned around and fought Russia. In the Crimea, where the rifle's accuracy led to the first trench warfare, Russia, Britain, and France had fought, and France alone had counted 90,000 dead. Turkey had fought Greece; the French had occupied Rome. And they never knew who their allies would be in the future. England and Russia had joined in fighting France in 1812; in 1855 the tables had been turned and England and France had joined in fighting Russia. In 1914 all three would be allies, fighting the Germans and Austrians, who in 1866 had fought each other.

The delegates listened to one another and to petitions presented by worried citizens' groups—the Belgian Society of Succur and the inhabitants of Antwerp. The delegates argued and negotiated with their former and future enemies and allies. They formed sides based on military power and form of government: democracies versus despotic powers, the large versus the small. An article in *Frazer's Magazine* charged that the great military powers were out to assert "the military right of a strong State to act against non-belligerent weak States according to its own discretion."[6] *Macmillan's* took a more sanguine view: "What Russia, Prussia, and Austria approve cannot be right; and thereupon it is assumed that the code put forward by Russia must be a code favourable to the interests of the despotic and military powers, and hostile to the interests of small states, who cultivate liberty and neglect their national defences."[7] Lieber's code, which had by then been adopted by Prussia, gave the delegates the grounds on which they could agree. His *Instructions,* carried to Brussels by the czar's representatives, formed the basis for the final declaration of the conference.[8] That declaration was never ratified. Perhaps the delegates had met too soon after the Franco-Prussian War, a war that attracts little attention today, but that at the time, according to Sir Henry (James Sumner) Maine, "probably never had a rival in the violence of the passions which it excited." The delegates went home and their governments rejected their declaration. History, though, has its tricks. A quarter of a century later, in 1899, the rejected declaration of the Brussels conference, almost word for word, became the Hague conference's Rules of Land Warfare. In 1907, with a few more modifications, the rules were signed and became treaty law.

Winston Churchill recalled the days before World War I as a time when "Nations and Empires, crowned with princes and potentates, rose majestically on every side."[9] The signatories include Edward, king of Great Britain and Ireland and of "the British Dominions beyond the Seas," emperor of India. Representatives signed for their majesties the kings of Serbia and Siam, the grand duke of Luxembourg, the emperor of China, the princes of Montenegro and Bulgaria. Franz Josef, besides being an emperor and the apostolic king of Hungary was "King of Bohemia, etc."[10]

The wording of the text has a strange quality, solemn and measured, yet dreamy and self-congratulatory, as though a pompous jurist dictated while dozing off. The signatories,

> Considering that, while seeking means to preserve peace and prevent armed conflicts between nations, it is likewise necessary to have regard to cases where an appeal to arms may be caused by events which their solicitude could not avert;

> Animated also by the desire to serve, even in this extreme case, the interests of humanity and the ever-progressive needs of civilization; and
> Thinking it important, with this object, to revise the laws and general customs of war . . . ;
> Have deemed it necessary to complete and render more precise in certain particulars the work of the First Peace Conference, which, following on the Brussels Conference of 1874, and inspired by the ideas dictated by a wise and generous forethought, adopted provisions . . . inspired by the desire to diminish the evils of war, so far as military necessities permit.

Inspired as these signatories were, seven years later World War I broke out and the final clause—"so far as military necessities permit"—showed its fierce teeth. Rather than diminishing after the Hague conventions, the evils of war increased. (In World War II they would enter the parlor.) The twentieth century learned to multiply death, piling bodies on bodies. Battles were fought in which the dead numbered more than the armies had in the Franco-Prussian War. At Gettysburg the Union Army had suffered 23,000 casualties; at the battle of Passchendaele in World War I, the British suffered 245,000 casualties—comparable to U.S. casualties in ten years in Vietnam. The great shock of World War I crumbled the edifice of the old regime. The czars and kaisers disappeared—more casualties—forced into retirement, exiled, or killed. "They are shooting us like sparrows off the roofs," moaned Archduke Francis Ferdinand. Communists would replace czars, Austria-Hungary would disappear. Because decades of conferences had not diminished the evils of war, a world order would dissolve. The world would be split on new lines. The twentieth century had begun in earnest.

These events might make the Hague conventions seem misguided, almost quaint. They are neither. When nations go to war some things change, but others remain the same. People still set their alarm clocks and get up to go to work. They shop for food and note that latest styles in clothes. They go to the movies, quarrel, study for exams, visit relatives, mow the lawn, and are convicted of felonies. The state of war modifies the life of the nation, but it does not create it anew. This normalcy applies in moral and legal matters as much as it does in others. As Lieber put it: "Men who take up arms against one another in public war do not cease on this account to be moral beings, responsible to one another and to God."[11]

War makes some acts permissible that in peacetime are impermissible, but it does not make everything permissible. The chief U.S. prosecutor at Nuremberg, Telford Taylor, emphasized this by saying that in most cases the term *war crime* is a misnomer. They are simply crimes: criminal in peace and criminal in war. Theft is theft, rape is rape, and murder is murder, regardless of the relations existing between nations. These are acts that "lie outside the area of immunity prescribed by the laws of war."[12] If this were not so, if in war everything were permissible, war could never be morally justified.

But where do we draw the line? Which uses of force are permissible? When is killing sanctioned? The Hague conventions offer partial answers to these questions. But should we credit these answers? Why take a legal document to be our moral guide?

Legality and Morality

It is a philosophical commonplace that legality and morality are not the same. What is legal may be immoral, and what is moral may be illegal. The law may allow a landlord to evict a tenant who is several months behind in her rent, even if it is winter and the woman has no place to go, even if she is the landlord's mother, and her son owns the building only because she gave it to him, even if she cannot pay the rent because she has lent the rent money to her son. Gratitude should preclude her son's evicting her, but the law might not notice this. It might treat the case as just another tenant's failure to pay the rent. The law does not try to be a perfect reflection of the moral universe or to make us perfectly moral. It governs certain aspects of our relations with one another and ignores others. Sometimes the ignored areas are crucial from a moral point of view: Ingratitude and selfishness are not criminal.

What is legal may be immoral. And what is illegal may not be inherently immoral. It may be illegal to walk on the grass in the park, but it is not immoral. In some parks it is encouraged. This divergence of law and morality is not a catastrophe. The British legal thinker, H.L.A. Hart, once asked, "Is the fact that certain conduct is by common standards immoral sufficient to justify making that conduct punishable by law? . . . Ought immorality as such to be a crime?"[13] His answer was that law and morality cannot coincide. Each has its own agenda. Law provides formalized machinery for settling certain sorts of disputes. Morality has other aims.

Because in principle law and morals are not the same, it might seem that the best course to take is to ignore legality and address only moral questions. If sometimes the two coincide, fine. Where they diverge, so much the worse for the law. Once we realize that the two are different, why should we allow questions of legality to distract us? Why not stick exclusively to moral questions?

This is what philosophers (and theologians) have done. The philosophical literature on war has generally ignored legal questions. When philosophers have mentioned the law of war, their comments have been disparaging. One has pointed out that the law of war forbids barbed lances, but not hydrogen bombs. So much for the law of war. Richard Wasserstrom, for example, wrote:

> The fact that countries have been able to agree upon certain conventions does not seem to me to be a matter of particular significance. At the very least, it is certainly a mistake to infer from this . . . that we have somehow succeeded in identifying those types of behavior that really matter the most. Indeed, it is at least as likely . . . that agreement was forthcoming just because the issues thereby regulated were not of great moment. And it is surely far more likely than not that agreement was forthcoming just because it was perceived that adherence to these laws would not affect very much the way wars got fought.[14]

This tendency of philosophers has been reinforced by the many law professors and political scientists who no longer see law as an embodiment of justice and equity.[15] They see law as designed to serve the interests of the class that frames and interprets it. "The law of armed conflicts," wrote Keith Suter, "has been devised over the past century in the sophisticated and elegant conference centres of Europe."[16] We picture cigar-smoking, mustachioed Edwardian generals and diplomats sipping cognac in splendorous pre–World War I paneled halls. They are on a mission from the crowned heads of Europe: Formulate the rules of war for the better class of people—people who go to war in formal dress and with the latest fashions in modern arms—and outlaw the sport for those who cannot afford the proper attire. Define the law of nations as it is derived, in the words of the Fourth Hague Convention, "from the usages established among civilized peoples."[17]

In this book, I intend to swim against this current and approach the moral questions that surround war through its law. If this sounds more typical of a late nineteenth century study than a late twentieth century one, so be it. The past is not merely something to be surmounted. There are old skills that are wisely preserved: the ability to start fires with sticks, for example, or to read a text closely. At any rate, the difference between legality and morality can be overemphasized. Law contains much that from a moral point of view is arbitrary, but law retains its roots in moral notions. Laws that seem no longer tied to morality lose their grip on our conscience; laws that seem to flout morality inspire rebellion.

The law of war is of some moment and significance. The Russians captured 130,000 German soldiers at Stalingrad, but because the law was ignored on the eastern front in World War II, only 5,000 of them returned to Germany after the war. Russian prisoners of war in Germany suffered at least as bad a fate. Millions of people are alive today because of the law, but where it has been ignored, hundreds of thousands have been needlessly lost.

Whatever its deficiencies and distortions, the law of war was not framed in a moral vacuum. It was framed in consideration of moral questions, even if other questions were at least equally important. This has nothing to do with the conscious or subconscious motives of the framers of the law: Even when their motives were self-serving (which was often) or cynical (less common), they instinctively grasped for moral justifications, and unlike many modern statesmen, they did this with a cultivated subtlety. Some vices involve corresponding virtues. Those who went to war wrapped in the cloak of honor and justice had a keen eye for moral proprieties. The old prohibition in the law of war against barbed lances, foolish as it might seem, is not a comic-opera joke. A nonbarbed lance will incapacitate an enemy soldier—all that needs to be done from a military point of view. To aggravate his wound by barbing the lance is to inflict unnecessary harm and so is forbidden. What seems at first glance an outdated eccentricity turns out to make sense and points to an important moral principle.

Moreover, the Hague conventions were formulated and signed by a wide variety of nations: small nations and large nations, Western nations and Eastern nations, rich nations and poor nations. Little Belgium, placed between two world powers, championed the rights of the neutral and the weak. Powerful Germany argued for "military necessity." The resulting compromises may not have been ideal for any particular country, but they were equitable enough to be accepted by most of the world's nations. This gives them a strong claim to our consideration.

It is true that the laws and customs of war are of European origin. Had they been based on the Japanese code of Bushido, they would have been quite different. But international law itself has a European origin:

> In the Middle Ages there had been a number of national or municipal courts which dealt with questions of what we should call international law, and a number of codes or collections of rules, especially for maritime questions, which were accepted as authoritative by these courts. . . . [But] their authority had narrow and almost fortuitous geographical limits, and for the most part each nation judged

> such matters according to rules of its own. There was little in the way of rules received by all nations.[18]

The intellectual foundations for an international code of law were laid in the sixteenth century and the early years of the seventeenth by Alberico Gentili and Hugo Grotius. The actual construction of the code began with the peace settlements at the end of the Thirty Years War (1684). From then on, one could talk about the *droits des gens de l'Europe*—the laws of the peoples of Europe.[19] A legal entity, the community of nations, had been born. In 1865 the Treaty of Paris admitted the Ottoman Empire to this community, and it ceased being exclusively Christian. By 1899, when the first Hague conventions were drawn up, Japan, China, Siam, and Persia had joined, taking up their responsibilities under the law of nations in exchange for the benefits they acquired. European law had become international. The process continued in the twentieth century as new nations subscribed to the UN Charter. International law, like the scientific revolution, was a European invention. But rather than being a Western imposition on less-developed countries, international law, also like the scientific revolution, has been voluntarily adopted by non-European people.

Finally, the laws of war were developed by soldiers, jurists, and diplomats, not by professors of moral philosophy. The laws of war are more a product of practice than of theory; they arose out of a consideration of details, not abstract principles. This can be an advantage. Examining them, we may discover moral principles that would not occur to us if we had approached the subject with our ethics textbooks in hand. Habits and customs may have a share of intelligence, and the moral discriminations implicit in the laws of war are sometimes more precise and perceptive than their bludgeoning civilian cousins. And we need to draw them out if we are to understand why wars are fought the way they are, for it is these principles military traditions instill. There is no one-to-one correspondence between morality and legality, but the law of war may still be a good guide to the moral issues raised by war. We cannot follow that guide, however, without becoming acquainted with a few preliminary points.

Sources of International Law

Laws, Treaties, and Customs

The Fourth Hague Convention contains a General Participation Clause, which says that the convention's provisions are "binding between Contracting Powers . . . only if all the belligerents are parties to the

Convention." These clauses are common in the law of war. The St. Petersburg declaration is binding only in wars between those who accept it. Nations are not bound to obey it unilaterally—they assume reciprocity.

In August 1917 Liberia, which had not signed the Hague conventions, announced that it had entered World War I—though it had no military forces to contribute immediately. Did this mean, in view of the General Participation Clause, that the Hague conventions no longer applied to the war? Even if Liberia did not engage in any hostile acts? It would seem so: "The effect of the clause was, in strict law, to deprive some of the Conventions of their binding force . . . as a non-signatory State, however insignificant, joined the ranks of the belligerents."

But though "in strict law" some conventions lost their binding force, in reality most did not. British courts ruled that "most of the substantive provisions of the conventions were [still] operative inasmuch as they embody rules of customary International Law."

In a footnote to this discussion, Lauterpacht,[20] the classic text on international law, approvingly quoted a British judge's characterization of the claim that the Hague convention no longer applied as "a quibbling interpretation of the Convention." The judge's point was that many of the provisions of the Hague conventions had the status of law quite apart from the Hague treaties. This made the General Participation Clause less important than it might seem: "Much ink has been spilled in discussing [General Participation Clauses]. . . . But the argument was essentially academic in nature, because the . . . instruments were declaratory, for the most part, of customary rules of law which would have applied to all parties to a conflict irrespective of the applicability of a Hague Convention."[21] The same view was taken by the tribunal at the Nuremberg War Crimes trials:

> It said: "The rules of land warfare expressed in the Convention undoubtedly represented an advance over existing International Law at the time of their adoption. But the Convention expressly stated that it was an attempt 'to revise the general laws and customs of war,' which it thus recognized to be then existing. . . . By 1939 these rules laid down in the Convention were recognized by all civilized nations and were regarded as declaratory of the laws and customs of war. . . . " For that reason the Tribunal found that although Czechoslovakia was not a party to the Hague Convention of 1907, the rules of land warfare expressed in that Convention were declaratory of existing International law and therefore fully applicable.[22]

International law comes in two types: treaty law and customary law. The distinction is vaguely similar to the distinction between statute law and common law. Treaty law is clear: Nations enter into formal agreements with one another, and they are legally bound to obey the terms of those agreements. We understand this because we understand promises as obligating us. Customary law is different. A custom can become so widespread that eventually everyone assumes it will be followed. This expectation shapes their actions. They do things they would not do if it were not for the custom, and they expect others to follow it as well. At that point, the custom can acquire the force of law, even though it is not mentioned in written law. It can be a crime to leave a restaurant without paying for one's meal, even if neither the law books nor the menu explains the relation between the name of the dish and the numbers to the right of the name. Even without a written law, one may be legally obligated to pay for one's meal. Similarly, customary maritime law binds all nations, regardless of whether they have signed maritime treaties, just as customary domestic law binds individuals apart from written law.

The line between mere custom and customary law is blurred; therefore, authors and documents may talk about "the laws and customs of war" or "the laws and customs of the sea." The distinction between treaty law and customary law can also be blurred. Customary maritime law may over time be incorporated into treaty law. And if enough countries become party to a treaty and abide by its terms, its provisions can in time become customary law.

The Hague conventions are treaty law and as such bind only the signatory nations. But the preamble to the Hague Convention on Land Warfare, by acknowledging a customary law of war as the basis for that convention, acknowledged that there are laws and customs of war apart from the Hague treaty. And the preamble specified that cases not covered by the convention are still covered by "the rule of the principles of the law of nations, as they result from the usages established among civilized peoples, from the laws of humanity, and from the dictates of public conscience." So "the Hague Conventions are binding on all belligerents to the extent that they represent customary law and are binding wholly in the event that all belligerents in a given war are signatories of the Convention in question."[23] A nation cannot legally excuse itself from obeying the laws of war simply because it has not signed the Hague conventions.

Counsels of Reason

There are laws that can be defended apart from the law, and laws that cannot. Under the Hague conventions, a belligerent who advances under a white flag has rights he would lack if his flag were red. The *white* flag signifies a desire to talk. But the color is not essential to the practice: If we decided that the flag should be red, nothing fundamental would change. Or we might put the green "Go" at the top of our traffic lights, and the red "Stop" at the bottom. As long as we are consistent (for the sake of those who are color-blind), we can do it either way. Some points of both customary and treaty law are conventions that serve a purpose. As long as that purpose is served, other conventions might do equally well—a yellow flag instead of a white one.

Others have a less arbitrary basis—a basis, sometimes, in "the dictates of public conscience." If we decide that the right of a soldier to harm the enemy is unlimited—that anything goes—something fundamental will change. It is because arbitrary conventions play a central role in law, but not in morality, that H.L.A. Hart thought that law and morality have different agendas:

> The rules of international law, like those of municipal law, are often morally quite indifferent. A rule may exist because it is convenient or necessary to have some clear fixed rule about the subjects with which it is concerned, but not because any moral importance is attached to the particular rule. It may well be but one of a large number of possible rules, any one of which would have done equally well. Hence legal rules, municipal and international, commonly contain much specific detail, and draw arbitrary distinctions, which would be unintelligible as elements in moral rules or principles. . . . It is possible, though difficult, to imagine that men with general beliefs very different from ours, might come to attach *moral* importance to driving on the left instead of on the right of the road or could come to feel moral guilt if they broke a promise witnessed by two witnesses, but no such guilt if it was witnessed by one. Though such strange moralities are possible, it yet remains true that a morality cannot (logically) contain rules which are generally held by those who subscribe to them to be in no way preferable to alternatives and of no intrinsic importance. Law, however, though it also contains much that is of moral importance, can and does contain just such rules, and the arbitrary distinctions, formalities, and highly specific detail which would be most difficult to understand as part of morality, are consequently natural and easily comprehensible features of law. For one of the typical features of law, unlike morality, is to introduce just these elements in order to maximize certainty and predictability and to facilitate the proof or assessments of claims. . . .
>
> It is for this reason that just as we expect a municipal legal system, but not morality, to tell us how many witnesses a validly executed will must have, so we expect international law, but not morality, to tell us such things as the number of days a belligerent vessel may stay for refuelling or repairs in a neutral port; the width of territorial waters; the methods to be used in their measurement. . . . Of course not all the

> rules of international law are of this formal, or arbitrary, or morally neutral kind. The point is only that legal rules *can* and moral rules *cannot* be of this kind.[24]

Even with purely conventional rules there may be a valid reason for preferring one convention over another. Most people are right-handed, and the gearshift knob is located on the transmission tunnel in the middle of the car. So driving on the right side of the road has an advantage. White flags are easier to spot than red ones, and white cloth easier to come by. But my focus will be on rules that have a more compelling claim on us and that express principles that can be defended on their own: Regardless of what the law of war says, it is immoral to inflict harm needlessly. We are looking for the moral dimension to the law; therefore, we must look for principles that make sense apart from the law.

A large and interesting group of laws do not fall neatly into either of these two groups. They are not arbitrary stipulations, but they involve considerations of prudence or humanity. Medical personnel are allowed to carry arms and to defend themselves and their patients. They cannot participate in an attack, though, or in a general defense. They can defend *only* themselves and their patients; in return, it is forbidden to attack them and their patients. These rules are humanitarian. A world under these rules is preferable to a world in which medical personnel are fair game. But if both sides agreed to waive these rules and treat medical personnel (or clergy) like other members of the armed forces, no fundamental breach of the moral order would occur, for it is not fundamentally immoral to shoot at military medical personnel. They do not have an inherent right not to be shot at, though the world may be better off if they are not.

The Domain of the Law of War

Statehood and Recognition

The international law of war does not apply to every armed conflict. It is *inter*national and has generally applied only to armed conflicts in which both parties are states.[25] It does not necessarily apply to every insurrection, revolutionary struggle, or secessionist rebellion. These may all, depending on the circumstances, be treated as the internal affairs of states. The law of war may apply to them, and it may not. It will if both parties to the conflict count as states.

There is disagreement over what this means. According to J. L. Brierly's *Law of Nations,* Lauterpacht thought that the criterion for statehood was recognition by other states. This seems to confuse recognizing a state with creating one. What states must be recognizing when they recognize something as a state is that it already is a state: "The better view is that the granting of recognition to a new state is not a 'constitutive' but a 'declarative' act; it does not bring into legal existence a state which did not exist before. A state may exist without being recognized, and if it does exist in fact, then whether or not it has been formally recognized by other states, it has a right to be treated by them *as* a state."[26]

Whether something is a state must be a question that can be addressed independently of whether acknowledged states recognize it as such. But Lauterpacht's view was not exactly that recognition creates states. In the 1920 edition of *International Law,* at any rate, he granted that unrecognized states can exist. His claim was that for a state to be acknowledged in international law, it must be recognized. Until it is recognized, the law takes no notice of it. Although it is a de facto state, it has no legal status.[27]

To Brierly, in contrast, international law applies to all states, not just recognized ones. William Edward Hall, the author of another famous text on international law, held the same view: "The marks of an independent state are, that the community constituting it is permanently established for a political end, that it possesses a defined territory, and that it is independent of external control. . . . So soon, therefore, as a society can point to the necessary marks, it enters of right into the family of states, and must be treated in conformity with law."[28] Lauterpacht claimed that states have no legal rights unless they are recognized; Hall and Brierly claimed that these rights belong to any state. In theory there is a great and deep-rooted difference between these views. In practice there is none, for a state that is completely unrecognized will, even if it has these legal rights, be unable to exercise them.

Criteria for Statehood

There is wide agreement on the criteria for statehood. As Brierly wrote: "A new state comes into existence when a community acquires, with a reasonable probability of permanence, the essential characteristics of a state, namely an organized government, a defined territory, and such a degree of independence of control by any other state as to be capable of conducting its own international relations."[29] The Confederacy during the U.S. Civil War provides a good example of all these requirements except permanence. The Union did not recognize it. Nonetheless, in the Confederacy, governmental functions continued to be served after secession, just as they had been before. Law suits were settled, criminals were prosecuted, land was bought and sold with titles duly transferred, taxes were collected, children went to school, and so on. There was what Lauterpacht called "orderly administration," regardless of whether the United States, or any other state, recognized the Confederacy. The Union, in its way, acknowledged this, treating captured Confederate soldiers as prisoners of war, not criminals.

Governments may, for their own reasons, grant recognition of statehood to groups that are not states, or withhold recognition from states. Libya might have recognized the Simbionese Liberation Army (SLA), but the SLA was never a state. The United States in 1955 did not recognize Communist China, which clearly was a state. Most Arab states do not recognize Israel, though it clearly is a state. The law of war, if we take the Hall-Brierly line, applies when the contending parties are states, regardless of whether they recognize one another.

This allows borderline cases. Is there a Lebanese Druze state? There is no clear answer to this question, though there are clear criteria: To the extent that the Druze handle their own affairs, live by their own laws, and represent themselves in the international arena, they could claim to constitute a state. The Palestine Liberation Organization (PLO) in Tunisia, however, is not a state. It is a guest of the Tunisians, subject to Tunisian law, in fact, not just in theory. Thus the notions of statehood and the administration of territory are inextricably linked. States have places where they exercise certain functions. Urban guerrillas do not constitute a state; guerrillas secure in their mountain bastions might.

States need time as well as space. A band of guerrillas that bursts into a town and reads the riot act to the inhabitants will not have constituted a state, not even a transitory one, even if the townspeople are willing. Orderly administration takes time. One can announce a legal code in the time it takes to read one's notes, but a legal code takes root bit by bit as its provisions are applied to actual cases. Announcing that something is the law is not the same as its being the law. Here too there will be borderline cases.

In addition to space and time, states must be independent in the conduct of their foreign affairs. Texas meets the first two requirements, but not this third one. This independence must be ultimately possessed by the state, though it can be contracted out in various ways and to varying degrees. At the end of the nineteenth century an Indian maharaja who had delegated to the British the right to conduct his state's foreign affairs (the state thereby becoming a British protectorate) got into another kind of foreign affair with an Englishwoman. The affair ended unhappily from her point of view and she tried to sue him for breach of promise in a British court. The court accepted the maharaja's claim that as he was a sovereign ruler, the court had no jurisdiction over him. He had, the court said, conditionally delegated some of his powers as a sovereign, but not renounced them.[30]

Finally, states must possess a number of what are called "physical capacities": "the ability to send and receive diplomatic agents, the capacity of its agents to conclude treaties in the name of the state, and the ability to apply to international tribunals in the event that grievances exist against other states. In addition, a state must assume responsibility for actions taken by any of its members acting as agents or in some other official capacity."[31] On these grounds some tiny countries do not qualify as states and thus are technically not members of the community of nations. There are island nations in the Pacific that fall into this category. They are too small to have representatives at the UN or to maintain embassies.

States and Governments

The state must be distinguished from the government. The state, not the government, is the major player, the legal person, in international law. Otherwise contractual obligations would always be at the mercy of politics. Treaty commitments would be checks on which payment could be stopped long after the goods had been consumed. So a change of government does not absolve a state of its former obligations—the new government inherits the obligations the state was under before the new government came to power. This is true even if the new government takes power under a new constitution—the French Fourth Republic assumed the international obligations that existed under the French Third Republic; revolutionary Russia assumed the obligations of the czarist empire:

> Internal changes have no influence upon the identity of a state. A community is able to assert its rights and to fulfill its duties equally well whether it is presided over by one dynasty or another, and whether it is cloaked with the form of a monarchy or a republic. It is unnecessary that governments, as such, shall have a place in international law, and they are consequently regarded merely as agents through whom the community expresses its will, and who, though duly authorised at a given moment, may be superseded at pleasure.[32]

This is so even if the government is unconstitutional. In 1923 U.S. Chief Justice William Howard Taft arbitrated a dispute between Costa Rica and Britain that centered on rights granted to some British companies by "one Tinoco," who had seized power in 1917 and enjoyed his office for two years. Costa Rica claimed Tinoco's regime had been unconstitutional under Costa Rican law and that Costa Rica was therefore not bound by contracts he had signed. Taft, in a decision Brierly said "clearly stated the law regarding this question,"

> held that if Tinoco's government was the actual government at the time when the rights were alleged to have been acquired, the restored government could not repudiate the obligations which his acts had imposed on the state of Costa Rica. He further said that this question must be decided by evidence of the facts. It was immaterial that by the law of Costa Rica Tinoco's government was unconstitutional. Even the objection put forward by Costa Rica that many states, including Great Britain herself, had never recognized Tinoco's government, was only relevant as suggesting, though it did not prove, that their government had not been the actual government of Costa Rica; but since Tinoco "was in actual and peaceable control without resistance or contest . . . " he held that his acts were binding upon Costa Rica.[33]

The normal understanding that the law of war applies only between states may seem unfair. Groups that do not qualify as states engage in armed conflicts with justice and right on their side. Why should they be denied the protection of international law? If members of such groups are captured, should they not be treated as prisoners of war, rather than executed as criminals? Of course they should. They should be given the reins of government. At the very least their grievances should be settled, and they should be given generous rewards, lifetime pensions, and sent home as heroes. In a morally perfect universe this would happen. But international law does not require it.

Therefore, this section ends on the note on which I began: morality and legality are not the same. Those who fight with justice on their side, but not as agents of a state, do not have the standard rights of international law. It is a harsh world, and the law of war does not extend its protection to every deserving person. But the law of war does, as we will see in the succeeding chapters, have its moral side.

The Status of International Law

The law we will be examining is the international law of war, and some people deny that international law really is law. They think that law must meet criteria international law does not meet and thus that international law is *law* in name only.

Even if these people are right, most of what I will say can still stand: first, because no one denies that there is national law, and national law can have the same provisions as international law. The U.S. Army's *Law of Land Warfare* (FM27-10), the current incarnation *uctions,* implies that those of its provisions that are of treaties the United States has signed are binding on courts. Many of its provisions come from the Hague ,, and because the United States signed those conventions, visions are law—U.S. law—even if international law is only onal "law."

over, what I will say can stand because I am not ultimately ed is what is or is not in accordance with real or nominal law. rested in the moral questions posed by the laws of war. Those are the same whether or not international law is really law. question is interesting: Is international law really law? Hart the reasons given for denying that it is law are not The most frequently cited reason comes from another thinker, John Austin. Austin thought that law differs from ls of morality" only in that law is backed by punishments Without that backing, he thought, a would-be law is only International law typically lacks this enforcement ma- Hart pointed out, on these grounds much of consti- d not be law: A constitution may establish a bicameral is not likely to provide penalties for the failure to

her happy with Hart's own view that, put crudely, hat something is law is that everyone treats it as iterion international law certainly is law: It is y nations. Even when they do not obey it or do uthority, states recognize that it is international ing or ignoring.

that international law really is law, others go They regard breaches of *international* law though a violation of international law is a a violation of domestic law. They think the international law gives it some higher, tran- ence.

domestic law there are misdemeanors and not on a par. First-degree murder is a more on the grass or driving one mile over the violations of international law are minor. on Prisoners of War specified that captured paid a monthly advance equal to twelve t signed those conventions paid eleven l law. But it would not have committed n end this discussion on a brighter note. of international law as sacred may take comfort in the thought that they may have committed offenses m serious than some breaches of international law.

Suggestions for Further Reading

Several books provide good introductions to our topic: Gerhard von G *Law Among Nations,* 2d ed. (Collier-Macmillan, London, 1970); Sir H Lauterpacht, ed., *Lassa Oppenheim's International Law: A Treatise,* 7th vol. 2 (Longmans, Green, London, 1952); J. L. Brierly, *The Law of Na* ed. Sir Humphrey Waldock (Oxford University Press, Oxford, 1963); Ge Best, *Humanity in Warfare* (Columbia University Press, New York, William Edward Hall, *A Treatise on International Law,* 8th ed., ed. A. Higgins (Oxford University Press, Oxford, 1924).

2

The 1907 Hague Conventions

Perhaps more than any other human activity war . . . introduces into every society in which it occurs a series of juridical and moral considerations which are often complex and equivocal. It is not necessarily proof of idealism or unreality to maintain that it is almost never desired, experienced or conceived as pure and unlimited violence, in a crude or elementary fashion. It exists enveloped in (and also masked by) a total conceptual system springing from custom, law, morality, and religion—an apparatus designed in principle to tame, orientate, and channel it. . . . [It] offers the historian or the sociologist an opportunity to study the relationships between reality and the ideal, between practice and ethics, and between fact and law.[1]

Responsibility and the Chain of Command

International law recognizes a distinction between lawful and unlawful belligerents: Only the former are afforded the protections of the Hague and Geneva conventions. Unlawful belligerents, according to the Hague conventions, are to be dealt with according to the laws and customs of the capturing country—which in some lands has traditionally meant summary execution without trial, though more recent additions to the Geneva conventions urge humane treatment and trials (of some sort) in all cases.

Lawful belligerents must meet four requirements. The first two constitute a sort of dress code—we will examine them in Chapter 5. The third requirement for lawful belligerents is that they must be "commanded by a person responsible for his subordinates" (Hague IV Annex, 1907, Article 1; Geneva, 1949 Article 13). A leaderless mob that opposes enemy troops is not protected by the law of war, which requires that belligerents be part of an organization in which some people are responsible for the actions of others. The organization, the leader, and the chain of command do not have to be recognized by the enemy power, but they must exist. If they do not, the law of war simply does not apply.

Why should there be such a requirement? The law itself does not tell us, but two considerations spring to mind. First, soldiers are not experts in international law, and courts will sometimes take that into consideration in assessing penalties. For example, the U.S. Army's rules of land warfare state that although neither ignorance of the law nor superior orders absolve soldiers of guilt for criminal acts, those factors may mitigate the punishment. But this is not a free grant for lawlessness: The price of some leniency at lower levels is increased responsibility at higher levels.

Second, though those who commit war crimes are punishable by the enemy if they are captured, they are punishable first and foremost by their own side: The primary responsibility for punishing offenders rests with the officers in command of the forces that have committed the offense. If these officers fail to do so, they themselves become subject to criminal charges.

Officers have been executed for crimes committed by their troops even though it could not be proven that those troops were acting on the officer's commands. Moreover, officers have been executed for crimes committed by their troops even though it could not be proven that the officer was aware of the crimes: It has been deemed sufficient to show that under the circumstances it was reasonable to expect the officer to have known what was going on. He cannot exercise command and deny responsibility.

If those in the field have no superiors responsible for their acts, they are not constrained by the major instrument for compliance with the international law of war, and so they are not protected by that law. But perhaps more fundamentally, the requirement of responsible leadership can be understood as a reflection of the requirement that in order for an entity to count as a state it must accept responsibility for those who act as its agents. An entity that disavows such responsibility cannot claim the rights of a state. Nor can the community of nations treat it as a state if the authorized agents of the purported state cannot be clearly distinguished from unauthorized agents. The right to exercise violence that soldiers have does not derive from their personal grievances nor from some informal agreement among themselves. It derives from rights that states have. It therefore presupposes that combatants act as agents of a state and that they are directed by officials who accept responsibility for the actions of belligerents.

Are soldiers who carry out war crimes criminal if they are obeying superior orders? In the public mind this seems to be a perplexing issue, and the view that superior orders excuse soldiers from guilt for participation in unjust wars has been widely held: St. Augustine said that if the lawful ruler "declared an unjust war, the sin was his alone, not his soldiers', since the duty of obedience rendered them innocent."[2] But that was a quesiton of the justness of the cause, not of the barbarity with which the war was fought. In the law that has developed since the Hague conventions, superior orders are no excuse for criminality. This is so clear that there is no need for a discussion of the legal question. Instead, I offer a string of quotations and cases.

> If the criminal law is violated by the execution of an order in the course of service . . . the subordinate obeying is liable for participating . . . if it was known to him that the order concerned an action the purpose of which was to commit a general or military crime or misdemeanor—1940 German Military Penal Code (*Militärstrafgesetzbuch*), Section 47.

> The fact that the law of war has been violated pursuant to an order of a superior authority, whether military or civil, does not deprive the act in question of its character of a war crime, nor does it constitute a defense in the trial of an accused individual, unless he did not know and could not reasonably have been expected to know that the act ordered was unlawful—U.S. Army's *Law of Land Warfare,* 1956, par. 509.

> The fact that a rule of law has been violated in pursuance of an order of the belligerent Government or of an individual belligerent commander does not . . . confer on the perpetrator immunity from punishment by the injured belligerent. . . . Members of the armed forces are bound to obey lawful orders only and . . . cannot therefore escape liability if, in obedience to a command, they commit acts which both violate unchallenged rules of warfare and outrage the general sentiment of humanity—British *Manual of Military Law,* ch. xiv. par. 433, amended 1944.

> In 1921 in The Case of Dithmar and Boldt the German Supreme Court found the defendants guilty of carrying out their submarine commander's orders to fire on survivors in lifeboats.

> No law of war provides that a soldier will remain unpunished for a hateful crime by referring to the orders of his superiors, if these orders are in striking opposition to all human ethics, to all international customs in the conduct of war—Goebbels, *Völkischer Beobachter,* May 28, 1944.

> He who violates the laws of war cannot obtain immunity while acting in pursuance of the authority of the State if the State in authorizing action moves outside its competence under international law—Judgment of the Nuremberg Tribunal.[3]

Whether the subordinate's crime is mitigated if he is under a serious threat for not obeying the order is a question best left to individual cases. The U.S. Army's code says that although having superior orders does not affect guilt, it may mitigate the punishment. The Nuremberg Tribunal said that "the true test" was "whether moral choice was possible" but did not explain further. Someone robbing a bank because the real criminal is holding a gun to his head or threatening his family is not morally responsible for his act. Someone embezzling funds from a bank because his boss told him that if he didn't he would be fired *is* morally responsible for his act.

The question of the commander's responsibility for crimes committed by his subordinates was addressed in the trial of the Japanese general Tomoyuki Yamashita, whose troops in the Philippines, when it became clear that they would have to retreat from the returning Americans, went on an orgy of atrocities. Yamashita had not ordered these acts—if he had, his responsibility would have been clear. But they were committed by troops under his command, and he was charged with failing to control them and thereby allowing them to commit these crimes. Yamashita appealed to the U.S. Supreme Court, on the grounds that he himself had neither committed nor ordered any war crimes and therefore had not violated the law of war. The court refused to review the case, explaining:

> The question . . . is whether the law of war imposes on an army commander a duty to take such appropriate measures as are within his power to control the troops under his command for the prevention of the specified acts which are violations of the law of war and which are likely to attend the occupation of hostile territory by an uncontrolled soldiery, and whether he may be charged with personal responsibility for his failure to take such measures when violations result. . . .
>
> It is evident that the conduct of military operations by troops whose excesses are unrestrained by the orders or efforts of their commander would almost certainly result in violations which it is the purpose of the law of war to prevent. . . . Its purpose . . . would be largely defeated if the commander of an invading army could with impunity neglect to take reasonable measures for their protection. Hence the law of war presupposes that its violation is to be avoided through the control of the operations of war by commanders who are to some extent responsible for their subordinates.[4]

Yamashita had claimed, in his defense, that in the chaotic conditions of the retreat he had lost communication with his troops and was in effective command only of the troops with him.

Justice Frank Murphy, in the minority, sided with the defense, saying, "These charges amount to this: 'We, the victorious American forces . . . charge and condemn you for having been inefficient in maintaining control of your troops . . . when we were so effectively . . . blocking your ability to maintain effective command.'"[5]

But the majority did not agree. Yamashita's lawyers had held that he was being subjected to "strict liability"—responsibility for his subordinates regardless of the circumstances. The court, however, did not believe that Yamashita was unable to control his troops. It said that "there is no contention that . . . the Commission held petitioner responsible for failing to take measures which were beyond his control . . . in the circumstances." The crucial question, then, was factual: Did Yamashita have the ability to communicate with his troops—to issue commands and to be aware of their activities? The legal point was clear: A commander must take those measures that are within his power to control his troops and ensure that they do not violate the law of war. Failure to do so is a crime of omission.[6]

The prosecutors did not claim that Yamashita knew about the atrocities. The Tokyo tribunal had stated that liability occurs not only if one has knowledge of crimes and does not stop them but also if defendants "are at fault in having failed to acquire such knowledge," and it added that crimes "notorious, numerous and widespread as to time and place are matters to be considered in imputing knowledge." The implication is that except for isolated incidents, it is a commander's responsibility to know what his troops are doing—a responsibility that is not always easy to carry out. What happens when an officer is unable to control his troops? He can resign his command.

Bombardment and Civilian Casualties

Belligerents, lawful or unlawful, are not the only legitimate objects of attack in war. The 1949 Geneva conventions, for example, recognize a class of nonbelligerents who are entitled to be treated as prisoners of war: "persons who accompany the armed forces without actually being members thereof"—military correspondents, for example. But the right of these persons to be treated as prisoners of war carries with it a liability: An air force can contract with a civilian company to maintain and repair its planes, bu the civilian status of that company's workers does not make them immune to attack. By the same token a civilian telephone-line repairman, working on the phone lines to a battalion command post, should not expect an enemy sniper to refuse to fire at him. One's function counts more heavily than one's status as a civilian.

The line between permissible and impermissible targets does not correspond to the line between soldiers and civilians. Still, there is a line: It is one thing to shoot a civilian laying telephone wire to a headquarters; it would be quite another to mow down a group of shoppers lined up at a bakery. The latter is murder, the former is not. This is not because the shoppers are, as the phrase goes, "defenseless civilians." The unarmed telephone repairman is a defenseless civilian but nonetheless may be a legitimate target. And civilians may be quite capable of defending themselves but still not be permissible targets.

The crucial question is not whether the person is military or civilian, defenseless or armed, but whether he is a source of danger. It is a violation of the law of war to shoot a prisoner or to refuse to give quarter to someone offering to surrender. These people are no longer threats. In contrast, it is not a violation to shoot an unarmed enemy soldier. The company baker, though momentarily unarmed, may at the next moment be armed, or he may, though unarmed himself, be capable of directing the fire of others. His being a soldier puts him in the class of combatants, even if at the moment he is not prepared for combat. So he is a permissible target under the law of war. (This is not to say that a patrol that has sneaked up on an enemy soldier and that is equally capable of killing him or of capturing him should open fire. The law of war permits actions that are immoral.)

In these cases fire is directed at observed individuals. More often soldiers are not under observation when they receive fire. An excerpt from *Just and Unjust Wars* gives Michael Walzer's approach to this situation:

> I am going to follow here a British journalist's account of the way the American army waged war in Korea. Whether it is an entirely just account I do not know, but I am more interested in the moral issues it raises than in its historical accuracy. This, then, was a "typical" encounter on the road to Pyongyang. A battalion of American troops advanced slowly, without opposition, under the shadow of long hills. "We were well into the valley now, halfway down the straight . . . strung out along the road, when it came, the harsh stutter of automatic fire sputtering the dust around us." The troops . . . dove for cover. Three tanks moved up, "pounding their shells into the . . . hillside and shattering the air with their machine guns. It was impossible in this remarkable inferno of sound to detect the enemy, or to assess his fire." Within fifteen minutes, several fighter planes arrived, "diving down upon the hillside with their rockets." This is the new technique of warfare,

> writes the British journalist, "born of immense productive and material might": "the cautious advance, the enemy small arms fire, the halt, the close support air strike, artillery, the cautious advance, and so on." It is designed to save the lives of soldiers, and it may or may not have that effect. "It is certain that it kills civilian men, women, and children, indiscriminately and in great numbers, and destroys all that they have."

Walzer's moral assessment of the action described is quite negative:

> Now there is another way to fight, though it is only open to soldiers who have had a "soldierly" training and who are not "roadbound" in their habits. A patrol can be sent forward to outflank the enemy position. In the end it often comes to that anyway, as it did in this case, for the tanks and planes failed to hit the North Korean machine gunners. "At last, after more than an hour . . . a platoon from Baker Company began working their way through the scrub just under the ridge of the hill." But the first reliance was always on bombardment. "Every enemy shot released a deluge of destruction." And the bombardment had, or sometimes had, its characteristic double effect: enemy soldiers were killed, and so were any civilians who happened to be nearby. It was not the intention of the officers who called in the artillery and planes to kill civilians; they were acting out of a concern for their own men. And that is a legitimate concern. No one would want to be commanded in wartime by an officer who did not value the lives of his soldiers. But he must also value civilian lives, and so must his soldiers. . . . Even if the proportions work out favorably, in particular cases or over a period of time, we would still want to say, I think, that the patrol must be sent out, the risk accepted, before the big guns are brought to bear.[7]

Walzer adopted a similar critical attitude toward the use of U.S. firepower in Vietnam.[8]

In doing so he asked far more of soldiers than the Hague conventions require. In the case he described troops were fired upon by automatic weapons and, I assume, pinned down ("the harsh stutter of automatic fire sputtering the dust around us"). The tanks fired back at the source of hostile fire on the hill, and an air strike was called in. This was all perfectly normal—a unit that did not reply in such a case with mortar or artillery fire or air strikes would be one that lacked these assets.

Walzer was correct in suggesting that the use of such assets decreases friendly casualties. Soldiers fight from cover whenever possible. According to Walzer, to avoid hitting unseen civilians, soldiers should not direct fire at enemy troops hidden by cover. Friendly riflemen would then have to leave their own cover and advance to root out the enemy. Those advancing riflemen would not have the protection of covering fire suppressing the enemy. They would advance under the conditions soldiers dread the most—exposed and fired upon while unable to return fire.

Walzer was also right in saying that the use of mortar, artillery, or air strikes causes civilian casualties that would be avoided if, instead of calling in artillery fire, riflemen crawled up and fired only at observed enemy troops. But the law of war does not require this: It allows troops under fire to fire back without ascertaining that there are no civilians mingled with the troops who are firing upon them. It allows troops under fire to fire back even if they know civilians are mingled with the enemy.

A case in point that Walzer discussed is the massive air and artillery support used in the World War II bombardment of the French town of St. Lô during the Normandy campaign that followed D day. Walzer suggested a number of alternatives that, on the grounds that they would have minimized civilian casualties, would have been preferable to the massive bombardment that actually took place:

> Perhaps the attack could have been redirected through some less populated area (even at greater risk to the soldiers involved). Perhaps the planes, flying low, could have aimed at specific enemy targets, or artillery could have been used instead (since shells could then be aimed more precisely than bombs), or paratroops dropped or patrols sent forward to seize important positions in advance of the main attack. I am in no position to recommend any of these courses of action, although, in the event, any of [them] might have been preferable, even from a military point of view.[9]

To anyone familiar with the Normandy campaign these suggestions are implausible.

Could paratroopers have been dropped or small units (I assume this is what Walzer means by "patrols") sent to seize important positions? The area was held by the Panzer Lehr Division, which though badly mauled from previous fighting, was probably the best division in the German army. To suggest that paratroopers or small units might do the job against an alert and elite enemy when regimental, divisional, and corps attacks had failed is like suggesting that if 10 people cannot lift the log, perhaps 2 can. Unless the enemy is incompetent, 30 men will not succeed where 30,000 have failed.

Could artillery and fighter bombers have been used? They were, and were not enough.

Could the attack have been directed through some less populated area (even at greater risk to the soldiers involved)? It could, but then there would have been no breakout: St. Lô was selected, not because it was a population center, but because the roads leading out of western Normandy ran through it. Towns and cities provide concealment and cover and tend to control transportation routes, as well as offering innumerable other benefits to the side that controls them. They are thus more difficult to attack than open country but are crucial military objectives, and the list of major battles of the twentieth century is, to a large extent, a list of towns and cities: Kiev, Bryansk, Berlin, Bastogne, Moscow, Kursk, Dunkirk, Aachen, Pusan, St. Vith, Hue, Khe San, Caen, Brest, Budapest, and so on. And when armies fight over the control of towns, civilians are always at risk.

At least one writer has concluded that modern warfare is inherently immoral: Donald Wells has declared that the notion of a just war becomes inapplicable "once we admit weapons that shoot further than the eye can see."[10] And according to Robert L. Phillips, the medieval church

> waged a long and generally successful campaign against ballistic weapons such as the bow and the slingshot. As one writer put it, "The arrow knoweth not whither it goes." In other words, if one releases a shower of arrows or stones, it is difficult to discriminate targets, and thus it is morally preferable to use only those weapons which can be wielded at close range where the target is visible, such as the sword or lance.[11]

On Wells's view, the bombardment of a civilian locale is itself immoral—one can fight a war morally only if one can direct harm *solely* at enemy soldiers. If one cannot fairly well guarantee that no civilians will be harmed, one fights immorally.

The Hague conventions do not see it that way. They allow the bombardment of areas defended by the enemy even if those areas are inhabited by civilians. They allow soldiers to put civilian lives at risk. The justification for this is "military necessity." But this phrase can cover a wide variety of extremely different cases. Let us see, in the case of St. Lô, what this meant on the ground.

When, on July 25, St. Lô was attacked by 1,500 heavy bombers, 380 medium bombers, and 550 fighter bombers, one of the largest air attacks in World War II was taking place (the famous attack on Hamburg involved barely 1,000 planes). The ground shook for miles around. Panzer Lehr was virtually wiped out, and the town, already heavily damaged by artillery fire, was turned to rubble. But in the next few days Americans, advancing through the hole created by the bombardment, drove more deeply into France than they had in the seven weeks that had passed since D Day, reaching the base of the Normandy peninsula at Avranches. They did not stop until they reached the German border. The bombing of St. Lô led to victory not only in the battle of Normandy but in the battle of France as well.

If Wells was right, the Hague bombardment rules are morally wrong, and the bombing of St. Lô was immoral. And the same could be said for the scores of assaults on defended cities and towns in the preceding weeks, for these assaults were almost always accompanied by artillery bombardments, and the artillery supporting the attack rarely fired on spotted targets (soldiers hide)—it fired on defended positions. If the whole town constituted a defended position, as at St. Lô, the artillery fired on the whole town, even if innocents were known to be present.

If these artillery bombardments and carpet bombings had been forbidden, there would have been no breakout from Normandy in 1944, and likely the invasion would have been defeated. For even with the massive artillery bombardments (U.S. Seventh and Nineteenth corps, attacking St. Lô, commanded approximately 800 artillery pieces) and the carpet bombings, Allied losses were almost unbearable. It is against these losses that we must weigh Walzer's question whether the attack could have been directed at a less populated area *even if it increased casualties.*

There are limits to what we can expect men to endure. In World War II, 150 days in the line was the average endurance level for a U.S. GI. Beyond that, combat troops were burned out. That limit was not often reached: "With a minimum daily casualty rate of 2 percent, the chances of keeping body and soul together for 150 days are slim."[12]

In an infantry division there may be 15,000 men, but the overwhelming majority of the casualties fall to 2,000–3,000 men in the rifle platoons who go forward to attack. They bear the heaviest burden, and as their casualties increase and the sight of violent death becomes pervasive, the division ceases to be an effective fighting force. There is only so much one can ask of men; when that is exceeded, they go into shock. The point at which this occurs varies, depending on morale and training, but in general: "a unit which suffers 33 1/3 per cent casualties in a short space of time is wrecked, and will remain so until it has been rested, reinforced, and reorganized. This is not an experience any unit, however good, can survive more than once or twice. It never recovers unless it is completely reconstructed, i.e. there is a new unit under the old name."[13]

How does this 33 1/3 percent figure compare with the actual casualties in the Normandy campaign? In the drive on St. Lô, the U.S. Thirtieth Infantry Division took over 90 percent casualties in its rifle platoons in fifteen days. Attacking in the hills around St. Lô, the Twenty-Ninth Infantry Division took 58 percent casualties in its rifle platoons, and the Thirty-Fifth took almost 40 percent. The U.S. Ninetieth Infantry Divison suffered 100 percent casualties in enlisted men, and 150 percent in officers: Statistically, every rifle platoon in the division had been wiped out and rebuilt with replacements *three times in six weeks.*

Commonwealth troops fared no better: In one three-day battle—Goodwood, which also began with a carpet bombing—the British and Canadians lost 36 percent of their tank strength in France. At the end of the war the commanding officer of the Gordon Highlanders reviewed his battalion's history:

> It occurred to me to count the number of officers who had served in the battalion since D Day. Up to March 27th, the end of the Rhine crossing, it was 102. . . . I found that we had had 55 officers commanding the twelve rifle platoons, and that their average service with the battalion was thirty-eight days, or five and a half weeks. Of these fifty-three per cent were wounded, twenty-four per cent killed or died of wounds, fifteen per cent invalided, and five per cent had survived.[14]

These casualties were largely caused by bombardment. In World War II, artillery accounted for 58 percent of all casualties—75 per cent in open terrain, 50 percent in towns and forest.[15] Small arms fire accounted for less than 10 percent of British battle wounds in World War II; artillery, bombs, and grenades accounted for 75 percent.

> Basically, World War II was fought with explosive missiles . . . whereas in the first two years of World War I approximately 80 per cent of all wounds were caused by gunshot, notably from machine guns. . . . The rifle by now was a subordinate weapon, mainly used by snipers or to keep the enemy's heads down. The pistol never had been of any use and even the machine gun had lost some of its old battlefield dominance because of the new emphasis upon dispersal and the widespread use of tanks and armoured personnel carriers.[16]

Extrapolating from these figures, one can assert that had the United States not bombarded towns in Normandy, German casualties in attacks against towns would have been halved, and U.S. at least doubled—a result that would have been completely shattering. As is, U.S. troops suffered horribly. As John Ellis recounted:

> By early 1945, 47 American regiments, spread over 19 divisions, had sustained 100 to 200 per cent casualties. Some examples from the Third US Army prove the point. By the end of the war the 90th Division had over 35,000 replacements; 5th Division over 30,000; 25th, 79th, and 80th

> Divisions over 25,000; 4th and 6th Armoured Divisions over 20,000. . . . The army made a survey of sample companies from 1st, 4th, 9th, and 29th US Divisons and came up with depressing results: [in the first seven weeks of the Normandy campaign] the rifle companies had lost 59.6 per cent of their original complement of enlisted men and 68.7 per cent of their officers. Equivalent figures for heavy weapons companies were 36.9 and 51.9 per cent. . . . The killing continued right through the battle for Germany.[17]

Nineteen divisions would normally contain fifty-seven regiments, so for those divisions the 100–200 percent casualty rate occurred in 82 percent of their regiments. Ellis quoted the experience of one replacement assigned that autumn to the Thirtieth Division at the time of the attacks on Aachen:

> Private Elmer S. McKay, a nineteen year-old mortarman replacement, recalls arriving in the 30th's lines during a bombing raid. . . . "I lined up with the rest of the replacements. I counted 33 men, which I thought was a rather large number of replacements for an infantry whose total complement was 190 men plus five officers. . . . " Little did the scared replacement realize it then, but by the time the battle for Aachen was over, he would be a platoon sergeant himself, the sole survivor of the men who had come with him, in charge of thirty men whose average age was just nineteen [i.e., fresh replacements].[18]

There is a point at which units are unfit for further service. A unit that takes 20 percent casualties in one action is at that point, with one in five men down, dead, or captured, a fair number of the remainder attending the wounded, and everyone dazed. The unit can be ordered to attack again, but likely it will only go through the motions if it does anything at all. If it really does attack, it is time to give out medals—those soldiers will have done more than one can reasonably ask of troops. In Normandy many U.S. combat units were worn down this way. Had they been deprived of artillery and air support, they would have been completely and irrevocably shattered.

It seems unlikely that it was morally permissible for the Allies to attempt to defeat the Germans, but morally impermissible to employ the means that had to be used if the war was to be won. The notion of "military necessity" lends itself to abuse, but every use of it is not abusive. It is not being abused if the alternative is to ask more of troops than we have any right to ask of anyone or than anyone can deliver.

By itself, though, this justification is unhappy, for it could be used to justify truly heinous behavior: One is not justified in using any means whatever so long as those means are necessary for victory. I suggest the following as a reasonable account of the limits: Innocents have certain moral rights, and it would be immoral for a rifleman who has an infant in his sights to gun the child down. But the rights of innocents are defeasible. If the indiscriminate shelling or bombing of a town is an attack on innocents, then armies are not under a moral obligation, in assaults, not to attack innocents. The rule is, I suggest, that the attacker may, given the presence of innocents in a combat zone, do anything that it would be permissible to do if there were no innocents there—subject to the restrictions entailed by the principle of proportionality (see below, "Proportionality and Utility"). This rules out discriminatory (selective) attacks on innocents but allows the indiscriminate shelling or bombing of defended areas containing innocents.

This view can be defended in a number of ways. It can be defended, for example, as approving certain risk preference assignments. In the Normandy campaign a rifleman in the Ninetieth Division could expect to last fourteen days before becoming a casualty. By contrast, in heavily bombed Germany, a civilian had only a one in seventy chance of being killed or seriously wounded by a bomb during the six years of the war. In France the odds of a civilian becoming a casualty were infinitesimal.

The law of war implies that soldiers are not obligated to raise their already high risks to even higher levels in order to lower further the risk to innocents in combat zones. This seems particularly reasonable in tactical combat, where civilians are usually free to leave the combat zone—indeed, in Normandy the Germans sometimes ordered them out. But even where this was not possible, as in the towns on Gold and Juno beaches where the British and Canadians appeared without prior notice on D day morning, the rights of innocents are defeasible when honoring those rights would push the soldiers' risks beyond what it is reasonable to expect any group to endure.

There are two more points that the St. Lô case can help elucidate. One critic has charged that the massive British and U.S. bombings of civilian areas in World War II were motivated by "villainous hatred." But St. Lô was French, not German, and the Allies had no desire to cause French civilian casualties. On the contrary, Allied leaders were concerned about minimizing French casualties. No hatred of the people of St. Lô played a role in the attack.

Second, because St. Lô was not an enemy town, though it was held by enemy troops, the permissibility of bombarding it had nothing to do with the presence of *enemy* civilians: The civilians were not enemy. Whether the town's inhabitants are enemy or friendly is irrelevant to the case that can be made for the bombardment of St. Lô. The Red Army, fighting to recapture Russian towns from the Germans, used artillery bombardments that were heavier than the bombardments the Germans had used to capture those towns in the first place.

Indeed, an appeal to military necessity is a subterfuge for what is actually a mere military advantage, and not a necessity at all, if the commander would cancel the attack were the casualties friendly. Where the perception of real military necessity is at work, a commander may, though with reluctance, engage in a practice even if the civilians who are being put in harm's way by it are friendly.

That an attack indiscriminately harms whoever is in the area—combatant or noncombatant—does not make the attack immoral.[19] I will return to this point in Chapter 6, for it is often claimed that nuclear weapons are immoral just on those grounds.

The St. Lô case was a bombardment of a *defended* locality in conjunction with an assault—a ground attack—on that locality. The Hague conventions permit this, and they permit the bombardment of defended localities even if no assault is contemplated.

They do not, however, permit the bombardment of undefended localities: "The attack or bombardment, by whatever means, of towns, villages, dwellings, or buildings which are undefended is prohibited" (Article 25). Article 25, like most of the Hague conventions, is a close adaptation of the corresponding provision in the Acts of the Brussels Conference of 1874. The provisions of the 1874 conference were never ratified and hence never became treaty law, but they are important because they formed the basis for the Hague Rules of Land Warfare. Article 14 of the Brussels conference rules said that one may neither attack nor bombard an open, undefended city. There is a clue to the rationale behind this rule in an objection raised against Article 14's wording by Colonel Brun, one of the Danish representatives. Brun objected to the word "attack" on the grounds that "one cannot attack that which is not defended."[20] "Attack" stayed, but his point was not disputed: Combat can be massacre only figuratively—military operations presuppose armed resistance. Slaughter is not a military operation but the butcher's task.

In the words of the Hague conventions: "The right of belligerents to adopt means of injuring the enemy is not unlimited" (Article 22). To the framers of the Brussels and Hague rules for land warfare the principle was clear: Undefended localities should be seized, not attacked. If they are undefended they are free for the taking, so to attack them is to cause unnecessary destruction. Such an attack would be punitive and vindictive because the legitimate military objective could be attained harmlessly. The bombardment of undefended towns was prohibited in the same spirit that prohibited the pillaging of captured towns.

When we turn to naval warfare, the law is different. We will consider this difference, and its significance, in Chapter 4.

Military Necessity

Military necessity has often been used to justify actions and policies that seemed morally or legally questionable. In August 1914 the German chancellor, Theobald von Bethmann Hollweg, defended the German invasion of neutral Belgium in an appeal before the Reichstag:

> We are now in a state of necessity, and necessity knows no law. Our troops have already entered Belgian soil.
>
> Gentlemen, that is a breach of international law. . . . France stood ready for an invasion. France could wait, we could not. A French attack on our flank on the lower Rhine might have been disastrous. Thus we were forced to ignore the rightful protests of the Government of Belgium. The wrong—I speak frankly—the wrong we thereby commit we will try to make good as soon as our military aims have been attained.
>
> He who is menaced as we are and is fighting for his highest possession can only consider how to hack his way through.[21]

Carried to its penultimate limit, the doctrine of military necessity would justify any act that was required for victory. Carried to its ultimate limit, it would justify any act that helped bring about victory, even if the act was not really necessary for victory. It would merely have to help. Every prohibition of the law would have to be rephrased: "It is forbidden to do X" would become "if it is of no military advantage to do X, it is forbidden to do X." This rule would still forbid harming the enemy out of pure bloodthirstiness, anger, or vindictiveness. The act would have to have a military gain. This would be a weak restriction, but still a restriction.

The law of war, though, goes much further than this. It rejects the claim that whatever helps bring about victory is permissible. It even rejects the claim that whatever is necessary for victory is permissible. It forbids some things absolutely: They are criminal even if without them the war will be lost. Yet it recognizes military necessity as a legitimate consideration.

According to the preamble to the Hague Convention on Land War, the wording of the provisions of the convention "has been inspired by the desire to diminish the evils of war, so far as military necessities permit." It has, as the U.S. Department of the Army's *Law of Land*

Warfare states, taken military necessity into account. Section (c) of Article 23, for example, prohibits without qualification killing enemy soldiers who have surrendered, whereas Section (g) forbids destroying or seizing enemy property *unless* "imperatively demanded by the necessities of war." The destruction or seizure of enemy property can sometimes be justified by military necessity under the Hague conventions. Killing prisoners, in contrast, is absolutely forbidden. Military necessity cannot be invoked to justify it.

The Geneva conventions have a similar stricture. Article 13 of the 1949 third convention says that POWs must "at all times" be protected against "insults and public curiosity." Article 17 says "no physical or mental torture, nor any other form of coercion, may be inflicted on prisoners of war to secure from them information of any kind whatever." But Article 53, 1949 Fourth Geneva Convention, echoing the Hague convention, allows the destruction of property in occupied zones if this is "rendered absolutely necessary by military operations." Thus, whereas the law of war acknowledges military necessity in some cases, it rejects it in others. It forbids torture, for example, under all circumstances.

From the legal point of view, then, military necessity can justify only what the law says it can justify. Military necessity does not conflict with the law of war, nor can it override that law. John Westlake, replying to a defense of the doctrine of military necessity under its German name (*Kriegsraison*), said the law of war is

> a code in which humanity to the enemy on the one side, and the essential needs of war on the other, have been considered. . . . The question raised under the term of *Kriegsraison* is not whether that code is defective or misconceived in any of its clauses, but whether a necessity, not of war but of success, is to be allowed to break it down. It is contended in effect . . . that the true instructions to be given by a State to its generals are: "Succeed—by war according to its laws, if you can—but at all events and in any way, succeed.". Of conduct suitable to such instructions it may be expected that human nature will not fail to produce examples, but the business of doctrinal writers should be to check, and not to encourage it.[22]

Reprisals

The primary responsibility for punishing soldiers who commit or order war crimes rests with the people who are superior to those soldiers in the chain of command. These superiors are themselves culpable for crimes committed under their command if they do not take disciplinary action to punish the offenders and prevent recurrences: The other side is not usually in a position to discipline enemy troops. If a violation of the law of war is committed, the offended side's first recourse is to contact the enemy commander and inform him of the violation. If that cannot be done or if the violations continue, the offended side can resort to reprisals—acts that would normally be violations of the law of war, but that are permitted in order to get the enemy to desist from unlawful acts. In a typical case, one side's planes might attack another's hospital ship, and the other side might retaliate by attacking the first side's ambulances.

Reprisals are legitimate only if they are undertaken to get the enemy to desist from an unlawful practice, and they must therefore be accompanied, whenever possible, with a communication informing the enemy commander of the circumstances leading to the reprisal. They are undoubtedly dangerous, for they may precipitate counterreprisals rather than compliance. But reprisals may be the only means of influencing the unrepentant: "It is a commonplace of human nature that evil-doers are checked by retaliation, and that those who are inclined to commit a wrong against others are often prevented by the fear of retaliation."[23] Reprisals are circumscribed by only a few restrictions: The 1949 Geneva conventions forbid reprisals against prisoners, and the U.S. Army's current *Law of Land Warfare* (1956) forbids the taking of hostages.

More than anything else, the acceptance of reprisals brings out the limitations of "the domestic analogy"—the attempt to understand the law of war by analogy from domestic situations and domestic law. Domestic law has no analogy for reprisals. It assumes that the malefactor can be handled within the framework of the law, and given a certain degree of social order, that assumption is warranted. But in war there is no police power to enforce the law, and any legal actions that might be available to punish the other side—a particularly heavy artillery bombardment, for example—are in general part of the course of war apart from any offenses: The bombardment would not be a punishment for an offense because bombardments are routinely mounted as a normal part of the conduct of war.

Reprisals can have another ugly side: J. M. Spaight said that it is a principle of the law of war that "for every offense punish someone; the guilty, if possible, but someone."[24] In 1965 South Vietnam executed three Vietcong prisoners, and the Vietcong executed two U.S. prisoners in reprisal, though the Americans were lawful belligerents.

A clearer case arose in August 1944 in France. The Germans had been executing captured partisans rather than treating them as prisoners of war, even when those partisans met the normal requirements for lawful belligerents by carrying their arms openly, wearing distinguishing badges, and so on. The Germans pointed out that under the terms of the armistice they had signed with the Vichy government in 1940, any French citizens who continued to resist would be considered insurrectionists rather than legitimate belligerents. France was no longer a belligerent power.

With the Normandy landings in June 1944, metropolitan France again became a battlefield, and FFI (French Forces of the Interior) operations against the Germans increased. In response, the German commander announced that "persons taking part in movements of rebellion directed against the rear of the occupying Power, have no right whatever to the protection which may be claimed by regular combatants" and that "such rebels will not be regarded as prisoners of war, but executed in accordance with martial law."[25] Despite protests against this policy by the provisional French government in Algiers, the Germans executed 80 prisoners. In reprisal, the FFI at Annecy then executed 80 of the 3,000 German prisoners they had captured.

The German actions seem themselves to have been illegal. The terms of the 1940 armistice could not deny the FFI the legal rights granted to legitimate belligerents under the Hague and 1929 Geneva conventions: Those conventions take precedence over the terms of any armistice.[26] And despite the terms of that armistice, the Germans routinely granted normal prisoner-of-war status to the Free French soldiers they captured in North Africa, Italy, and France.

But the FFI executions were also illegal because Article 2 of the 1929 Geneva Convention Relative to the Treatment of Prisoners of War expressly forbade reprisals against prisoners.[27] Military necessity, as we have seen, cannot legally justify an action that the law of war absolutely forbids. Though reprisals are acts otherwise unlawful, the choice of which otherwise unlawful acts are permissible as reprisals is constrained by law. Under the 1907 Hague conventions, killing prisoners of war is forbidden; under the 1929 Geneva conventions, killing prisoners of war even in reprisal was explicitly forbidden.

Walzer argued that the execution of the German prisoners was not only illegal but also morally wrong—that to kill helpless prisoners is murder. But the alternative he offered is not satisfactory either:

> The partisans might have attempted to raid the prisons or camps where their comrades were being held. Such raids were not impossible, though they would have involved risks entirely absent when one shoots down captured soldiers. . . .
>
> To argue against the executions isn't to deny the partisans a last resort. It is only to say, for example, that military raids are their last resort.

If such raids had been good ideas militarily, they should have been mounted in any case, and if they were bad ideas, then the partisans would be responding to the German action by putting themselves at greater risk—hardly a course of action likely to gain compliance or end the German practice. The partisans would have been ill advised to think of this as a recourse. So Walzer's advice really seems to be that the partisans had no recourse, for he allowed them no course of action that they would not have had open to them if there had been no executions—save announcing that when the war was over, the guilty, if they were still alive, and if they could be identified and arrested, would be punished.

We can take a more generous view of the Annecy executions. The French had an obligation to their own fighers and to their own cause, which would be harmed if every would-be volunteer had to mull over the fact that he would be executed if he were captured. The execution of the German prisoners was a terrible act, but when the Germans did not reply to the French protests, nor to the French threats of taking reprisals on captured Germans, the responsibility for those deaths passed to the Germans, who had left the French with no other effective means of ending the executions. (As it turns out, after the partisans had killed the German prisoners, the Germans stopped executing captured partisans—the reprisal worked.) The eighty dead Germans should be added to the eighty dead Frenchmen as the result of German decisions. When a criminal act by one belligerent leaves the other no effective means of compelling the first to desist except another act of the same kind, responsibility lies, not in the hands of those who have been placed in the dilemma, but of those who created it.[28]

Proportionality and Utility

Two general principles have been widely seen as underlying the particular provisions of the law of war.[29] In Chapters 4 and 5 I shall discuss the principle of discrimination, which distinguishes between people who are and are not legitimate objects of attack.

The principle of proportionality is said to require that the harm done by military action be in proportion to the military gain. However, when we examine the law of war we find that this principle has a very low profile. Article 28 of the Fourth Hague Convention reads, "The giving up to pillage of a town or place, even when taken by assault, is forbidden." The Geneva conventions require enemy troops incapacitated by wounds or illness to be cared for. Article 23 of the Fourth Hague Convention lists as "especially forbidden" several things that are cited as evidence for the law's adherence to proportionality:

(c) to kill or wound an enemy who, having laid down his arms, or having no longer means of defense, has surrendered at discretion;
(e) to employ arms, projectiles, or material of a nature to cause superfluous injury;
(g) to destroy or seize the enemy's property, unless such destruction or seizure be imperatively demanded by the necessities of war.

The intention of several of these rules is to limit damage to enemies who are able and willing to resist. Once a town has been declared open (undefended) or has been captured, its reduction is gratuitous, so the bombardment of an undefended town is prohibited. For the same reason the pillaging of a captured town is forbidden: It can serve no direct military purpose though it may serve indirect ones—intimidation, for example, or pleasing the troops. In former times these practices were accepted. Julius Caesar would capture a city and have all the men killed and the women and children sold into slavery, to encourage other towns not to resist. I know of no ancient writer who criticized these practices.[30] Today they are rightly criminal. Looting was an accepted source of income for soldiers throughout most of history; it too is now criminal.

Once a soldier surrenders, he is no longer a threat, so harming him is forbidden.[31] Article 23 (c) thus joins (e) in forbidding *superfluous* injury—injury that does not reduce the military strength of the enemy.

All these prohibitions presuppose a *principle of utility:* They forbid gratuitous or superfluous harm—harm that does not serve to bring about a military benefit. But to require that the harm bring a military benefit is not to require that the harm be proportional to that benefit. It is only to establish the much weaker principle that the harm must bring *some* military benefit. It allows inflicting a great deal of harm to obtain a modest benefit. The rules of bombardment, for example, allow the bombardment of defended localities and forbid the bombardment of undefended localities. These rules do not additionally require that the bombardment be proportional either to the strength of the defense or to the military value of the town. They allow the intensive bombardment of a town that is only lightly held by enemy troops or that occupies no crucial bit of terrain and possesses no great intrinsic value.

In Chapter 1, I quoted H.L.A. Hart on the difference between law and morality: Law requires strict guidelines in a way in which morality cannot. For the law to require that the harm be proportional to the military gain would establish a very inexact criterion and would raise questions about the legality of countless individual bombardments—questions that would usually be difficult to settle. A town might be lightly defended, but it might be vital to take the town quickly and that might justify a major bombardment. It might be heavily defended but of no consequence. The raising of all these questions every time a commander calls for an airstrike or artillery support would not, in practice, result in a gentler approach to bombardment. It would result in endless charges of criminality. So the law takes a different tack: It absolutely forbids bombardments if the town is undefended and allows it in all other cases.

From a moral point of view this solution is unsatisfactory. We cannot morally condone the destruction of a major city for the sake of a minor military gain. The law, within its limitations, stands on moral principles, but those principles by themselves are morally inadequate. I shall return to this point in Chapter 4.

Postscript: The State of War

There is a good deal of confusion about what a state of war is. In *An International Law of Guerrilla Warfare,* Keith Suter claimed that it is illegal under international law to declare war. To get around this, he wrote, "states now fight each other without formal declarations of war": "The word 'war' is now rarely used since war officially no longer exists: hence the use of the phrase armed conflict."[32] According to Suter, jurists and diplomats, attempting to place constraints on war, have only restricted the use of the word *war*—a poor reward for their efforts. It is not, however, illegal to declare war. In fact, the Hague conventions require a warning, declaration, or ultimatum before signatories go to war, and no subsequent development in international law has made compliance with this provision illegal.

Nor do wars require declarations of war. A war can occur between two nations even if no one has declared war. Hague convention signatories that go to war without declarations of war or of intent or warning violate the treaty, but that does not mean they are not at war. In the words of one legal text:

> The absence of a declaration, while it will involve the breach of a treaty obligation, will not of itself render the ensuing conflict any the less a war. . . . A state of war will arise upon the commission of an act of force, under the authority of a State, which is done *animo belligerandi* [in a belligerent spirit], or which being done *sine animo belligerandi* [without a belligerent spirit], the State against which it is directed . . . elects to regard as creating a state of war.[33]

In general, a state of war exists if a nation uses force against another, and the second resists with force. This does not require a declaration of war.

Confusions arise because authors mistake (1) the state of war and the legal state of war; (2) declared war and the legal state of war; and for the United States, (3) declared war with legal war.

The first distinction arises because two states may in fact be at war without a legal state of war existing between them. They may choose to maintain normal diplomatic and commercial relations—particularly if the fighting is localized or intermittent. The Falklands War is an example. Whether a legal state of war exists between two nations engaged in war is a matter for courts to decide.

The second distinction arises because whether a legal state of war exists between two states cannot be decided simply by seeing whether they have declared war on each other. They may not have declared war, yet a court, on the grounds that a loss claimed was due to a state of war, might reject an insurance claim. Did a captain's insurance policy, which excluded death due to war, cover his death in the Japanese attack on Pearl Harbor on December 7, 1941? Neither Japan nor the United States had declared war at the time of the attack, but a court ruled (*New York Life Insurance Company versus Bennion,* United States Circuit Court of Appeals, Tenth Circuit, 1946, 158 F.2d 260) that nonetheless his death was excluded: "When one sovereign nation attacks another with premeditated and deliberate intent to wage war against it, and that nation resists the attack with all the force at its command, we have war in the grim sense of reality. . . . To say that courts must shut their eyes to reality and wait for formalities, is to cut off their power to reason with concrete facts."[34] Declarations of war are not necessary for a legal state of war to exist.

Nor is the declaration of war a sufficient condition for a legal state of war. Though World War II ended in 1945, Britain and the United States did not sign peace treaties with Germany until many years later. British courts have ruled that the legal state of war between Britain and Germany ended when hostilities ended in 1945—though the declaration of war remained in effect until the peace treaty was signed and replaced the 1945 armistice of surrender. U.S. courts, in contrast, ruled that a legal state of war still existed between Germany and the United States in 1948.[35] It is irrelevant to our concerns to inquire into the legal state of war in this sense which bears more on the status of commercial contracts and insurance regulations than on any moral questions.

More to the point: When states engage in armed conflicts with other states, they are at war and the law of war applies. Whether they issue declarations of war or whether there is a legal state of war is irrelevant. The law of war is the law of war, not the law of declared war or of legal states of war. If both sides want to regard an armed conflict as less than a war, its legal status can suit their wishes. They can retain diplomatic relations with one another, and other nations can go on conducting normal business with either or both. But they are still bound by the law of war, which applies to all armed conflicts between states.

The third distinction is a matter for U.S. constitutional law. Throughout U.S. history, presidents have used armed force without declarations of war. It is frequently claimed that this violates the Constitution, because the Constitution grants Congress the right to declare war. The Supreme Court, by refusing to judge the issue, has left the question in the hands of Congress and the presidency. It has said in effect that it is up to Congress to restrict or allow the president war powers, that it is not a constitutional question but a legislative one. By not acting, the Supreme Court has refused to rule these undeclared wars unconstitutional; thus it seems they are not. If that is so, a U.S. war may be legal (not unconstitutional) but undeclared.

The issue is confused because, first, there are uses of compulsory means in retorsion and reprisal that legally are acts short of war: the embargo of foreign merchant ships or the freezing of a country's assets. Second, even acts of armed force (naval blockades, bombardments, and uninvited troop landings on foreign soil, for example) can be acts short of war—when, for example, they are done to protect endangered nationals. Calling a war something else will not change its legal character, but neither is every use of armed force an act of war. The Israeli raid at Entebbe was not an act of war directed against Uganda,[36] whereas what was going on along the border between Iran and Iraq during the 1980s was a war.

However, a naval blockade or armed intervention even done *sine animo belligerandi* becomes an act of war if the other side chooses to regard it as one and uses force to oppose it. It is a *casus belli;* whether it is an actual act of war depends on the response.

Though the issue might seem purely terminological and legalistic, it is not. There are circumstances in which a nation that starts a war is morally at fault, and it can matter very much whether that nation really did start *a war.* Technically a state of war (though with an armistice) existed in the 1980s between Israel and Syria. But if either attacked the other unprovoked the attacker would be morally guilty of starting a war.

(Consider a case I shall discuss in Chapter 3. A sends troops into B purely to protect A's citizens in B—a job that B has proven incapable of doing. B's troops clash with A's, and the two are at war. Who started the war: A, whose acts constituted a casus belli, or B, who turned an incident into a war?)

Even if there is fighting between the troops of two nations, there may not be a war. Suppose that because of an insulting remark soldiers of two states have an armed clash at a border outpost. If their governments honestly regret the incident, exchange urgent notes of explanation, and quickly make sure the fighting ends, no war will have taken place.

The character of war is brought out most clearly if we realize that even if the soldiers of two nations fight each other *with* the authorization of their governments, there may not be a war. A UN General Assembly report on defining aggression says that the Security Council might decide that a country that initiated a use of armed force was not guilty of a war of aggression because the incident lacked "sufficient gravity."[37] The idea is that because an act of aggression might not have sufficient gravity, every *act* of aggression does not amount to launching a *war* of aggression. Imagine that the prime minister of A orders one of his soldiers to throw a snowball across the border at one of B's soldiers, and the soldier from B retaliates in kind. The snowball attack is an act of aggression, and the incident might lead to war, but it would be exaggerating to say that the authorized flight of the snowball, even with the counterstroke, constituted a war.

In the last quarter century the Soviet Union and China have had several serious armed border clashes—not just snowball fights—but they have not fought a single war with each other. Every armed clash between two states is not a war, and it would be wrong to charge a state with initiating a war if in fact it had only initiated a border clash.

So nations can fight one another without being at war. In the Sino-Soviet border disputes each side, by its willingness to use force, showed its unwillingness to bow to the other. Yet because neither side resolved to settle the location of the frontier by force, these clashes did not become wars. An armed clash becomes a war when one side attempts to settle—not merely make a point about—a dispute through armed conflict. Had the Soviet Union or China decided to obtain the borders it wanted through armed struggle there would have been a war. Because each side was content to use force to demonstrate its rejection of the other side's claims, there was not.

Even in an age of limited wars, there is wisdom in Lauterpacht's traditional definition of war as "a contention between two or more States through their armed forces, for the purpose of overpowering the other and imposing such conditions of peace as the victor pleases."[38] The General Assembly report was sensible in not bringing full charges against a state that commits a much lesser offense. A war is limited if, for one of the combatants, the issue is not worth its full effort. But what makes even a limited war a war is the decision to settle the issue by force.

This sheds semantic light, if not legal light, on the U.S. Constitution. The Constitution reserves for Congress the right to declare war. But a foreign warship might fire on a U.S. ship, and the president order a retaliatory strike, without there being a war. As Aristotle said, "One swallow does not make a spring." Israel's raid on Entebbe to free its hostages was not a war—not even a very brief war. Israel has never fought a war with Uganda. The United States has taken casualties in Beirut but has not been at war there. The control of armed conflicts that fall short of war is in the hands of the president—the commander in chief. Short of a constitutional amendment, Congress cannot legislate new meanings for the Constitution's words on the division of powers. War in the Constitution means war in common parlance—not sixty days in a hot spot.

In Korea and Vietnam the United States really was at war, without Congress having issued declarations of war. Some defenders of presidential powers contend that precisely because these wars were undeclared, they did not violate the constitutional provision. In other words, because the Constitution allows only the Congress to declare war, and these wars were undeclared, the respective presidents complied with its terms.

This makes a mockery of the constitutional provision. It would mean that the Founding Fathers wished to reserve for Congress only a right of nomenclature—the right to declare certain wars *wars.* Surely that is not what the Founders had in mind. They intended a real restriction, not a semantic one. They were establishing a division, not of authorized vocabularies, but of powers.

The Founders meant that only Congress can declare a war in the sense in which governments can declare elections. To declare an election not to proclaim an episode of voting officially entitled to be called an *election.* It is to decide that there will be an episode of voting. Congress's power "to declare the punishment of treason" under Article III is the power to decide the punishment of treason, not the power to make a declaration of what another branch of government has the power to effect but not declare.

Just as Congress cannot legislate uncommon meanings for the Constitution's words on division of powers, the executive cannot pronounce constitutional reservations of powers to be rhetorical. If the Constitution allowed the commander in chief to engage the country in undeclared wars, Congress's power to declare war would be virtually no power at all. It would only be a power of public pronouncement—on a level with the ability to declare National Pickle Week.

In fact, through such vehicles as the Gulf of Tonkin Resolution, Congress authorized the Korean and Vietnam wars, satisfying the constitutional requirement. Declarations of war do not have to begin "we declare." An ultimatum or statement of intent will do. In 1939 Neville Chamberlain acknowledged, rather than declared, war with Germany: Germany had failed to reply to Britain's ultimatum and Chamberlain told the British people, "consequently this country is at war with Germany." Would anyone want to argue that if the president involved the country in a war with congressional approval, the war would still be unconstitutional unless Congress passed a resolution whose subject was "the Congress," and whose operative verb was "declare" taking the object "war"?

Suggestions for Further Reading

The treaty texts are short and are presented together with interesting discussions in A. Pearce Higgins, *The Hague Peace Conferences and Other International Conferences Concerning the Laws and Usages of War: Texts of Conventions with Commentaries* (Cambridge University Press, Cambridge, 1909). Morris Greenspan, *The Modern Law of Land Warfare* (University of California Press, Berkeley, 1959), gives an account of all the topics discussed in this chapter, whereas in Peter D. Trooboff, ed., *Law and Responsibility in Warfare* (University of North Carolina Press, Chapel Hill, 1975), there are at times heated, Vietnam-era discussions of the law of bombardment. Lord McNair and A. D. Watts, *The Legal Effects of War* (Cambridge University Press, Cambridge, 1966), covers the legal state of war.

3

The Justification of War

The shield he has is newly built, a perfect round;
On it a two-fold emblem, cleverly contrived:
A full-armed warrior is displayed in hammered gold;
A woman leading him goes modestly before.
"Justice" she says her name is, as the lettering
Will show.

—Aeschylus
Seven Against Thebes

The Historical Context

"Stalin is a university graduate and a man of great studies. He is a man, who, when he sees a great mistake, admits it and corrects it. Today in Russia, Communism is practically non-existent," said Tryphosa Duncan Bates-Batcheller, addressing the 1942 national convention of the Daughters of the American Revolution.[1] Mrs. Bates-Batcheller's wishful thinking when her gaze turned to the international arena was not without precedent in the years that led to World War II. In the 1930s, in what was perhaps the most successful mass antiwar movement in history, thousands of college students in Britain and the United States signed the Oxford Pledge, vowing that they would never go to war.

A few years later almost all those signatories were in uniform, their pledges withered and scattered in the swirling autumn winds as the German and Soviet armies crossed the Polish border that last September of the decade.[2] "The gathering storm," Churchill called those days, and when the dark thunderhead clouds swept over Europe and the first raindrops fell, the ink ran on the paper currency of college idealism. Like the Confederate money people have used to wallpaper their dens, its value was decorative, not redemptive. The pledges had promoted the heady, self-congratulatory air of youthful idealism and moral superiority—a short-lived pleasure for which many would soon pay dearly.

This move toward pacifism began as a response to the great bloodbath of World War I and ended in discredit as World War II drew near. Immediately after World War II pacifism showed some signs of resurgence as a movement toward world federation, but it was doused again by the cold war. In the 1960s and 1970s it revived in the more moderate form of a movement, not against war, but against nuclear war—a movement to restrict, rather than abolish, war. In this section I shall follow the movement's history; in the next two sections I shall examine its parallel legal and moral threads.

The Industrialization of War

In New York City, across from the Plaza Hotel, one can rent a horse-drawn carriage for a jaunt through Central Park. At the end of the workday the carriage operators, obeying a constraint that for thousands of years limited the size of armies, drive the horses back to the barn. Horses in the wild spend the day grazing. Work horses have other things to do, so when the day's work is done their owners must feed them. There is not enough time left in the day for the horses to get their caloric needs through grazing. (Horses sleep at night.) The trade is food for labor.

The Central Park horses wear one of the great technological breakthroughs of the Middle Ages—the modern yoke, which distributes the load to the horse's shoulders. In the ancient world horses were harnessed with ropes that were tied around their necks. The heavier the load, the more the horse choked itself as it pulled; therefore, carts were slow and lightly laden. The military cart, inevitably weighed down with the personal gear that makes a soldier's life tolerable, was a luxury fast-moving armies could not afford. Philip of Macedon forbade carts in his army. In Afghanistan his son, Alexander the Great, ordered the carts and their contents burned, starting with his own. Scipio Africanus the Younger, given command of a Roman army, had a more prudent solution: He ordered the carts sold.

The pack animal, not the cart, was an army's normal transport, particularly away from roads. As a pack animal, a horse can carry about 200 pounds, day after day. But at the end of each day, the horse still has to be fed, and on a journey there will be no waiting barn. The horse must carry its own food—20 pounds per day. If grass is plentiful along the route, the driver can reduce the horse's food requirement to 10 pounds of grain a day and let the horse forage for the remainder. The driver has to eat too: During the U.S. Civil War the normal allotment was 3 pounds per person per day. Assuming that water is available along the route (and does not have to be carried too), at the end of a ten-day journey, the horse and driver will deliver 70 pounds of supplies. They consumed the other 130 on the journey.

The people of Imperial Rome owed their bread to the fleets of grain ships that carried the harvest surplus from the fertile Nile Delta to Italy—the largest ships the ancient world knew, the largest ships seen in the West until the modern age. But until the Industrial Revolution, overland supply lines were remarkably short. Grain and other bulk cargoes could be carried long distances only by ship. On land, caravans transported precious cargo low in weight and high in value: spices and silk, jewels and gold. Away from the sea and navigable rivers, an army found its supplies in the area that stretched a few days' march around it. This was still the norm two thousand years later in Napoleon's time, though the yoke and cart were improved, and this norm accounts for Napoleon's disastrous retreat from Moscow in 1812. Armies lived off the surrounding countryside, and when the countryside was incapable of supplying them, as the interior of Russia was that winter, the armies starved.

The limited area from which preindustrial armies could obtain supplies constrained the size of those armies. Another constraint shortened the supply line further. In theory Alexander the Great's army could have been supplied over a twenty-five-day overland journey, but on a track wide enough for pack animals to travel 4 abreast, this would have required a caravan seventy-five miles long with over 100,000 animals. Aside from the difficulty of obtaining so many animals and feeding them, the length of the caravan would itself pose "an interesting logistic problem," as the Macedonian army was known to march more than nineteen miles a day. At sundown the exhausted soldiers would be settling into the new day's camp, while two-thirds of the baggage train would still be waiting to start out.[3]

All this changed in the late nineteenth century. In the U.S., Civil War armies were supplied by railroad for the first time. By 1914 rapid industrialization had brought about exponential growth of armies. The German army called up for World War I was 900 percent larger than it had been in the Franco-Prussian War just forty years earlier. The mobilizing Germans used 550 troop trains a day to rail their army across the Rhine. The French used 7,000 trains in sixteen days to transport 3,781,000 soldiers—at times trains "succeeded one another at the rate of one . . . every eight minutes."[4]

Alexander the Great's army had numbered about 25,000; in World War I 56 million men served under arms. In both time and space, war became continuous, as the railroad allowed armies to grow larger. In earlier times the campaigning season had ended when the harvest was taken in and the army went into winter quarters; the railroad allowed armies to be supplied in the field through the winter. And earlier armies were local presences, marching from town to town to find one another and do battle; in World War I the armies stood on a continuous front stretching from the English Channel to Switzerland.

Another change was even more momentous. Modern armies fought with missile weapons. Weapons for hand-to-hand combat—the sword, pike, or thrusting spear—survived only in the vestigial form of the bayonet, clipped to the rifle as an afterthought. Earlier armies had used missile weapons too—the sling-propelled rock, the arrow, and the throwing spear. But the victor retrieved the missiles after the battle. Arrows were too expensive to "fire and forget." By 1914 armies were fighting with explosive missiles that self-destruct on use. Only the launchers—rifles, artillery pieces, torpedo tubes—were durable, and they are useless without the missiles. Munitions had to be constantly delivered to the front if the troops were to remain a fighting force. At the start of World War I Britain produced 30,000 artillery shells a month. A year later it was 1.2 million. A Roman legion needed only a few tons of supplies a week, but

> by 1916 a British division in the line needed some twenty [railroad] wagons of food and thirty of ammunition each day. . . . British gunners fired 1,723,873 rounds in the preliminary bombardment on the Somme in 1916—each of the 18-pounders began the battle with 1,000 rounds on the gun position. Even this was dwarfed by the 4,282,550 shells fired in the early stages of the Third Battle of Ypres the following year: this bombardment . . . represented a year's production by 55,000 munitions workers.[5]

Motorization carried the process further:

> The mechanization of armies had far-reaching consequences. J.F.C. Fuller pointed out that, although an army's requirements for petrol would grow as motor vehicles replaced horses, petrol was less bulky and more easily transported than fodder. He lent weight to his case by noting that though the British had shipped 5,253,538 tons of ammunition to France during the First War, the greatest single item of tonnage was oats and hay—5,438,602 tons of it. Horses munched their way through fodder even when resting: motor transport used fuel only when running.[6]

Trucks and trains brought a drastic change in the relation between the forces in the field and the civilian population at home that now fed them. The Roman legion needed only occasional instructions and replacements from Rome, but had the Germans cut the road to Verdun, over which a French truck passed every fourteen seconds during the great World War I battle that was fought there, the French would have lost the war. The modern army was far too large to supply from local sources:

> The scale of operations [in World War I] was incomparably so much greater than anything men had experienced that the generals and general staffs were beyond their depths when they started. Like the schoolboy who merely reads about the massing millions, they were awed by what they saw approaching. But they could not fathom it. France at mobilization had 4,000 artillery pieces. This was thought to be enough for victory. She had to build another 36,000 before the war ended. Her 2,500 automatic weapons were a token of the 315,000 machine guns to come.[7]

The fighting forces had become parasitical off the industrial strength of the homeland—off its manufacturing ability and its transportation system. The artillery shell made in London went by truck to a train station, by train to a port, by ship to another port, by train to a depot, and by truck again to the battery, whose guns sent it on the last and shortest leg of its journey. Break this chain and the army would break; weaken it and the army would be weakened.

Industrialization made armies larger and more destructive. Never before had so many men been intent on doing grievous harm to one another or been so well prepared to do so. This increased capability, drawn from the industrial base to the rear, was purchased at the price of increased dependence on the hinterland. Food, munitions, weapons, gasoline—all had to be produced or imported and constantly conveyed to the front. This new dependence of the army on the noncombatant population, which by World War I could be called "the home front," would by World War II draw the interest of military thinkers.

In August 1914, as six million soldiers groped toward each other, Kaiser Wilhelm told his departing Imperial German troops: "You will be home before the leaves have fallen from the trees." His brave public words hid another response he had exhibited a week earlier when, returning from a cruise, he realized that Germany was headed inexorably toward war: "On the station platform he cried out to Bethmann-Hollweg: 'How did it all happen?' Pale of face, utterly cowed, the Chancellor admitted to the Kaiser that all along he had been deceived by [Austrian Foreign Minister] Berchtold and forthwith offered his resignation. Wilhelm replied: 'You've cooked this broth and now you're going to eat it.' "[8] Thus began the Great War for hegemony over Europe. Over the next four years almost ten million people would die in the struggle, and Germany would not be denied its victory until troops from the New World entered the fray.

It was a war in which combat troops suffered ghastly and incomprehensible losses in campaign after campaign. Previous wars had seen great suffering, but nothing on this scale, nor with so little, year after year, to show for it. The continuous entrenched front deprived the combatants of the ability to maneuver, throw the enemy off balance, and produce quick and relatively painless victory—as would happen time after time in World War II. To attack meant to go right at the enemy. But the machine gun, and the assembly-line efficiency with which it was used, made that impossible. The guns were sited to create overlapping fields of fire; their operators trained to traverse their weapons back and forth at a drilled rate. They did not aim—that was unnecessary. The rate of traverse, the overlap of fields of fire, and the rate of fire of the guns themselves had all been calculated to ensure a hail of bullets that no man could penetrate—a "killing zone." Later in the war the machine gun lost its battlefield dominance to its natural enemy, the artillery piece. But for the infantry on the attack, nothing had improved. Death by artillery shell replaced death by machine gun. Only toward the end of the war, as the tank came into use, did the attacker regain an offensive ability.

It would be pointless in a book like this to recount the history of the war. But to understand the postwar mood requires some familiarity with the conduct of war in a conflict that began in high spirits and ended in a dark and somber melancholy. I will briefly recount two of its most important battles.[9]

In February 1916 Germany opened the battle of Verdun, a French fortified area whose loss, the Germans thought, would shatter French morale. The theory was that though Germany did not have the manpower to fight a long war against the enemies allied against it—eventually the weight of numbers would tell—it did have numerical superiority over France. If that superiority could be used to bleed France, France would break and the alliance would crumble.

In preparation, the Germans deployed hundreds of artillery pieces in the Verdun area and built five rail spurs to feed them ammunition. By the eve of the battle the Germans had brought up 3 million artillery rounds. The attack began on February 21 with a twelve-hour bombardment, during which more than 100,000 shells an hour—about 1,600 per minute—were hurled at the six-mile front. The next morning the bombardment continued.

On February 25 a major French fort fell, and it began to look as though the German plan might succeed. But that day Philippe Pétain took over and organized the defense of Verdun, and French reinforcements began moving there. The Germans had temporarily exhausted their ammunition supply. While they built it up, Pétain, realizing that the existing railways could not supply the half-million French troops in the area, got together 3,000 trucks to establish the first motorized supply system in military history—*la voie sacrée* (the sacred way). The attack supplied by rail was countered by truck.

The Germans began a new round of attacks on March 6 against aptly named Dead Man Hill, and a third round on April 9. Shortly thereafter, the French began counterattacking, which they continued to do during the summer. It was almost Christmas before the Verdun front grew quiet again. By then the French had recaptured the ground they had lost in February. The battle, indecisive as a military operation, caused 900,000 casualties.

While the French were slowly pushing the Germans back at Verdun, the British opened an offensive on the Somme, where the German Second Army had been weakened to provide troops for Verdun. When the Second Army's commander, Fritz von Below, told the German commander, Erich von Falkenhayn, that the British would attack, "Falkenhayn told him it was a wonderful hope. Having splintered his own army by throwing it against the unmovable object, Falkenhayn couldn't imagine that the enemy would be equally stupid."[10]

The attack began at 7:28 on the morning of July 1, 1916, after a week-long barrage that had involved 1.5 million artillery rounds. A half hour after his troops had gone over the top, General Sir Douglas Haig, the British commander, wrote in his diary, "Reports . . . most satisfactory." His optimism was unfounded. By evening more than half of his 110,000 attacking troops were casualties. In that one day the British army suffered about a fifth of the casualties that the United States took in ten years in Vietnam. No important ground had been won.

These battles were not unusual in World War I. At First Ypres the British and French lost almost 250,000 men and Germany, 130,000. Third Ypres (Passchendaele), preceded by a three million–shell, two-week bombardment, cost the British 30,000 the first day, and 250,000 in all. On the Somme 1 million men fell in an area seven miles by seven. The Nivelle offensive on the Aisne in April 1917 cost the French 187,000 casualties in eleven days. The five-week battle of Arras that began on April 4, 1917, cost the British 160,000 for a gain of 7,000 yards on a twenty-two-mile front. In three week's fighting in the Meuse-Argonne the United States averaged 1,000 battle deaths a day. "Being shelled," a soldier observed, "is the main work of an infantry soldier."[11]

In battle deaths it was as though the entire U.S. Civil War had been fought over and over again every three weeks for four years.[12] The blood of these men would fill 2,250,000 five-gallon gerry cans. If it were gasoline, it could fill the average car's fuel tank a million times on a 225 million–mile journey. Forty-five thousand tons of blood—the weight of 18,000 automobiles. Enough blood to float a battleship or fill a medium tanker. Enough blood to cover a football field eight feet deep.

Pacifism Between the World Wars

The 1921 *Encyclopedia Americana* article on the western front by John Bassett of Smith College could still rise to an optimistic viewpoint reviewing the battlefield carnage. Granting, for example, that Third Ypres was a failure (British losses were heavier than those of Germans, and in three months only the objectives for the first two weeks had been taken), Bassett could still say:

> But the struggle was not all lost. It served to reduce the manpower of the Germans and to push them back on the east from dangerous proximity to Ypres and Hazebrouck. They were by that much—five precious miles—further away from the Channel than they would have been when in April 1918, they made their last great drive in that direction, and nearly reached the hills southwest of Ypres from which the glistening waters of the Channel can be seen on a clear day. In finding the balance of loss and gain the conclusion may be that the operations were worth all they cost in death and miserable living.[13]

The British had "worked their way forward across lines of defense that seemed beyond human ability to take . . . but pluck and courage had triumphed." They captured the high ground; the Germans were pushed back.

The desire to make the best of a bad thing that we see in this passage did not hold up for long in the postwar years. Not many people would see depriving the Germans of a view of the English Channel's glistening waters as worth a quarter of a million casualties. Disillusion set in—it was already forming in the last years of war—and mingled with prewar religious pacifism. In the 1930s, pacifism was combined with the class antagonism of the depression in the claim that the rich arms manufacturers had led the world into the Great War to increase sales, much as an oil company might promote summer travel.

Daddy Warbucks became a cartoon figure in the newspapers; *Merchants of Death* by Carol Engelbrecht Helmuth and Frank Cleary Hanighen became a Book-of-the-Month Club selection. In the Senate, Gerald Nye of North Dakota headed a committee investigating wartime profiteering in the munitions industry. Republican isolationists joined Communists in denouncing the industrialists and imperialists who, they claimed, had misled the United States into the Great War. Revisionist historians attacked the moralistic pretenses of the war, while philosophers proclaimed there was no truth or falsity at all on moral questions. A *Literary Digest* poll in 1935 indicated that 80 percent of U.S. college students would not serve in the military if the United States invaded another country, and 16 percent would not serve even if the United States were invaded.[14]

These sentiments contrasted with events in Europe, Asia, and Africa, where aggressive powers were on the march. Austria, Czechoslovakia, Ethiopia, and China were being absorbed at the point of a gun, and the newsreels made pacifism look like an increasingly utopian position. After the capitulation of the democracies to Adolf Hitler in the Munich agreement, one prominent pacifist agreed that "those people are probably right who think the four-power deal . . . is unlikely to accomplish any good. They lapse into sentimentalism, however," he added, "if they think war would accomplish more. There is only one course that will not lead to practically certain disaster: It is a renunciation of the game of power politics."[15] Another prominent pacifist, Oswald Garrison Villard, went further. "Great armaments," he wrote, "bring with them increased worship of the State, increased nationalism, increased State service, and therefore play into the hands of . . . Hitler and Mussolini."[16]

But if the democracies abandoned armaments and renounced the game of power politics, who would be left on the field and who would be declared the winner? The tide was turning, and Reinhold Niebuhr, a pacifist in the 1920s, spoke for many when in 1937 he asked whether "peace is always preferable to the exploitation of the weak by the strong."[17]

The embarrassing struggle between the demands of the real world and the proclamations of pacifists reached a high point in the twists and turns of the U.S. Communist party in the prewar years. In the mid-1930s the party had opposed war as a capitalist phenomenon. But in 1938 Moscow sought defense treaties with the Western democracies, and the party abruptly switched its views. Its youth groups renounced the Oxford Pledge. A year later Moscow, rebuffed and distrusted by the democratic powers, signed an alliance with Germany, and the party again reversed course. It created the American Peace Mobilization and denounced the war in Europe, precipitated by the Moscow-Berlin pact, as an imperialist struggle. (In France the Communist party urged French soldiers to refuse to fight in the "imperialist war" with Germany.)

In the spring of 1941 the American Peace Mobilization's antiwar campaign got into high gear with the proclamation of National Peace Week, aiming to keep the United States out of the war in Europe. National Peace Week began on the first day of summer, with antiwar demonstrators picketing the White House. As fate would have it, that very day three German army groups crossed the partition line separating German- and Soviet-occupied Poland, and Russia was at war. This required another reversal of party policy—the fourth in five years. The American Peace Mobilization was quickly renamed the American People's Mobilization. Its goals were now just the opposite of what they had been on June 20: "National Peace Week, of course, was never mentioned again."[18]

The frequent and cynical reversals of Communist stance in the late 1930s and early 1940s caused them some embarrassment and lost them a great deal of sympathy among the non-Communist Left. But the Communists were always true in their fashion. They were not ideological pacifists (that is, they were not really pacifists at all). Their pacifism was a matter of convenience, of tactics rather than principle. When pacifism seemed in the interest of the Soviet Union (and hence of the workers' world revolution), they were for it; when it seemed not in Russia's interest, they were against it. They understood the priorities and held to them consistently, though in the process they abused the faith some well-meaning people placed in their pronouncements of principle.

The self-inflicted humiliation suffered by the Communists was peculiarly public, but the same forces were whipsawing all pacifist groups: International aggression was on the march, and it was difficult, to say the least, to see the sense of "opposing" it with nonresistance. Not while Hitler was occupying Austria, Czechoslovakia, and Poland. Not while Russia was swallowing the Baltic states, the western Ukraine, and southeastern Finland. Not while Italy was settling into Greece and Ethiopia. Not while Japan was taking over Indochina.

Political reality in the form of armies on the march was shattering the U.S. peace movement. Pearl Harbor completed the process: "In December, 1941, just nineteen months after the Methodist Church, the largest Protestant denomination in the United States, proclaimed that it would never 'officially support, endorse or participate in war,' its bishops voted that 'the Methodists of America will loyally support our President and our nation.'"[19]

The serious pacifism of the 1930s leaned in the direction of Mohandas Gandhi's pacifism, holding that war is immoral and that citizens should refuse to participate in it. It foundered as international aggression made the case for defense. It was, after all, one thing to practice nonviolent resistance against the relatively civilized British; it would have been quite another to practice it against the Nazi SS or the Imperial Japanese Army. (Gandhi's advice to Jews in Nazi-occupied lands was that they should commit suicide.) I shall assume without any argument that this sort of pacifism is misguided: People sometimes have the right to defend themselves and others with deadly force. Under certain conditions they may have a moral duty to do so.[20]

World Federation

After World War II U.S. pacifism came to be dominated by a new theme, which reached its peak of popularity in the late 1940s when the United World Federalists, spurred on by the *Saturday Review*'s Norman Cousins, attained a membership of 50,000.[21] A nation settling down to peace and presented with the awesome threat revealed at Hiroshima and Nagasaki found some of its desires answered with the vision of a war-free world under the banner of a strengthened UN, rather than as a consequence of millions of individual decisions of conscience. "Nations," Cousins argued, "should retain the right to maintain their own cultures and political institutions . . . but the U.N. should have authority in matters related to world security and world development."[22]

In a book written during the war in Vietnam, Donald A. Wells said that he had considered blaming war on mankind's "invincible stupidity" and "ineluctable depravity": "How else can we account for the fact that the human race has known how to solve its problems so much longer than it has been willing to have them solved? We confront international anarchy and knowing that it leads to war, we fear to part with this last vestige of international license."[23] Wars are caused by "inept, unthinking, and callous statesmen and citizens."[24] The answer is a federal world government. After all, he pointed out, the United States has avoided internal wars (with one notable exception from 1861 to 1865) by federating. Why not do the same for the whole world?[25] We will not go to war with others, the idea seems to be, if we officially define those others to be ourselves. With a single world government, there would be no one left to fight. War becomes not just unlikely, but impossible.

Carl Sagan's 1985 novel, *Contact,* offers a recent popular example of this thinking. Sagan imagined that orbiting satellite stations have become retirement homes for the wealthy who, from their vantage point in space, see that the earth is a single planet:

> National boundaries are as invisible as meridians of longitude, or the Tropics of Cancer and Capricorn. The boundaries are arbitrary. The planet is real.
>
> Spaceflight, therefore, is subversive. If they are fortunate enough to find themselves in Earth orbit, most people, after a little meditation, have similar thoughts. The nations that had instituted spaceflight had done so largely for nationalistic reasons; it was a small irony that almost everyone who entered space received a startling glimpse of a transnational perspective, of the Earth as one world.
>
> It wasn't hard to imagine a time when the predominant loyalty would be to this blue world.[26]

After a few years these people, supported by the scientists of all nations, communicate their vision to those below—to the politicians and the common people (those who have neither riches nor doctorates). And the people who go to war even though the planet is blue, and not the patchwork quilt of orange, yellow, red, and purple we see on maps, see the error of their ways.

Just how this would work, however, is unclear, for in a federation the UN would still be, as it is now, a cacophony of divergent interests, and as the Lebanese, Congolese, Ethiopian, Chinese, Nigerian, Greek, Spanish, Russian, Cuban, Sudanese, and Cambodian civil wars have shown in the twentieth century, a common government does not prevent war. In the absence of substantive agreement among the factions within the country, a common government produces civil war. It is not because the U.S. states have a common federal government that they are unlikely to go to war with one another. It is the other way around: The states have a common government in part because they are unlikely to go to war with one another—though perhaps they are more likely to go to war with one another than with Canada. The bloodiest dispute in the nation's history, the Civil War, would not have occurred if the North and South had *not* formed a single government.

The difficulties become glaring if we consider taking a mild dose of world federalism. Forming a single world government would involve transcending scores of international conflicts—Greece and Turkey, Iran and Iraq, Afghanistan and the Soviet Union, Britain and Argentina, Israel and Syria, Cambodia and Vietnam, India and Pakistan, China and Vietnam, Argentina and Chile. Suppose we minimize the problems and just federate with one or two problem countries: with Libya and perhaps Iran. It worked for Connecticut and Massachusetts. Needless to say, it would not work. It is like suggesting that two people who cannot stand each other get married, on the grounds that if they were married they would get along.

Federation suggests that the nations of the world, though members of a single world state, could remain pretty much as they are now: About the only thing that would change is that war would be abolished. But what would it mean for nations to retain "their own cultures and political institutions"? Might one state be an Israel and another a Nazi Germany? The people of some of the federated states would be allowed uncensored access to the debates going on in the world government, whereas others would hear only what their local governments wanted them to hear. Would these states still have an equal say in world governance? Would the federal world government be a single-party dictatorship or would it be a Western-style democracy? Would its deliberations be secret or open? Would world newspapers be government organs on the lines of *Pravda* or independent on the lines of the *New York Times?*

All this, and much more, is swept under the rug with the word *federation,* as though war could be abolished through a formal proclamation, while all the serious differences and conflicting interests that lead nations to war could remain, rendered impotent by the power of the word. It presupposes that a world government could exist that had no moral or political principles, composed of any nations whatsoever, regardless of their ways.

The fact is there is not enough commonality of ways between Americans and the Italians, let alone the Russians or Libyans, to allow confederation. And if Sagan is impressed that national borders do not show up from space—that nations are not really different colors the way they are on political maps—others are equally impressed by the number of East Germans who have died, and continue to die, trying to cross that electrified imaginary color line, guarded by packs of attack dogs, land mines, machine guns wired to fire automatically, and trigger-happy border police, that locks them in. The East Germans would have a far easier time trying to cross many of the natural features that do show up from space: sailing across the Bering Strait in an inner tube or climbing the Rocky Mountains on all fours. For the Danish and German Jews in the 1940s the "arbitrary" line between Denmark and Germany was the difference between life and death even though Denmark and Germany are not really two different colors.[27]

Wells was wrong to think that wars are caused by "inept, unthinking, and callous statesmen and citizens." The cause of war is not that politicians and commoners lack the good sense and sound humanitarian values of Carl Sagan or Donald Wells. Nations do sometimes blunder into war: World War I is often cited as an example. But just as often, nations blunder into peace—the Versailles Treaty ending World War I, for example, and blunder by *not* going to war, as France did when the Nazis occupied the Rhineland. Nations blunder, period, just as philosophers and astronomers do, though the blunders of nations have more serious consequences. But they do not blunder into war any more than they blunder into or out of anything else.

The "what fools these mortals be" approach convinces only college freshmen. As Michael Howard said, "Whatever may be the underlying causes of international conflict . . . wars begin with conscious and reasoned decisions based on the calculation, made by both parties, that they can achieve more by going to war than by remaining at peace."[28] Sometimes they are right. Whether what they do is also morally right is, of course, a different question.

The Legal Context

In the twentieth century, pacifism has been cultivated in hothouse forms—strange and exotic growths incapable of surviving in the wild and weedy world beyond the fragile, sheltering glass. But between the two world wars a hardier variety escaped the greenhouse and put down roots in the real world.

The Paris Pact

In 1928, on the initiative of the French and U.S. governments, the General Treaty for the Renunciation of War (more widely known as the Paris Pact or the Kellogg-Briand Pact) came into existence. By now it has been signed by more than sixty nations and is a fundamental document in international law. It is little known by the general public because too much was expected of it, and when it did not meet those expectations, it suffered a normal fate: dismissed as a disappointment, while its merits were ignored.

The disappointment arose because many people thought it outlawed war,[29] and many of those people thought in turn that if war were outlawed, wars would not occur. They were wrong on both counts. Had the pact outlawed war, that would not have meant there would be no wars—robbery is illegal but still occurs. Making a practice illegal need not abolish it. And the pact did not outlaw war in the first place:

> Article I. The High Contracting Parties solemnly declare, in the names of their respective peoples, that they condemn recourse to war for the

> solution of international controversies and renounce it as an instrument of national policy in their relations with one another.
>
> ART. II. The High Contracting Parties agree that the settlement or solution of all disputes or conflicts, of whatever nature or whatever origin they may be, which may arise among them, shall never be sought except by pacific means.

This does not forbid war between nonsignatories or with nonsignatories. And it was never understood to outlaw self-defense.

The pact's preamble says that its benefits are denied to a signatory that resorts to war "to promote its national interest." In the interpretational correspondence that led to the pact, this was understood, as Article I states, to forbid war as an instrument of *national* policy while allowing war "as a measure of collective action for the enforcement of international obligations by virtue of existing instruments."[30] A nation, though not acting in self-defense, might under the terms of the pact be justified in coming to the aid of another nation that had been attacked or in joining other nations to enforce a legal obligation. This allows collective action to right an international wrong—a wrong that might exist even if no hostile acts have occurred. Finally, the pact does not preclude to that end acts of force that legally fall short of acts of war. Naval blockades, for example: "Though measures of force short of war are compulsive means, they are still pacific means."[31]

The pact, in short, forbids the use of force to change existing international legal relations, but not to enforce them. Even aside from these restrictions, the pact may seem a failure. Not only did it fail to abolish war, but even the types of war it did outlaw have continued to take place. The Argentinean invasion of the Falklands, for example, was an attempt of a nation acting on its own to change existing legal relations by force.

Suppose nation A commits a grave offense against nation B, an offense that traditionally is a casus belli, but that falls short of being an act of war. What is nation B to do? The pact tells B that it may not go to war to enforce its rights, but offers B no alternative unilateral means of securing its goal, and guarantees no effective collective means. A nation that feels itself sufficiently aggrieved may decide that violating the pact is a lesser evil than allowing the status quo to continue. Sometimes this claim is defensible. In its most basic aspects this is a very enduring problem: To outlaw war may be to freeze the status quo and hence to legitimate grave injustices.

Moreover, the Paris Pact had no enforcement mechanisms and established no alternative means by which nations could resolve the disputes that lead to war. Nations initiating wars almost always claim to be acting in self-defense in one way or other: World War II began with the Germans staging a pretend Polish attack on a German radio station. Hitler claimed this attack gave Germany the right to invade Poland. The Paris Pact allowed nations to determine for themselves whether the situation warrants resorting to war as a means of self-defense, and it is difficult to imagine nations abrogating that right. But the pact also established no procedure for overruling that claim or for punishing the aggressor.[32]

This is so serious a flaw that some authorities on international law have declared the pact to be moot—on the grounds that a document so widely and lightly disregarded is not really law. Gerhard von Glahn wrote that he

> does not believe that war, except in self-defense, was outlawed by the Pact of Paris. He believes, instead, that it represented nothing more than a moral preachment, despite the trappings of a treaty surrounding the document. The states which had signed it denied validity to the doctrine, and armed conflicts in the ensuing decade were both more numerous and more serious than they had been between 1919 and 1928. . . .
>
> Treaty law . . . is a particular international law based on general international law. When the particular treaty rules, created in derogation of general law, cease to be effective, they are replaced, automatically and instantly, by the relevant or corresponding rules of general international law. Hence the return of the community of nations to traditional notions of neutrality and of warfare appears to have been well founded.[33]

If it is law, it is bad law. Behind it is the assumption that, except for collective action or self-defense, the avoidance of war is always the greater good. That, I will argue below, is a doubtful proposition. In 1971 India invaded East Pakistan to end the massacre of Bengalis by Pakistani troops. It is certainly arguable—I think it is evident—that the invasion was preferable to the killings, rapes, and mutilations that were taking place, even though India was acting unilaterally and even though it was not acting in self-defense (though, of course, it claimed at the time that there had been incidents).

The Paris Pact has been a failure in many ways; it has been ineffective and misguided. But that should not blind us to its virtues. It was also a milestone. War has traditionally been the means whereby changes in the relative *power* of nations were translated into changes in the *rights* of nations. If Germany grew stronger and France grew weaker, war provided the means for Germany to expand at France's cost, for the terms of a new peace treaty establish a new legal status quo. Victory in war could give Germany title to Alsace-Lorraine. This is the meaning of Karl von Clausewitz's dictum that war is the continuation of politics by other means. But in the aftermath of World War I's tremendous casualties and horrors, a new sensibility grew, a feeling that war had grown too monstrous to be an acceptable recourse when negotiations fail to satisfy a nation's ambitions. As a treaty reflection of this new postwar sentiment, the Paris Pact comes into its own. A revolution in attitudes toward war had taken place. It has been the subject of surprisingly little discussion.

Jus ad Bellum

Questions about the rightness of the manner in which a war is being conducted go under the heading of *jus in bello* (proper conduct of war). But a nation may fight according to the rules of war even if it is not morally justified in fighting at all, even if the war itself is immoral. Questions about the rightness of the war itself, rather than of the way it is fought, go under the heading of *jus ad bellum* (justification of war).

As a moral issue *jus ad bellum* is an ancient topic. It goes back at least as far as St. Augustine in the fourth century A.D. and was further developed in the Middle Ages by thinkers like St. Thomas Aquinas and Francisco Suarez. Today it is usually summed up in the following set of conditions.[34] According to the theory, *all* of these conditions must be met for a war to be just.[35]

1. Legitimate Authority. In the Middle Ages private, feudal wars were common. The requirement of legitimate authority grants the right to make war only to those authorized to act for the public good: Just as the sovereign can use the sword to maintain domestic peace, he can use it to defend the commonwealth against external enemies.[36] Its modern counterpart is the understanding in international law that wars are conflicts between states.[37]

2. Just Cause. Augustine thought that if a Christian were assaulted he should try to turn the other cheek, but not if the victim were some other innocent person—Christians should defend the innocent. Augustine thought the defense of others, as opposed to self-defense, was a moral obligation. He had private acts of violence in mind, but his statement can be seen as a modification of a principle of Roman domestic law: Vim vi defendere omnes leges omniaque iura permittunt (all laws and legal systems permit force in defense against force.)[38]

The defense of the common good represented by the state is an extension of this obligation to defend the innocent. But the medievals (and the Romans) interpreted just cause more broadly than merely as defense against attack. Augustine had said just wars avenge the wrong done when another state refuses to make amends for wrongs done by its citizens or restore what has been unjustly taken. Gratian's Decretum cites "prior injury." St. Thomas said there is just cause if those who are to be attacked are attacked because they deserve to be attacked because of a fault. All three formulations require a prior offense; none requires that offense to be an attack. Today the defense of important human rights is frequently listed as providing a just cause for war.

3. Last Resort. A state might have a grievance that would justify going to war, yet not be justified in going to war. If it is possible to settle the grievance by less destructive means, the state is morally obligated to attempt such a settlement. The just grievance is not a pretext for war, but a justification that can be claimed only if other remedies are ineffective. War is the injured state's last resort, not its first resort.

This does not mean that every alternative short of armed force has actually to be pursued, a requirement that would make it impossible for states ever to use force to undo a wrong. States are not required to pursue avenues of settlement that experience has shown offer little or no hope of success or of the timely settlement of an urgent crisis. And, of course, it does not mean that states cannot initiate wars.

The criterion is widely misunderstood. One writer recently asked why, if war should only be declared as a last resort, "will we not forswear 'first use'" of nuclear weapons.[39] This confuses a willingness to use nuclear weapons to stop an advancing enemy attack with an unwillingness to negotiate in order to avoid war in the first place.

4. Proportionality. The harm the war will bring should not be disproportionate to the cause. If the cause is just, yet minor, whereas the suffering the war will produce is great, the war is not justified.

5. Right Intention. Even if all these criteria are met, the war will be unjust unless there is right intention. The intention should be to rectify the wrong that constituted the just cause and to conclude the war with the institution of a just and fair peace: The war must be intended as a means for reestablishing this peace. Even if the cause is just, if the intention is to exterminate the enemy, or to deprive the enemy of what is rightfully its, the war will be unjust. In the traditional formulation, a war motivated by hatred cannot be just.

6. Reasonable Probability of Success. Finally, there must be a reasonable probability of success to justify the harm created by war. This criterion does not interpret success as necessarily requiring military victory: A sacrificial defense against hopeless odds may succeed in asserting a crucial moral principle, even if there is no chance of a military success. The armed resistance of the Danish palace guards to the German invaders in 1940 established the Danish opposition to the invasion in a way no mere statement could.

Though the doctrine of the just war has played an important role in philosophical and theological discussions, international law has largely ignored it. The 1907 Hague conventions govern how states may fight wars, not why or when they are justified in doing so. The conventions do not ask who is right; they treat both sides as equal, regardless of who started the war or what the reasons were.

The classic defense of this neutrality is in William Edward Hall's *Treatise on International Law.* The book is not widely read today, though the last two lines of the following passage are often quoted. Alone they give the impression that Hall thought neutrality was desirable—that the law should not concern itself with which belligerent is right. That was not quite his view:

> As international law is destitute of any judicial or administrative machinery, it leaves states, which think themselves aggrieved, and which have exhausted all peaceable methods of obtaining satisfaction, to exact redress for themselves by force. It thus recognises war as a permitted mode of giving effect to its decisions. Theoretically, therefore . . . it ought to determine the causes for which war can be justly undertaken. . . . It might also not unreasonably go on to discourage the commission of wrongs by . . . subjecting a wrong-doer to special disabilities.
>
> The first of these ends it attains to a certain degree, though very imperfectly. It is able to declare that under certain circumstances a clear and sufficiently serious breach of the law, or of obligations contracted under it, takes place. But in most of the disputes which arise between states the grounds of the quarrel, though they might probably be always brought into connexion with the wide fundamental principles of law, are too complex to be judged with any certainty by reference to them . . . and sometimes they are caused by collisions of naked interest or sentiment, in which there is no question of right, but which are so violent as to render settlement impossible until a struggle has taken place. It is not therefore possible to frame general rules which shall be of any practical value, and the attempts in this direction . . . result in mere abstract statements of principles, or perhaps of truisms, which it is unnecessary to reproduce.
>
> The second end international law does not even endeavor to attain. However able law might be to declare one of two combatants to have committed a wrong, it would be idle for it to affect to impart the character of a penalty to war, when it is powerless to enforce its decisions. . . . When a state has taken up arms unjustly it is useless to expect it to acquiesce in the imposition of penalties for its act. International law has consequently no alternative but to accept war, independently of the justice of its origin, as a relation which the parties

to it may set up if they choose, and to busy itself only in regulating the effects of the relation. Hence both parties to every war are regarded as being in an identical legal position, and consequently as being possessed of equal rights.[40]

The UN Charter

After World War I attitudes began to change.[41] In the years between World Wars I and II, the Paris Pact and the Charter of the League of Nations condemned the initiation of war under certain circumstances, and after World War II at the Nuremberg trials one of the categories of crimes listed in the tribunal's charter was "crimes against peace"—the "planning, preparation, initiation or waging of a war of aggression, or a war in violation of international . . . assurances."[42]

The Charter of the United Nations continued the process of trying to outlaw aggressive war, restricting not only war but any use of (armed) force, and not just use of force, but even the threat of force. According to Article 2: "All members shall settle their international disputes by peaceful means in such a manner that international peace and security, and justice, are not endangered. All members shall refrain in their international relations from the threat[43] or use of force against the territorial integrity or political independence of any state or in any other manner inconsistent with the Purposes of the United Nations." Where, then, does the law stand? For example, was the U.S. naval intrusion across Libya's "line of death" in March 1986 in violation of Article 2? Some political commentators at the time said so. They argued that by sending a powerful fleet into an area claimed by Libya, the United States was using the threat of force to contest Libya's claim to the Gulf of Sidra, contrary to Article 2. A similar case came up when the UN was just getting into business.

The Corfu Channel Case. Between Corfu and Albania lies the Strait of Corfu, less than six miles wide for some of its length, and wholly within the territorial waters of Greece and Albania. Nonetheless it is an international waterway, traveled by right of innocent passage.[44] During World War II the Axis powers mined the strait, leaving a mile-wide mine-free channel for their own ships—the North Corfu Channel.

On May 15, 1946, the British Royal Navy cruisers *Orion* and *Superb,* passing southward through the channel, were unexpectedly (and rather erratically) fired upon by an Albanian coastal battery. Twelve rounds of what the British thought were four-inch shells fell astern of the cruisers, which did not return the fire.[45] In the exchange of diplomatic notes that followed the incident, Albania said that it did not wish to interfere with navigation in the strait so long as the "necessary formalities" were observed and the permission of the Albanian authorities obtained. Britain's note of August 2 replied:

> The rule of international law regarding straits gives both to ships of war and to merchant vessesls in time of peace as well as in time of war a right of innocent passage through straits which form routes for international maritime traffic between two parts of the high seas. His Majesty's Government recognize no right on the part of the territorial Power concerned to demand fulfillment of conditions before entry into such waters is permitted. . . . Should Albanian coastal batteries in future open fire on any of His Majesty's vessels passing through the Corfu Channel fire will be returned by His Majesty's ships.[46]

On October 22 Britain sent the cruisers *Mauritius* and *Leander,* accompanied by the destroyers *Saumarez* and *Volage,* through the channel after a week's port call at Corfu. Their guns were trained in the normal fore and aft positions, but their crews were at action stations.[47]

The Albanian guns were silent, but at 1453 there was a loud explosion, and smoke and flames were observed coming from the *Saumarez,* dead in the water. It had hit a mine. Admiral H.R.G. Kinahan, on the *Mauritius,* ordered the *Volage* to go to the aid of the *Saumarez.* By 1600 the *Volage* had the badly damaged *Saumarez* in tow by the stern, but at 1615 the *Volage* itself hit a mine and lost sixty feet of bow.[48] Thirty-five sailors were lost on the *Saumarez,* and nine on the *Volage.* Forty-two more were wounded. The *Volage* was eventually repaired; the *Saumarez* was a total loss.

The channel had been swept and found to be free of mines in October 1944 and again in January and February 1945; nothing indicated that it had been subsequently mined until the *Saumarez* and *Volage* discovered that fact. The Royal Navy, looking for "the smoking gun," swept the channel again in early November, despite Albanian protests. The navy found twenty-two German-made mines and took two to Malta for examination. The mines were found to be "free from marine growth; the paint was fresh, the mooring wire was still loaded with grease, there was no rust on the mechanism plate, and the horns unscrewed easily."[49] The navy concluded that the mines had been laid quite recently—a few days before the *Saumarez* and *Volage* struck them.[50]

The British took the case to the UN Security Council, where a Soviet veto blocked action. But both parties agreed to the council's recommendation that the case be taken to the International Court of Justice, which eventually upheld the British transit on the grounds that it was "designed to affirm a right which had been unjustly denied." That the ships were at action stations the court was ready to understand:

> In view of the firing from the Albanian battery on May 15th, this measure of precaution cannot, in itself, be regarded as unreasonable. . . . The intention must have been, not only to test Albania's attitude, but at the same time to demonstrate such force that she would abstain from firing again on passing ships. . . . the Court is unable to characterize these measures taken by the United Kingdom authorities as a violation of Albania's sovereignty.[51]

Implicitly, then, the court affirmed the right of a state to adopt an aggressive defensive posture—threatening the use of force—in exercising a threatened just right.[52]

Defining Aggression. Article 2 of the UN Charter, read in isolation, is misleading. It is qualified by the right of defense granted in Article 51: "Nothing in the present Charter shall impair the inherent right of individual or collective self-defense if an armed attack occurs against a Member of the United Nations, until the Security Council has taken the measures necessary to maintain international peace and security."

How are Articles 2 and 51 related? Article 2 prohibits uses of force (and the threat of force) inconsistent with the UN's purposes. On the *strong interpretation,* Article 51 gives us the one case in which the use of force is consistent with those purposes, so the two articles together forbid the use of force except in defense. Lauterpacht, who said the comprehensiveness of Article 2 "can hardly be surpassed," held this view. He thought the charter forbids attacking another state's territory in anticipation of an enemy attack or to obtain redress, even "without the intention of interfering permanently with the territorial integrity of that State": "The Charter confines the right of armed self-defense to the case of an armed attack as distinguished from anticipated attack or from various forms of unfriendly conduct falling short of armed attack."[53] Because there must be an actual armed attack, and not just an anticipated one, we are led to the principle of priority: The side that fires the first shot acts inconsistently with the charter.

Georg Schwarzenberger took the same view:

> The combined effect of the Kellogg Pact and the Charter of the United Nations (Articles 2 (4) and 51) has been to resolve the dilemma arising from the coexistence of a limited right to apply forcible reprisals and of an unlimited right to resort to war. Under this international quasi-order, forcible reprisals have become illegal. At the same time, any other threat, or use of force save in self-defence against armed attack, has been prohibited . . . [except for] collective defence.[54]

More recently Keith Suter concluded that "it is now legal only to use force in self-defence or in a collective defence measure authorized by the UN."[55]

On the *weak interpretation,* Article 51 spells out one case in which force is consistent with those purposes but does not imply there are no others. The "if" in Article 51 is not an "if, and only if."[56] On this second interpretation the charter does not limit the use of force to repelling armed attacks: A state, though not attacked, may use or threaten force in a way consistent with the UN's purposes.[57] The ambiguity that allows these two readings led Gerhard von Glahn to comment sardonically: "Today it can be asserted with some degree of validity, even though perhaps rather academically, that under the provisions of Article 39 of the Charter of the United Nations, the planning, preparation, and launching of a war not strictly in self-defense *may* be regarded as unlawful."[58] Article 39 says that the Security Council should determine whether any acts of aggression have taken place. Obviously that depends on what constitutes aggression, and the strong and weak interpretations gave different answers—hence von Glahn's "may." On the strong interpretation, aggression is any use of force that is not in defense against armed attack. On the weak interpretation, aggression is any use of force inconsistent with the charter's purposes, and although defense is consistent with those purposes, so are some other uses of force.

In 1974 a UN General Assembly committee on the question of the definition of aggression in the charter reported that "aggression is the use of armed force by a State against the sovereignty, territorial integrity or political independence of another State, or in any other manner inconsistent with the Charter." That was just a restatement of Article 2. But the report went on to say:

> The first use of armed force by a State in contravention of the Charter shall constitute *prima facie* evidence of an act of aggression although the Security Council may, in conformity with the Charter, conclude that a determination that an act of aggression has been committed would not be justified in light of other relevant circumstances including the fact that the acts concerned or their consequences are not of sufficient gravity.[59]

This sides with the weak interpretation: Because priority is only prima facie evidence of contravention and can be overridden, defense against an actual armed attack cannot be the *only* legitimate justification for resorting to force.[60]

This raises several questions. What are the "other relevant circumstances" (beside the one mentioned) that can weigh more heavily and be consistent with the charter? As the first use of force may be consistent with the charter, Articles 2 and 51 are not consistent unless we deny that every attack against a nation is an attack against its territorial integrity or its political independence. When is an attack on a nation an attack against its territorial integrity or political independence? And even when a nation is acting in *self-defense,* must it avoid using armed force against the aggressor's territorial integrity and sovereignty? In the twenty-one years of meetings that led to this report, delegates addressed a number of these questions.

Minor border incidents need not by themselves provide a justification for war, as the Soviet delegation had said in the early 1950s. To label them *aggressions* would give wronged states a legal right to go to war, claiming self-defense. If the incident really was minor, this would be an exaggerated response. Hence the reference to "sufficient gravity."[61] A Dutch representative, Mr. Röling, agreed that not every use of armed force constitutes aggression.[62] De minimius non curat lex, another delegate pointed out seventeen years later, following up on the point—the law does not take pains over trivialities: "a use of force . . . so limited in nature and in duration of time could not be described as an act of aggression."[63]

This led some delegates to ask whether the question of intention is not so important as the question of priority. A police patrol might cross a border or might fire at a fleeing suspect who had just crossed the border. These acts lack *animus aggressionis* and hence are not acts of aggression—there is no intent to harm the other nation: "If, as a result of an emergency . . . aboard an aircraft, bombs had to be jettisoned . . . over the sea and they damaged a ship on the high seas or an oil installation in a State's territorial waters, how would it be possible for the Security Council to determine, without examining the objective or purpose of the act, whether or not there had been armed attack."[64]

And on the third question some delegates appealed to the principle of proportionality, which even in self-defense prohibits a war of revenge.[65] That a nation is responding to an attack does not give it a carte blanche.

But we will not find the answer to these questions in the reports. Their ambiguity is intentional—a deliberate consequence of having to accommodate the opinions of delegations with widely differing interests.[66] The 1974 report was itself a compromise: The delegates repeatedly said that its great merit was that its wording was acceptable to all. Proponents of the strong interpretation got something: The first use of force is prima facie evidence of aggression. Proponents of the weak interpretation got something: The first use of force is *only* prima facie evidence of aggression. No agreement could have been attained on what the "other circumstances" were—it took after all, twenty-one years to get the modest statement itself. It was left to the Security Council, in discussing particular crises, to decide for itself what these circumstances were. The foregoing is a misleading statement, and makes sense only internally to the UN. The Security Council, whose permanent members have veto powers, does not formulate guidelines for itself. Its members argue and vote. They do not have to agree on guidelines.

The Moral Context

Moral criteria for the justness of a war do not lend themselves neatly to a formal system of legal adjudication. What clear legal criteria could there be for just cause, or right intent?[67] As a consequence, international law traditionally was silent when it came to deciding which side was right in a war. The result seemed (and was) an abdication of responsibility for a most important question, an abdication that could be blamed on the inadequacy of international law or on the inadequacy of just war theory:

> In a state of practically uninhibited auto-interpretation of legal obligations, assertion necessarily stood against assertion. As international customary law provided, if anything, too ample a scope for the exercise of the right of self-defence and the right to apply forcible reprisals, it was impossible to settle with any legal finality which of the parties had acted in self-defence or in the exercise of a right of self-help. Thus, probably inevitably, the Doctrine of international law resigned itself to treating war of any kind as legal.
>
> This situation made it impossible to conceive of international law as a consistent legal system. If a State was free to wage even aggressive warfare, there was little point in attempting to refine the law relating to the use of force in the exercise of either the right of self-defence or that of self-help.[68]

With the memory of World War I strong, and later World War II, international law took a new turn. Rather than beg the question of which side was right and confine itself to whether each side fought in accordance with the laws of war, it was now prepared to discuss *jus ad bellum*. It would do so by replacing the traditional question of whether a war is morally justified with the simpler, quasi-juridical question of whether a war is aggressive.

This seemed to provide a clear and straightforward criterion for assigning blame, and after all, everyone is against aggression. But to a large extent it was an illusion: The criterion of aggression is straightforward only if we take the simple view that the aggressor is the one who fires the first shot. The 1974 report indicates that things are not that simple.

Once we grant that a nation can fire the first shot and start a war without being the guilty party, we abandon the simplicity of the aggressive-war criterion. A nation is no longer culpable merely for breaking the peace. We must examine the circumstances that led that nation to war, and we may decide, in view of them, that even though state A initiated the war, A was justified. The questions raised by traditional just war theory then reappear when we examine those circumstances. One of them, proportionality, is already implicit in the "sufficient gravity" criterion. A minor border incident would not justify a full-fledged war.

The moral complexities of the real world forced the 1974 report. The problem that Schwarzenberger identified proved intractable and chronic. Nations sometimes have a moral right to resort to force even if they have not been attacked. Inevitably the other side will charge aggression. And there is no simple legal formula to decide who is right.

In *Just and Unjust Wars* Michael Walzer examined the circumstances that he thought justified war even in the absence of armed attack.[69] I turn now to the first of these.

Preemptive War

In late November and early December 1941, at a time of great tension between the United States and Japan, a Japanese carrier strike force with all six Japanese fleet carriers secretly sailed 3,000 miles across the Pacific, arriving on December 7 at a position 275 miles north of Pearl Harbor—within strike range.[70] Had they been on an exercise, there would have been no need for them to come so close to Hawaii, placing the U.S. Pacific Fleet in grave danger. The only plausible interpretation of the force's movement was that the Japanese intended to attack the Pacific Fleet.

Suppose they had been detected. The United States would then have known that the Japanese had gone to great trouble to get their carriers in a position to strike Pearl Harbor. Would the Americans still have had to wait for the Japanese to strike first, lest an attack on the Japanese carriers be an act of aggression? Or would "the discovery of a large Japanese fleet a few hundred miles from America's principal naval base . . . in itself have been sufficient *casus belli,* regardless of whether the Japanese actually attacked or not."[71]

On the weak interpretation of the UN Charter (which, of course, did not exist in 1941), a strike against the Japanese task force at that point could be an act of defense. In 1956 at the UN committee's second meeting, the Dutch representative used this very example: "In exceptional cases the factual direction of the armed forces of a State against another might, even without actual contact, constitute such a use of armed force as would constitute an armed attack under Article 51, for example, when the Japanese . . . were approaching Pearl Harbour."[72] He suggested that armed attack in Article 51 should be understood to mean any use of armed force (it need not be an actual attack) that required the other state to use military means to preserve its territorial integrity and independence.[73] He had argued the same point in a different way at the 1953 session when he said that in order for the *threat* (as opposed to the use) of force to constitute aggression, and hence authorize the use of force in self-defense, the threat must be imminent.[74] If the *threat* of force can constitute aggression, the first use of force can be a reply to a prior aggression (the threat itself). The approach of the Japanese carrier force to within strike range of Pearl Harbor constituted a use of armed force creating an imminent threat. On the weak interpretation, a U.S. strike at the Japanese at that moment, even though the Americans would be striking first, would be a defensive act. Intent overrides the prima facie evidence of priority. There is hostile intent on the part of the Japanese, as shown by their fleet movements; the intent on the U.S. side is to defend itself from the danger created by those fleet movements.

Walzer suggested that there is sufficient threat to justify a preemptive war if there is "a manifest intent to injure, a degree of active preparation that makes that intent a positive danger, and a general situation in which waiting, or doing anything other than fighting, greatly magnifies the risk."[75] The Pearl Harbor case certainly illustrated the third and involved an active preparation that posed a positive danger. Whether there was a manifest intent to injure is a more difficult question, but one that is answered, in view of the political situation at the time, by the course set by the Japanese fleet. Its movement into strike range exhibited a manifest intent to injure. There need not be a prior manifest intent to injure if the action in question itself poses a grave danger "such as only a determined enemy would hope to bring about."[76] In 1940, in circumstances that were probably not covered by Walzer's criteria, British Prime Minister Winston Churchill appealed to anticipatory self-defense to justify the Royal Navy's sinking of the French fleet—lest it fall into German hands.[77]

Another case led Princeton University's Richard Falk, a prominent expert on international law, to change his understanding of aggressive war.[78] On May 15, 1967, the Egyptians put their armed forces on maximum alert and began deploying in force on the Israeli border in support of the Syrians, whose artillery fire against Israel the previous month had led to an air battle between Israel and Syria. Over the next few days, Gamal Abdel Nasser had the UN remove its peacekeeping force in the Sinai, closed the Strait of Tiran to Israeli shipping,[79] announced a joint military command with the Syrians and Jordanians, and declared that he wanted "the rights of the people of Palestine—complete," rights he claimed were denied them by the very establishment of Israel. Additional military units arrived from other Arab countries, while bellicose radio broadcasts all over the Arab world announced that the time had come for the destruction of Israel—a message Nasser delivered to a trade union congress on May 26. Meanwhile, Israel repeatedly insisted it did not want war and called for mutual military pullbacks.

Nasser said the Israelis did want war and that Egypt was ready. Poised as they were, at any moment the Egyptians could attack. The Egyptians had 100,000 troops and over 1,000 tanks on the Israeli border and could afford to keep them there indefinitely. The Israelis, with a population only a fraction of Egypt's, had a standing army of only 30,000 and had to contend with the Syrians and Jordanians as well as the Egyptians. To counter the Egyptian threat, the Israelis would have to mobilize their reserves, and if they kept their reserves mobilized for any great length of time, their economy would collapse. Nasser may have thought that he could reduce or at least demoralize the Israelis by forcing them to stay mobilized or to live in a permanent and imminent crisis—that he could win without firing a shot. If so, he miscalculated. The Israelis appealed to their allies and to the UN. When they decided they could wait no longer, they struck the first blow, defeated their adversaries, and demobilized.

Though they had not been attacked, they had been placed in great and immediate peril. And though the Egyptians did not start the war, and perhaps did not intend to start a war, the Israelis seem justified in resorting to force. For even without an Egyptian intention to conduct an armed attack, the Egyptians had used armed force to place Israel in imminent danger. The Israelis acted to defend themselves from that danger.

I mentioned that Nasser made numerous threatening remarks, but in going over the Pearl Harbor case, I did not say anything about the intentions of Japan's leaders. It was not necessary, and frequently it is not possible: States do not always broadcast their intentions; and even when they do, their statements may be misleading. Intent is judged by military acts—the location of the Japanese carrier force or the deployment of the Egyptian army—not by psychoanalysis. A question of intent is about an element that emerges "from the facts, and not a question of the secret or psychological motivations of Governments."[80]

States can defend themselves by initiating a war—by striking the first blow—and the UN statement is right to imply that first use of armed force is not the sole determinant of whether a war is a war of aggression. A state's territorial integrity, sovereignty, and political independence can be blatantly, intentionally, and seriously threatened without a shot being fired, and these are threats states have the right to respond to with force. To insist that the threatening state must be the first to use force is excessive legalism—like insisting that the person holding a gun on you must pull the trigger before you can shoot at him. The mere fact that he is holding the gun on you makes your act self-defense—particularly because once he pulls the trigger, it is too late.

The first use of force may sometimes be justified by a threat against *another* state. Nations do not have a right only to self-defense; they have a right as well to collective defense—to defend others as well as themselves. And if preemptive strikes are sometimes justifiable on the grounds of self-defense, they must also be justifiable on the grounds of collective defense. In the right circumstances nation A may be justified in launching a preemptive strike on C, if C places B in imminent peril.

Protection of Citizens Abroad

In 1964 Belgian paratroopers intervened in the former Belgian Congo to protect Europeans who were being killed by Congolese rebels:

> Within four days, this operation had been completed and two days later all paratroopers had also been removed from the Congo. This intervention resulted in widespread criticism from African members of the United Nations and an unsuccessful attempt was made by eighteen of them to have the Security Council condemn the rescue operation as "armed aggression." In retrospect, however, the episode presents one of the clearest modern instances of true humanitarian intervention and should be viewed as lawful in character, in view of the conditions then existing in the "target state" and of the total inability of the incumbent government to protect the refugees in question.[81]

A state's inability to protect foreign nationals traditionally legitimates armed intervention, though such inability does not threaten the national survival of the intervening state. The intention is not to go to war with B, but to fulfill an obligation B is unable to fulfill. A's intervention is, in the legal phrase, *sine animo belligerandi* (see Chapter 2). A intends no harm to B but merely to protect A's citizens.

This type of intervention traditionally constitutes a use of armed force short of war. A has no intention of going to war with B and does not regard itself as going to war with B. If B agrees, there will be no war. B may, however, chose to view the intervention as a casus belli. B may, for example, feel that it is capable of handling the situation itself and resent the violation of its sovereignty caused by the uninvited presence of foreign troops. B may not trust A's motives. B may oppose the intervention with armed force or even declare war on A. Whether a use of armed force short of war creates a war depends on how the other side responds.

In this case is the aggressor B, who fired the first shot and initiated the war, or A, whose troops entered B uninvited, creating the casus belli? The principle of priority might be interpreted either way: as branding B for firing the first shot or A for crossing the border. In the examples I presented earlier, this distinction did not matter, so I took priority to mean priority of fire. But here priority of fire does not work. We would not say that in 1939, when Germany invaded Poland, the Poles would have been the aggressors if the Germans, having crossed the border, had held their fire until they were fired upon. To cross a frontier with soldiers and occupy foreign soil is to use armed force, even if no shots are fired. This is why there is a category in international law for uses of armed force short of war.

A, then, seems to be the aggressor, for A undertakes the prior use of armed force, though B has not placed A in imminent danger. However, A's intent is honorable, and as A intends B no harm, it seems odd to label A's intervention as an aggression against B. A is not acting *against* B at all. A is merely rescuing its own citizens. The truth may be that in this case there is no aggressor. There is merely a war caused by B's suspicion of A. Wars do not require aggressors.

If B's failure to fulfill its obligations to foreign nations is willful rather than originating from incapacity, the situation is more serious. B cannot claim a right to mistreat foreign nations, and A may feel obligated to protect its citizens abroad. The casus belli in this case is on A's side.

Intervention to protect one's own citizens might be subsumed under the heading of defense—defense of citizens abroad, though not of the national territory or sovereignty. But the connection between justifiably initiating war and national defense would become tenuous at that point. In the next sort of case it becomes even more tenuous, and in subsequent cases it disappears entirely.

The Right of Self-Help

There are international wrongs that are not forms of armed attack. A state might renege on an international commercial obligation or refuse free passage through an international waterway. This need not threaten anyone's safety, let alone national survival; it might only cause mild economic harm. (The closing of the Strait of Tiran is an example.) Yet traditionally such international wrongs have been taken to justify the use of force as an act of self-help for the enforcement of international rights and duties.[82]

The elimination of this unilateral right of forceful self-help was one of the aims of the Paris Pact. The intention was that states should retain a unilateral right to use force only in self-defense. Forceful self-help other than in defense would be a right that could be exercised only collectively. If the wrong did not involve the use of armed force, the right to use force unilaterally to restore the prior situation was denied. Or, more correctly, the right to go to war to right the wrong was denied. There are, we have seen, uses of armed force that are short of war: "Whatever the earlier position taken toward the *jus ad bello,* in the twentieth century reconstruction of *bellum justum,* war is no longer a means generally permitted to states for the redress of rights that have been violated. Still less is war considered a legitimate means for changing the status quo."[83] Nations retained the right to peaceful self-help. In particular, they retained the right to retorsion, retaliation, and other forms of pacific though compulsive settlement.

Retorsion consists of legal but unfriendly acts in response to prior legal but unfriendly acts. In response to B's arrest of one of A's journalists, A might require B to reduce the size of its diplomatic mission. In response to B's harassment of tourists from A, A might place tourists from B under similar restrictions. In response to Soviet restrictions on travel by U.S. diplomatic staff, the United States put Disneyland off limits for Soviet diplomats. At a more serious level, A might suspend trade with B or break off diplomatic relations.

Reprisals are far more serious.[84] Acts of reprisal are acts that normally are illegal, but are legal as a response to prior illegal acts, as a means of encouraging the original offender to desist. (There is no question of illegality with retorsion, because the offense and the reply, though unfriendly, are legal.) Nations commonly retaliate by freezing the funds of other nations—as the United States did with Iran after the Iranians took the U.S. Embassy hostage—or by refusing to honor agreements.

Rarer is an embargo, which may forbid ships of the other nation from leaving the injured nation's ports.

The most serious form of compulsion short of armed intervention is pacific naval blockade, which can easily become war if the blockaded nation uses force to break the blockade. As a naval blockade does not ipso facto create a state of war, it is technically not a resort to war and hence not forbidden as a form of self-help under the Paris Pact. To include such acts, the UN Charter refers to "acts of force" rather than "war." A naval blockade is an act of force, even if it is not an act of war.

Unfortunately, nonforceful means of self-help often are ineffective, and the rejection of the right of forceful self-help was not accompanied by the substitution of reliable alternatives. Action by the UN Security Council is subject to veto by the council's permanent members, and the International Court of Justice can only consider a case if both parties to the dispute agree to submit it to the court, and parties to a major dispute are unlikely to hand over their fate to the court.

If a nation that is illegally wronged has no hope of relieving the situation short of armed force, what is the harmed nation to do? If it agrees with the proposition that war is justified only in response to actual or imminent attack—that "no provocative action other than an armed attack across an international frontier warrants the use of military force by one nation against another"[85]—it has no alternative but to lick its wounds and complain. In many cases this may be the wisest response—every wrong does not have to be righted, and the cost and dangers of taking action may exceed the expected gain.

But we will be in a difficult position if we grant that force, or the threat of force, may never be used against a malefactor. If the alternatives short of armed force do not deter the unfriendly nation—and if it has enough to gain by its breach of law such alternatives will not be a deterent—we will have tied our hands. The wronged nation would have no effective recourse, and the nation that stands to benefit from the wrong will know that. Over the long run this would be conducive neither to friendly relations nor to the promotion of the cause of peace. It would increase the occasions for international crises, and eventually those who gain from these acts might be emboldened to the point that those who suffer would feel compelled to take forcible counter-action. The U.S. air attack against Libya in April 1986 indicates that this point has already been reached in U.S. policy toward state-supported terrorism.

There is a point to restricting the right of forceful self-help, and its use, for example, to force states to honor debts has now disappeared. That disappearance, one of the great legacies of the Paris Pact, can be defended on the grounds of prudence, proportionality, or abuse of the privilege. At any rate, nations now assume that investments and loans to foreign countries are at the lender's risk—they no longer expect to collect bad debts at the point of a bayonet. War has ceased being an instrument for the enforcement of commercial contracts—a role it can serve only if lives are cheap.

The right of forceful self-help has not, however, completely disappeared. If it had, we could not regard denial of free passage as a legitimate casus belli. In fact we do. The exercise of forcible self-help presents very serious and obvious dangers. The lesson of the 1970s and 1980s is that so may its nonexercise.

Humanitarian Intervention

Preemptive war is a defense against armed attack, even though it is undertaken before the attack is launched. In *Just and Unjust Wars* Michael Walzer discussed three circumstances that he thought justify armed intervention even though *no* attack is threatened.

One of these occurs "when the violation of human rights . . . is so terrible that it makes talk of community or self-determination or 'arduous struggle' seem cynical and irrelevant, that is, in cases of enslavement or massacre [humanitarian intervention]."[86] The oppressed in these cases do not have the power to end their oppression. If help comes, it must be from the outside world. The example Walzer discussed is the Indian intervention in East Pakistan in 1971.

When India gained independence from Britain, widespread religious hostility and fighting led to a partition. Pakistan, predominantly Moslem, was created out of the northwestern (West Pakistan) and northeastern (East Pakistan) provinces, separated by predominantly Hindu India. The East Pakistanis and the Bengalis of northeastern India spoke the same language and shared a common culture, though their religions differed; East and West Pakistanis, in contrast, shared a common religion, but were linguistically and culturally different.

In 1971 West Pakistanis dominated the government of Pakistan, and massacres of East Pakistani Bengalis by West Pakistani troops were taking place. This violence induced a large number of Pakistani Bengalis to flee to India, where these refugees were a financial burden and caused resentment among non-Bengalis, although they had the sympathy of a great many Indian Bengalis.

India, claiming that Pakistani planes had raided its territory—a charge the world took with a grain of salt—invaded East Pakistan, defeated the Pakistani troops there, and ended the massacres. India then allowed the East Pakistanis to decide their own future. Thus the new nation of Bangladesh came into existence.

Undoubtedly there was some self-interest involved on India's part. It was in India's interest to end the massacres and thereby solve the refugee problem. And it was fortunate for Indian foreign policy that ending the massacres meant breaking the West Pakistani hold on East Pakistan, creating a situation in which East might secede from West. So the Indian invasion could have been justified on grounds of national self-interest. And perhaps India would not have invaded had that not been so: Nations are usually reluctant to help others if it is not in their own interest. Still, India did intervene to end the massacres. Humanitarian concerns and national interest can coincide.[87]

There are cases of humanitarian intervention. In the most interesting ones the invader is trying to help people who are not its own nationals—protecting citizens of other countries from their own government or from some third government. These are the cases I have in mind in this section.

North Vietnam might have claimed that its invasion of Cambodia fit this pattern, but this justification was lost when Vietnamese troops, having deposed the brutal Khmer Rouge regime of Pol Pot, took up occupation duties that continued for a decade. The Vietnamese were in Cambodia as an occupying army and clearly had no desire to let the Cambodians set up a government of their own choice. If humanitarian concerns played any role at all in this intervention, they long ago ceased to apply once Pol Pot's forces were restricted to border camps. By contrast, the Indians let the East Pakistanis sort out their own affairs.

The claim that an intervention is humanitarian, without a prompt evacuation, rings false. The Indian intervention was in India's national interest and was humanitarian as well. What tips the scales in India's favor is that once the humanitarian justification ceased to apply, India ceased the intervention. India pursued its interests only so far as humanitarian considerations would have allowed it to act anyway. That acting on those considerations was in its own interest was viewed as a fortunate coincidence—as fortunate for the East Pakistanis as it was for India.

Humanitarian interventions have always been viewed as potentially dangerous: "International law professes to be concerned only with the relations of states to each other. Tyrannical conduct of a government towards its subjects, massacres and brutality in a civil war, or religious persecution, are acts which have nothing to do directly or indirectly with such relations. On what ground then can international law take cognizance of them?"[88] But it does take cognizance of them—most notably at the Nuremberg War Crimes Trials. German slaughter of foreign nationals in World War II was criminal under existing international law. This posed no special legal questions. The murder of Germans by Germans, though, was a different matter.

International law, we saw in Chapter 1, is aimed at regulating the relations between states. What a state does to its own citizens has been generally taken to be outside the province of international law. But to many people Nazi crimes were so great and egregious that international law could no longer restrict itself to the treatment of foreign nationals. These people wanted a new category of crime introduced into international law: crimes against humanity. This new category would apply even in cases where the victims were not citizens of another state. "Crimes against humanity" thus appeared in the charter of the tribunal at Nuremberg. "Murder, extermination, enslavement, deportation, and other inhumane acts committed against *any* civilian population" were declared to be criminal.[89] The tribunal thereby claimed the right to judge crimes committed by Germans against Germans—crimes that were not international in character.[90]

What goes on within a state is traditionally its own affair, and the category of crimes against humanity goes against this tradition. It treats as an appropriate matter for international law actions that would previously have been thought to be the internal affairs of a state, thus sanctioning intervention in that state's internal affairs. The principle of nonintervention has served the community of nations well, and its dilution is a matter for concern. But states have intervened on humanitarian grounds—to stop massacres—without being condemned by the world community. And if a state's barbaric practices toward its own citizens is serious enough to justify a war of intervention by another nation, and the loss of life that might involve among its troops, then it seems reasonable to say that those practices are criminal.

There are, at any rate, two different questions here. The question raised by crimes against humanity is not whether states have a right to intervene in the affairs of other states to stop barbaric internal practices, but whether they have a right to prosecute those responsible for such practices as criminals. One could justify humanitarian intervention without claiming that those responsible for the massacres should be subject to criminal charges. One can intervene, end the massacres, and not put anyone on trial. This is how the nineteenth century sometimes handled the problem, and this is what India did in 1971.

Ignoring the question of the criminality of the perpetrators, is genuinely humanitarian intervention justified? The U.S. invasion of Grenada is an interesting case. The U.S. government offered several justifications for it—an embarrassment of justifications. One was the right to rescue U.S. citizens, which might justify getting onto the island

and getting U.S. citizens out but not using that opportunity to depose the government. A second amounted to a claim to a preemptive strike: Grenada was planning aggression or support of armed subversion against its neighbors, and the U.S. invasion was preventive. Here, too, the U.S. case was weak. Grenada did possess an inordinate quantity of small arms for a small Caribbean state, but a few hundred rifles would not pose a danger to a U.S. ally, and there is no evidence that any of these weapons were ever provided to non-Grenadans. Finally, their mere possession by Grenada hardly constituted an imminent threat to any state: The weapons were in sheds, not in the hands of a trained amphibious assault force.

A more plausible reason for the invasion was U.S. national interest, as Grenada had allied itself with Cuba. But this alone could not morally justify the invasion. It becomes more plausible when we add that not only had Grenada become Cuba's ally, but it had also introduced another innovation—the execution of the opposition. This must have made its neighboring governments nervous, and it lends some moral force to U.S. claims. Whether it is sufficient to justify a claim to humanitarian intervention is, however, another question. The Indians did not invade East Pakistan in response to the execution of a single political leader, but in response to massive brutality.

The question turns on what legitimates governments. Political scientists tend to be tolerant in this regard, and there is a long-standing tradition among them of treating a government as legitimate if it is homegrown and if it seems to have at least the acquiescence of the population. To say that a government is "legitimate" in this sense is not to give it any moral praise: A government might be legitimate and reprehensible. It is to say that the government is a native growth, that there is "a certain 'fit' between the community and its government."[91] The government can be taken to be the agent of the state and to express the will of the state, rather than being an alien imposition. To put this another way, to a large number of political scientists, a government is legitimate whenever the resistance is not a serious threat to it. (Again, this has nothing to do with moral approval of the government.)

The right of states to self-determination allows them their own form of government. The form may be a multiparty democracy, but it need not be: It might be a monarchy, a council of elders, or a brutal dictatorship. The English monarchy of the late Middle Ages was the legitimate government of England, even though it did not involve universal suffrage. Americans are taught that democracy is the best form of government. In another time or land, with different customs, institutions, and different conceptions of the sources of political allegiance and the roots of obedience, democracy might not work. Perhaps dictatorship is the only form of government that can command the allegiance of the people. Perhaps they would not respect, understand, or obey a government that tolerates dissent. Perhaps they would interpret that as weakness, and they do not give their loyalty to weak rulers. Perhaps they want to be led, not to lead. Perhaps they expect opposition to be crushed and do not want a freer society. "There is no right," said Michael Walzer, "to be protected against the consequences of domestic failure, even against a bloody repression."[92] Not, at least, apart from a political consensus for such a right.

On this view, humanitarian intervention is not justified by political repression or by the occasional execution of opposition leaders—that may just be their normal way of doing business. Walzer deferred to the principle of self-determination, and unless we want to remake the world in our image we must agree with him. Humanitarian intervention is justified only by widespread atrocities like mass murder or enslavement, which presumably do not have the approval of those who are exterminated or enslaved, and which are so excessive that we cannot write them off as the unfortunate and regressive ways of the natives—not without paying a great moral price ourselves. The Tanzanian intervention in Uganda to depose Idi Amin might fit this bill; intervention in Cambodia to end the extermination of Cambodian people by the Cambodian Communists certainly would. The U.S. intervention in Grenada does not.

Others dispute this viewpoint.[93] On their view, a government that, although not engaging in mass extermination or enslavement, keeps itself in power by repressing the opposition has no claims to legitimacy—it is not an expression of the people's self-determination; it stays in power by denying the people self-determination. In the words of David Luban, "The government fits the people the way the sole of a boot fits a human face: after a while the patterns of indentation match with uncanny precision."

These two sides, though, can be reconciled. For the existence of repression does not by itself show that the fit is real or not real. If it is real, that will eventually manifest itself in a tendency toward resistance to the intervening troops, or it will reestablish itself when the intervening troops are withdrawn. If the fit is due to misfortune, the population will attempt to keep it from reestablishing itself.

In a 1980 article Walzer wrote that if the citizens of a country in which an intervention is taking place do not defend the country, or if they make a pretense of defense but surrender at the first opportunity, the state is not really defended and the invasion is a lesser crime or no crime at all.[94] This was what happened in Grenada. The real resistance did not come from the tens of thousands of Grenadans, but from the few hundred Cubans who were there.

Criticism of the operation must then be tempered by the welcome the bulk of the islanders gave the U.S. forces. This caused those Americans who initially opposed the operation to let the issue die quickly. Opposition to the invasion became academic in tone—no one was really angry. How do you stay indignant when the natives are cheering? This answers our question about humanitarian intervention: If the invaders are greeted as saviors, intervention is difficult to criticize. The practice is extremely dangerous but hard to oppose if the risks are small and the benefits great.

Counterintervention and Neutrality

The second type of intervention Walzer defended is counterintervention, when one nation intervenes in a civil war to offset an intervention by another nation, "when the boundaries have already been crossed by the armies of a foreign power, even if the crossing has been called for by one of the parties in a civil war."[95]

In this case intervention is justified as a defense of the principle of self-determination. Nations have the right to work out their own destinies. If this leads a nation into civil war it is *its* civil war. When another nation intervenes on behalf of one of the participants, its intervention tips the scales in favor of that participant, which is more likely to be victorious than it would be if only the desires of the populace were at work. Intervention is thus seen as upsetting a process akin to natural selection: The side favored by the intervention acquires power out of proportion to the wishes of the people. Counterintervention is justified in order to neutralize that imbalance, or so the argument goes. The counterintervention in theory reestablishes the circumstances necessary for self-determination.

The justification for counterintervention is the reestablishment of the status quo ante: the situation that existed before the first intervention. The purpose of counterintervention must be to reestablish the balance that would have existed had there been no intervention, not to enable the favored party to win. If the aid bestowed by the counterintervention exceeds the aid provided by the first intervention, the counterintervention goes beyond neutralizing the first intervention and creates an imbalance in favor of the other side—it neutralizes the original intervention and then in effect goes on to establish a new intervention in favor of the second side. This is no more conducive to self-determination than the original intervention was. (It is also likely to cause the original intervention to be increased, in order to neutralize the new disparity.)

When we speak of intervention here we are talking about military intervention. The question is the following: When are nations justified in resorting to the use of armed force even though they have not been attacked? Much lesser degrees of involvement are often denounced as "interference in another nation's internal affairs": criticism of a nation's human rights policies or other internal affairs, statements favoring one political candidate over another, and so forth. None of these amounts to intervention in a legal sense. The intervention in another state's internal affairs that international law abhors is dictatorial intervention. Criticisms and recommendations do not restrict sovereignty.

There is another kind of intervention that, though milder than the use of armed force, does come under our heading: selling or giving arms to other nations. The nations bestowing the arms is not a direct party to the conflict, but its actions may favor one side as much as the loan of a brigade would. (But so, if we followed that argument, might the supply of food or medicine under the right circumstances.) This form of intervention is milder than military intervention, for the arms are only useful to the recipients if they have people willing to use them, whereas military intervention may prop up a government that has no popular support. Yet the milder form of intervention can be decisive.

Here international law is on murky grounds. Its intention was to allow neutrality to be compatible with conducting normal commerce with belligerents. In World War II Sweden, for example, continued to supply steel to Germany. The law forbids neutral *governments* from giving or selling arms to belligerents but allows their citizens or companies to do so. The United States could thus remain neutral in a conflict even if the Northrop Corporation were selling arms to a party to that conflict. In an age when many weapons manufacturers and dealers are partly or wholly state owned or regulated, or when international arms sales may require governmental approval, this distinction makes little sense, and it seems, in fact, to be falling into disuse. As I write, France has been selling arms to Iraq for years without becoming a party to the Iran-Iraq war of the 1980s.

Another requirement of neutrality is impartiality. A nation that supplies arms to one side, but refuses to supply the other, in strict law loses its right to claim neutral status. This too seems to be falling by the wayside: The USSR has supplied arms to Iraq without Iran's considering itself to be at war with it; the United States in the Yom Kippur War supplied arms to Israel without Egypt's considering itself to be at war with the United States. What seems to be evolving, then, is a new status: the ally that is not quite a belligerent.

Of course, it is not illegal to become a party to an international conflict—nations are not obligated to be neutral. But nations are forbidden from providing arms to insurgents. (In an insurgency, the rebels do not control territory.) Insurgency, as opposed to war, is an internal affair, and supplying arms to insurgents is an unlawful intervention.

Here, too, the status of international law can be questioned. Since the end of World War II this provision has been violated so often that one can question whether it is still in force. If the arms supplier is a superpower or its client state, the dangers and costs of trying to enforce the law become so great that rival nations are reluctant to take forceful action. The law then atrophies through neglect.

National Liberation

Walzer's third case occurs "when a particular set of boundaries clearly contains two or more political communities, one of which is already engaged in a large-scale military struggle for independence; that is, when what is at issue is secession or 'national liberation.'"[96] The case he discussed is the attempted Hungarian secession in 1848 from the Austro-Hungarian Empire—an attempt the Austrians, aided by a Russian army, suppressed. Walzer cited John Stuart Mill's view that England ought to have intervened when Russia did. As Walzer pointed out, Mill thought of this as a counterintervention to the Russian intervention, rather than as an intervention to help the Hungarians gain independence from the Austrians.

But Walzer believed that the drift of Mill's argument allows him to be cited this way, for Mill said that "the Austrian in Hungary was in some sense a foreign yoke." "The clear tendency of his argument," Walzer wrote: "is to justify assistance to a secessionist movement at the same time as it justifies counter-intervention—indeed, to assimilate the one to the other. In both cases, the rule against interference is suspended because a foreign power, morally, if not legally alien, is already interfering in the 'domestic' affairs, that is, in the self-determinations of a political community."[97] In a footnote Walzer qualified this approval of the right of self-determination: "The will and capacity of the people for self-determination may not establish a right to secede if the secession would remove not only land but also vitally needed fuel and mineral resources from some larger political community."[98]

Once we grant that, though, we will have to go on to grant more. In the late 1930s the ethnically German population of western Czechoslovakia (the Sudetenland) was, with Germany's encouragement, agitating for secession from Czechoslovakia and union with Germany—

a wish that was granted at the infamous Munich conference in 1938. Though there were terrorist acts by secessionist Sudeten Germans, there was no "large-scale military struggle for independence," so the Sudetenlanders' "liberation struggle" does not meet Walzer's criteria for intervention. But we can imagine that there had been: Suppose the Sudetenlanders had organized a military resistance and expelled the Czech army from a portion of the Sudetenland. Would Germany have been justified in intervening on behalf of the rebels?

The Sudetenland had no vital natural resources, but it had something else that was vital to Czechoslovakia: mountain ranges. Mountains are natural defensive strongholds, and the Czechs had further strengthened the Sudeten mountains with a network of formidable fortifications. If Czechoslovakia lost control of the Sudetenland, its central plains would be exposed to Nazi Germany, whose aggressive and expansionist tendency was becoming evident. The Sudetenland was Czechoslovakia's defensible border.

A second factor is that although there was some discrimination in Czechoslovakia by ethnic Czechs against ethnic Germans, there was not nearly the level of harm that would normally be thought to justify humanitarian intervention: no massacres or enslavement. Hitler, in fact, had to encourage the production of "incidents" to make the problem seem worse than it was.

Given these two considerations, the Sudeten Germans had a weak case. The loss of the Sudetenland in the circumstances of the time would threaten—indeed, led to—the dissolution of Czechoslovakia. This might be a price we would be willing to countenance if the Czechs had treated their ethnic Germans in a barbaric manner, but they had not. The Sudeten Germans may have been subject to some discrimination, but if so, it was in the form of petty annoyances—not in a lethal form or even a form that prevented their living the same sort of lives as their Czech compatriots.[99] That would not, it seems to me, justify their secession at the cost of endangering the national existence of Czechoslovakia.

The desire, no matter how strong, of a group to secede does not by itself make the secessionist case right. We have to consider not just the desire, but whether the circumstances that are invoked to support it carry enough moral weight to justify the loss the state will suffer. If that loss is serious, and if the grievances of the rebellious group are exaggerated, their "right to secede" can be overruled.

In the 1970s the International Committee of the Red Cross (ICRC) convened a series of conferences in Geneva to update the humanitarian law of war, culminating in the 1977 Diplomatic Conference on the Reaffirmation and Development of International Humanitarian Law

Applicable in Armed Conflicts. The idea was to develop two new protocols: Protocol 1, for international armed conflicts, and 2, for internal conflicts. The conferences were dominated by Third World representatives, with (nonvoting) representatives of several "national liberation movements" (NLMs) also attending. The result was the insertion, by a vote of 70 to 21 to 13, of a passage in Protocol 1 that said, "armed conflicts in which peoples are fighting against colonial domination and alien occupation and against racist regimes in the exercise of their right of self-determination" are international in character. Though the protocol has not been ratified by the major powers, it is still of considerable interest.

The insertion owed more to political considerations than to legal reasoning. The Third World wanted to support national liberation movements and could do so by extending the law of war to cover them. This extension has been supported by Keith Suter:

> The distinction between international and non-international conflicts is no longer feasible. In this light, the growth of "national" movements in the last few years seems an anachronism, for these movements, in an increasingly interdependent world, draw some of their strength from emphasizing the "national" uniqueness of the territory which they wish to liberate from foreign control. . . . The movements . . . to win a national war . . . need international help. This weakens still further the distinction between international and noninternational conflicts, for it is an example where a national war involves other people and other governments.[100]

He thought that the dependence of liberation movements on outside help and support makes these conflicts international in character. In one sense he was right: If a revolutionary group is supported by a foreign government, then politically the conflict is internationalized. But this does not show that the conflict is international in a *legal* sense: The armed conflict is not between the opposing governments. When, in the Yom Kippur War, the United States was sending tanks to Israel and the USSR was sending tanks to Syria, the United States and the USSR were not at war. Suter's analysis, in fact, replaced legal reasoning with political considerations: The political reality may be that revolutionary movements have foreign support but, legally, revolutionary movements may still be internal struggles.

We could defend the extension by arguing that in these struggles the native population is trying to throw off the yoke of *foreign* domination. As those who are doing the dominating—the colonialists, racists, and aliens—are not part of the native population, the conflict can be taken to be (really) between that population and the alien state. In some way this must have been the intention of the Third World bloc. Why else should they specify "colonialists," "racists," and "aliens," which suggest outsiders? The wording lends itself to condemning ruling groups if they are not of indigenous stock, but not if they are. So if the Ibo rebel against the Hausa, or the Tamils against the Sinhalese, or the Biharis against the Bengalis, these are not struggles against alien occupation—the Hausa, Sinhalese, and Bengalis are indigenous, at least in the larger area.

If the wording had every national liberation struggle as international, even if the ruling groups are neighbors, every Third World secessionist movement could claim to be engaged in an international struggle. The Sikhs and the Eritreans, for example, could claim to be opposing alien Hindu and Ethiopian domination. This would not suit many Third World countries, rent as they are with internal divisions.

Roughly, the rule is that if the oppressors have arrived by ship, they are alien; otherwise, not. This distinction may make sense politically, but not morally. One can argue that the harm done by racial laws to blacks in South Africa is far less than the harm that has been done to blacks by blacks in African nations ruled by blacks: In some African countries tens of thousands of members of the wrong tribe have been maimed and massacred by members of the dominant tribes. We hear very little about this in international forums. These forums—the UN, for example—are places where government voices speak, and the governments that have committed these crimes have no desire to allow their victims access to microphones. But surely those people, if their voices could be heard, would think that being paid a discriminatory wage and disenfranchised by aliens is preferable to being disemboweled, albeit by your own kind.

The 1977 protocols have not been ratified by the major powers. If they ever become law, their effect will be drastic: Some armed conflicts will be international in character even though one of the parties to the conflict is not a state. By way of contrast, Protocol 2, for internal conflicts between states and

> dissident armed forces or other organized armed groups which, under responsible command, exercise such control over a part of its territory as to enable them to carry out sustained and concerted military operations and to implement this protocol . . . shall not apply to situations of internal disturbances and tensions, such as riots, isolated and sporadic acts of violence and other acts of a similar nature, as not being armed conflicts.

Paradoxically, Protocol 2 for *internal* conflicts grants lawful belligerent status only to those with a prima facie claim to statehood ("exercise such control . . . "), whereas Protocol 1, for *international* conflicts, is silent about this requirement. Some of the delegations that accepted Protocol 1 specified that they did so assuming that the exclusions of Protocol 2 applied equally to Protocol 1.

Suggestions for Further Reading

Besides Walzer's book, for historical depth one should read James Turner Johnson's *Ideology, Reason, and the Limitation of War: Religious and Secular Concepts, 1200–1740* (Princeton University Press, Princeton, 1975). William V. O'Brien's *The Conduct of Just and Limited War* (Praeger, New York, 1981) and Robert L. Phillips's *War and Justice* (University of Oklahoma Press, Norman, 1984) defend just war theory. C. A. Pompe's *Aggressive War: An International Crime* (Martinus Nijhoff, The Hague, 1953) is the fullest study of the notion of aggressive war, but I find Yehuda Melzer's *Concepts of Just War* (A. W. Sijthoff, Leyden, 1975) more enlightening. The reports of the UN Committee on Defining Aggression (see my Bibliography) are more interesting than one would expect.

4

Strategic Air War

Unfortunately we have to make war as we must and not as we should like to.

—Lord Kitchener[1]

The most crucial and troubling development in twentieth century warfare is the extent to which civilians have been placed in harm's way. In part this change has been due to the widespread adoption of guerrilla tactics. I shall discuss this factor in Chapter 5. Here I examine the other factor: the development in World War II of strategic warfare against the enemy heartland.

As remote as this kind of warfare might seem from current problems, it is central to them. When Hiroshima and Nagasaki were subjected to atomic attack, the weapons were new and revolutionary, but the havoc they wrought on enemy cities was not. Nuclear weapons provided a more effective means of carrying out a strategy that was already widely and vigorously pursued through conventional bombing: "It was not thought that any irreversible threshold was being crossed."[2]

When the war ended, that strategy remained almost by default; the new weapons were simply integrated into it. In the words of one writer, "present nuclear strategies are an institutionalization of Second World War methods of waging war."[3] Post–World War II nuclear strategy is a legacy of that war.

The Historical Context

War in the Sky

Industrialization brought the means as well as the motive for attacking the enemy's home front. At the end of the eighteenth century soldiers took to the air for the first time as hot-air balloons began to be used as floating observation platforms. In 1849 the Austrians, inventing the cruise missile, launched unmanned bomb-carrying balloons at Venice in the first air attack in history.

The balloon took war into the skies, but the balloon could not set a course; it drifted with the wind. In 1908 Germany solved that problem by adopting the propeller-driven dirigible as a weapon—a true airship, rather than an air raft. These early giants caused panic when, on the last night of May in 1915, they lumbered over the British capital and released their bombs. The very idea of a person's leaving work and discovering enemy soldiers buzzing about overhead was a novelty that produced considerable consternation among the English: "It is particularly humiliating to allow an enemy to come over your capital city and hurl bombs upon it. His aim may be very bad, the casualties may be few, but the moral effect is wholly undesirable. When the Zeppelins came to London they could have scored a galling technical triumph over us if they had showered us with confetti."[4] Thirty years earlier the author of a study of military uses of the hot-air balloon had noted that "it undoubtedly produces a depressing effect to have things dropped on one from above."[5]

Air war began with the zeppelin and the balloon. In 1915, though, the zeppelins suffered increasing losses as the British organized anti-aircraft gun and fighter defenses against the slow, fragile, and unwieldy lighter-than-air ships. The next year the raids petered out. By then planes had taken up the battle. Austrian bombers struck Ravenna, Venice, Padua, Naples, and other cities; the Italians bombed Ljubljana and other Austro-Hungarian cities. In German territory, Freiburg and Karlsruhe suffered, blast furnaces were attacked, and the rail network radiating from Metz was the object of a prolonged bombing campaign. Paris, close to the front lines throughout most of the war, was subject to repeated air attacks: As early as 1914 searchlights and machine guns were mounted on the Eiffel Tower. In 1917 the Germans initiated the first serious strategic bombing campaign the world had seen, as Gotha and R bombers—the latter monsters carrying 2,000-pound bomb loads—again brought the war to London.

But the small numbers, poor accuracy, and low payload of World War I bombers kept the damage they inflicted low compared with the investment needed to build and operate the bomber fleets. By the end of the war it was obvious that planes could attack the enemy's homeland—the British alone counted 1,400 dead in the bombings of 1917. It was not obvious that the results achieved by such attacks justified their cost.

Nonetheless, in the 1920s and 1930s a number of writers and military thinkers prophesied a new form of warfare: a lightning war in which great fleets of bombers would devastate the enemy's cities in just a few hours, creating an almost instantaneous demand in the stricken nation for a cessation of hostilities. This possibility had been anticipated even before the twentieth century:

> As early as 1893, Major J. D. Fullerton of the Royal Engineers had presented a paper at a meeting of military engineers in Chicago in which he prophesied that the impact of aeronautics foreshadowed "as great a revolution in the art of war as the discovery of gunpowder," that future wars might well start with a great air battle and that "the arrival of the aerial fleet over the enemy capital will probably conclude the campaign."[6]

A 1923 British Air Staff memorandum said that winning a future air war would require "bombing the enemy's country, destroying his sources of supply of aircraft and engines and breaking the morale of his people." A 1929 British cabinet paper claimed that air power enabled a nation to defeat another without defeating its armed forces first: "Airpower . . . can pass over the enemy Navies and Armies and . . . attack the centres of production, transportation and communication in which the enemy war effort is maintained." And in 1938 the Air Corps Tactical School's bulletin, ACTS, proclaimed, "The possibility for the application of military force against the vital structure of a nation directly and immediately upon the outbreak of hostilities is the most important and far-reaching development of modern times."[7]

Though this vision of "the knockout blow" far exceeded the technological abilities of the time and remained an illusion until the nuclear era, in the popular mind the vision took hold. Journalists charge generals with fighting the last war; the generals might charge the journalists with fighting the next war. In the late 1950s films like *On the Beach* portrayed the destruction of human life on earth through nuclear war—an ability the arsenals of the time possessed only in the public imagination. In 1936 the movie *Things to Come,* based on an H. G. Wells novel, portrayed a world bombed into the Dark Ages when war breaks out in 1940. Magazines and newspapers, books and motion pictures, popularized this notion of cataclysm from the skies, the instantaneous obliteration of major cities and the destruction of European civilization by the warplane. On the ground the elite mobile infantry pedaled bicycles.

The Strategic Air War in Europe

When World War II broke out, all the major combatants were leery of using the airplane in a strategic bombing role—at least as long as the enemy seemed to have the ability to retaliate in kind. President Franklin D. Roosevelt appealed to the belligerents not to bomb civilian population centers. Hitler agreed, and the British and French bombers were forbidden by their governments to carry bombs over Germany at all. That first winter of the war the Royal Air Force (RAF) confined its strike missions to attacks on German warships. Even then, for fear of hitting civilians, the British were ordered not to attack ships in dry dock. British and French bombers also spent the winter of 1939–1940 dropping leaflets on Germany, "leaflets designed, in Churchill's discontented words, 'to rouse the Germans to a higher morality.' Sir Arthur Harris [Chief of Bomber Command], on the other hand, considered that the purpose they chiefly served was 'to supply the Continent's requirements of toilet paper for the five long years of the war.' "[8] When the German assault on the Low Countries began in May, Allied bombers were used to harass and interdict German military formations, but not to bomb cities.

The Germans, too, kept their bombers on a leash. It is true, and Allied propagandists made much of the fact, that the German air force (Luftwaffe) had taken part in a prolonged and extensive bombardment of Warsaw, causing a great deal of destruction to the city. The Germans hit Warsaw with about 5,000 tons of bombs. But this air campaign was in support of the German siege and assault on a resisting Warsaw, and the use of air bombardment in support of an attack on a defended city could hardly be faulted as a war crime when, as we saw in Chapter 2, the Hague conventions specifically allow the bombardment of defended places: Where artillery and naval bombardment is permissible, air bombardment cannot be criminal. The same can be said for the Luftwaffe's subsequent attack on Rotterdam, which killed about 1,000 people (though the Dutch initially claimed 30,000 dead): It too was launched in conjunction with ground operations, and the Germans were willing to cancel it if the Dutch declared Rotterdam an open city.[9] The attack on Rotterdam induced the Dutch to surrender. Not until Hiroshima and Nagasaki would air attack have such an effect on a nation again. After the fall of France, during the opening stages of the Battle of Britain, the Luftwaffe and the RAF concentrated on ports, shipping, and airfields, all understood to be valid military targets. Except for these installations, enemy cities were spared.

But it soon became apparent to both sides that even if as Stanley Baldwin, then former prime minister, put it in a speech to Parliament in 1932, "the bomber will always get through," the cost might be unacceptable. The bombers got through, but many did not make it back home, and the ratio of those lost to those launched was prohibitive. Antiaircraft guns and fighter planes exacted a heavy toll, a toll made more unbearable by the great cost of the bomber. Bomber losses exceeded the ability of the combatant nations to replace them—a trend that signaled failure for daylight bombing campaigns. Prewar predictions had exaggerated the power of the bomber and underestimated its vulnerability.

For the RAF's Bomber and Coastal commands there were indications of this weakness from the start of the war. On September 4, 1939, when the war was only three days old, a flight sent to bomb German warships at Wilhemshaven lost four of its five planes. That day Bomber Command lost 23.3 percent of its sorties. The British ran no more attacks against German warships for twenty-five days. When they did strike again with two flights of bombers, eleven planes in all, one flight of five was wiped out, with eighteen of its twenty-four airmen killed. The next day the British sent five light bombers on a daylight reconnaissance mission over Saarbrucken—none returned. The next month they abandoned daylight reconnaissance missions. (The light bomber was the Fairey Battle, "described by one of its pilots as 'that gentle old tin swallow.'"[10])

Two attacks in December proved particularly telling. On the fourteenth, Bomber Command again went after German naval targets near Wilhelmshaven. Flying at 200 to 1,000 feet under heavy clouds, 50 percent of the attacking planes were shot down. The air staff attributed these heavy losses to the effectiveness of flak against low-flying planes and decided to try another approach.

Therefore, when four days later, on a perfectly clear day, the bombers returned to Wilhelmshaven, "the height of the attack had accordingly been raised and the action [was] . . . fought at high altitude around 15,000 feet."[11] But the loss rate did not go down: Of the twenty-two Wellingtons attacking, twelve were shot down. This "loss of fifty per cent of the force dispatched, and nearly fifty-five per cent of that engaged, was at least ten times the casualty rate which Bomber Command could ever afford as a regular drain on its crews and aircraft."[12] And this time the losses were mainly due to fighters. (Though the British did not know it, the Germans had used radar for the first time to direct the interceptors.) The lesson of the two attacks posed a dilemma: in low-level attacks, flak was murderous; in high-altitude attacks, German fighters were deadly.

The British began to reevaluate their strategy. They had planned to attack the Ruhr, "the industrial nerve centre of the enemy,"[13] if a German offensive endangered France. Now there were second thoughts:

> For a long time the Commander-in-Chief, Bomber Command, Sir Edgar Ludlow-Hewitt, though in many respects aware of the limited power of his force, had nourished the hope that the plan would succeed. . . . Soon after the outbreak of war, however, the Commander-in-Chief began to reach different conclusions and thereafter the more he thought about the plan, the less he liked it. Writing to the Commander-in-Chief, Fighter Command, Sir Hugh Dowding, on 12th October 1939, he said that he could not measure the effectiveness of the Ruhr defences, nor could he predict what the Bomber Command casualties would be if an initial attack was made by a hundred bombers. . . . "We cannot afford," he said, "to contemplate losing a large part of it [Bomber Command] in one operation, however successful. . . ." Finally . . . in December, these somber forecasts were confirmed by experience when small formations of Wellingtons, operating in daylight over the North Sea, were engaged by the enemy and very severely mauled. . . .
>
> This confirmation of his worst fears caused Sir Edgar Ludlow-Hewitt to disavow the Ruhr plan. On 28th January 1940 he sent a new appreciation of the prospects to the Air Ministry. This raised considerable doubts about achieving the necessary degree of destruction with the small force . . . which could take part. If the attack was made from high level the bombing accuracy would not be adequate, and if from low level the bombers might run into a smoke screen and balloon barrage. Casualties might amount to fifty per cent of the force attacking. Such losses, apart from the serious psychological effect, would reduce the efficiency of the force by eighty per cent for months to come. . . . In his covering letter to the Air Ministry, the Commander-in-Chief concluded, "In view therefore of the risks involved and the doubt which must exist as to the possibility of achieving success, I suggest the urgent necessity to reconsider the whole question and in particular to study the possibility of devising some other means of employing the bomber strike force to the best effect without committing the whole force to such grave risks of heavy loss as is involved in the plan under consideration."[14]

Meanwhile the leaflet-dropping night bombers were suffering much lower losses: From September 3, 1939, to April 9, 1940, Bomber Command's loss rate on night sorties was 2.6 percent versus 4.8 percent for daylight missions. According to Britain's official history of Bomber Command, "If Bomber Command was to remain in the war it had no alternative but to fight in the dark."[15]

But in December 1940 the lesson was still not perfectly clear. One more possibility remained for daylight raids: In the December 18 attack the bombers that had flown in particularly tight formations, presenting the Messerschmidts with more intense defensive fire, suffered much less than the others. Perhaps if the planes could stay in a close formation, the tide could be turned.

On May 10, 1940, the Germans launched their assault on France, and RAF bombers based on the Continent, the Advanced Air Striking Force (AASF), were flung at the advancing columns in a series of desperate actions. In attacks by thirty-two light bombers, the British lost thirteen, and all the rest were damaged: "The storm of fire that came up from the ground made each of these missions tantamount to suicide—yet they continued until the squadrons were practically wiped out."[16] On May 11, "of eight Battles sent off in bad weather to attack German columns near Luxemburg only one returned, badly damaged: 100 per cent loss, and 'there is no indication that the bombers ever reached their target areas.'"[17]

The next day, No. 139 Squadron lost seven out of nine Blenheim bombers, and Bomber Command's No. 2 Group lost ten out of twenty-four. No. 12 Squadron was asked for volunteers to attack the bridges over the Albert Canal (attacks on these bridges had already cost the Belgians ten out of fifteen planes). The entire squadron stepped forward to volunteer, so the mission was composed of the first crews on the duty roster. Five planes were sent; one returned. At the canal captured British flyers were given a tongue-lashing by a German officer for pressing their attack in the face of the deadly flak barrage. A fighter pilot who had visited No. 12 Squadron said that its bomber crews were "pathetically confident in their tight formation with their fire-concentration tactics. . . . We admired their flying and guts, but although we gave them as much . . . encouragement as we could, we privately didn't give much for their chances."[18]

In two days the Advanced Air Striking Force had lost 63 of its 135 bombers. On May 14, the British managed to get off 71 bomber sorties, but lost 60 percent of the force. Three days later "Air Marshall Barratt decided that except in dire emergency the AASF bombers would not again be used in daylight. This meant that the only remaining daylight strike force was No. 2 Group of Bomber Command in England."[19] A month earlier an Air Staff directive had ordered Bomber Command's new commander in chief, Air Marshal Charles Portal, to fly the bulk of his missions at night.

The following summer attacks on naval targets, which could only be attempted in daylight, proved the point again: An attack on the Scharnhorst resulted in the loss of five Halifaxes out of fifteen. Another attack prompted Churchill to write: "The loss of seven Blenheims out of seventeen in the daylight attack on merchant shipping and docks at Rotterdam is most severe. . . . The losses in our bombers have been very heavy this month, and Bomber Command is not expanding as was hoped. While I greatly admire the bravery of the pilots, I do not want them pressed too hard."[20]

If the RAF wanted to conduct a daylight bombing campaign, it had to overcome two problems. First, Britain needed larger, sturdier bombers, with more defensive gunfire and safety features that were costly in weight, like self-sealing fuel tanks. Second, Britain needed fighter escorts to protect its bombers. But the fighters of the time did not have the range. It would be half a decade before the North American P-51 Mustang would overcome the problem; and until long-range fighters proved themselves in combat, no one could know that the problem could ever be solved. In theory one might assume, as Portal did, that the long-range fighter would always be at a disadvantage facing a short-range fighter: The larger size and greater weight of the long-range fighter, due to its fuel requirements, would make it, all other things being equal, less maneuverable and slower.[21]

By fall 1940, Bomber Command had essentially become a night-bombing force—a change that radically decreased bomber losses, but at the price of radically decreasing bomber accuracy. Daylight attacks were reserved for naval targets and for tactical air strikes against enemy ground troops.

In the skies over Britain the Luftwaffe was learning the same hard lesson. With air supremacy on the Continent, the Luftwaffe's bombers had not suffered the RAF's losses. When the Luftwaffe was fighting over Britain, things were different. From advanced bases in Normandy and the Pas de Calais, German single-engined fighters, the Me-109s, could range over southern England, providing an escort the British bombers had lacked in their raids. But the Me-109's range was so short that loiter time over England amounted to only a few minutes, and the German fighters were never able at that range to acquire air superiority. In consequence German bomber losses were so heavy that the Germans, too, were forced into night missions: The only all-out daylight attack on London occurred on September 7. From then on, the blitz was a nocturnal event. Ten days later "the last great daylight battle" over Britain took place.[22] Fighter-bombers (Me-109s and twin-engined Me-110s) would attack in daylight, but the Luftwaffe's devoted bombers "practically vanished from the daylight skies."[23]

The consequence of the change from day to night missions was, in retrospect, almost inevitable. On the night of August 24, Luftwaffe bombers, attempting to bomb the London docks, bombed central London instead. Churchill ordered a retaliatory raid on Berlin. Hitler replied with an all-out raid on London that was carried out on September 7. The gloves were off.

These attacks ushered in a momentous change in the strategic air war, which from then on would be directed to a large extent at cities. Some writers have alleged that Churchill, realizing that the diversion of Luftwaffe attacks from aircraft factories and airbases to British cities was to the military advantage of the hard-pressed Fighter Command, seized on what he knew was an accidental bombing as a pretext to attack Berlin, knowing that Hitler would order the Luftwaffe to counter: "There was little doubt, even at the time, that the bombing was unintentional. And later analyses indeed proved that the attack programs of the Luftwaffe over the next few nights called for no raids on London; instead they were focusing their attention on such vital industrial centers as Liverpool and Birmingham. But Churchill was delighted to believe otherwise—and to act accordingly."[24] This looks like a case—not the only one in this chapter—of interpreting the actors of the time as if they already knew what subsequent events have taught us.

Why should Churchill have known any of these things? How were those on the ground to tell an accidental bombing from an intentional one? There was no apology from the Germans. How was Churchill to know that the diversion of the Luftwaffe to London was to Britain's advantage? At the time, estimates of the damage that such a campaign would produce were greatly exaggerated, and an air assault on London was hardly a matter for eager anticipation. Studies of bombing in World War I and the Spanish Civil War had led to estimates of 50 casualties for every 2,000 pounds of bombs: the Air Staff believed a bombing campaign against British cities would produce 60,000 casualties in the first week alone.[25] Some estimates were even more pessimistic: "There was no doubt that the generation of 1939 was stunned and horrified by the spectacle of Warsaw in flames. It seemed to fulfill perfectly the most dire predictions that Douhet and other military Cassandras had been making for years. . . . Some 'experts' had written that 5,000 tons [of bombs] was sufficient to raze a city the size of Paris."[26]

The October 9, 1939, issue of *Time* magazine had reported from Warsaw: "The corpses of men and horses [were] rotting in almost every street of Europe's fifth largest capital. More than 500 separate fires were blazing . . . covering the city with a choking lid of smoke and flame. The reservoirs were blasted and dry, the power plants smashed, and Nazi bombers had methodically blown to bloody smithereens all Warsaw hospitals, crammed with wounded."

How was Churchill to have known that these predictions would not come true—that this scene would not be duplicated in London? The

Dutch had claimed 30,000 dead at Rotterdam—and Rotterdam had been struck by a mere fifty Luftwaffe planes. The British Chiefs of Staff viewed their own slender bomber resources with similar awe. In a 1939 paper on the plan to attack the Ruhr they said that the population of the Ruhr "might be expected to crack" under Bomber Command's onslaught. The paper was approved by the War Cabinet. World War I bombers had caused a panic in London that shocked the British government. How would Londoners respond to World War II bombing? And assuming that the best policy for the Germans was not to strike at British cities, how could Churchill have known that Hitler, in a pique, would foolishly abandon it?

At any rate, although Hitler had ordered that central London not be bombed until he gave the word, he had not had the same reservations about other British cities. On the same day central London was accidentally bombed, a hundred homes were destroyed in the suburb of Bethnal Green, and residential areas in Portsmouth and Ramsgate were attacked. And on the following night, as British planes were flying to their first raid on Berlin, German bombers were heading for Birmingham and Coventry.[27] On the night of August 28, Liverpool was heavily bombed, without any special permission having been necessary from Hitler. The bombing of Portsmouth, Bristol, Liverpool, and Manchester would have given Churchill any excuse he might have needed for bombing Berlin even if London had never been bombed: Churchill could not treat the bombing of London as calling for reply while ignoring loss of life in northern and southern cities.

The fact is, as was proven over and over again during the war, that the night bombing of the period was so inaccurate that when it was conducted in the vicinity of a city, the difference between bombing the city itself and bombing military installations or docks in or near the city was a theoretical difference rather than a practical one. In the words of the British official history of Bomber Command, "It may be a crime to attack a cathedral, but it is only war to miss a railway station."[28] The inaccuracy of the bombers began to be noted in 1940, when Air Marshall Sir Richard Peirse concluded that:

> "On the longer range attacks only one out of every five aircraft which he [Peirse] despatched actually reached the target. On the short-range attacks, he thought one in three found the target." On November 12, the chairman of a Group Navigation Officer's conference in Bomber Command (Wing Commander L. K. Barnes) pronounced his conclusion that only 35 per cent of all bombers despatched were reaching their primary targets. These gloomy perceptions were not generally well received in 1940, and certainly not for wide consumption; in due course

> they would receive striking confirmation . . . in May 1941 it was accepted that approximately 50 per cent of the Command's bombs were falling in open country.[29]

These were only impressions. But by summer 1941, the RAF had developed a night photographic reconnaissance ability that enabled it to survey the results of the June and July bombing attacks—the first time a systematic attempt was made to assess bombing campaign results:

> Air-staff calculations continued to give aiming error in hundreds of yards; now the extensive photographic analysis of the summmer of 1941 would supply a more reliable indication of bombing accuracy, and as it turned out, a thoroughly disheartening one. The Butt Report, which incorporated the findings, put the proportion of bombers that placed their payloads within five miles of the target as about one-fifth. In the Ruhr, with its special challenges to the night bomber [smog and dense flak concentrations], perhaps seven planes in a hundred released their bombs anywhere within the most general neighborhood of the objective.[30]

Read in detail, the Butt report was even more discouraging than this account indicates. Butt's statistical analysis of the photographs revealed that over Germany for every four planes recorded as attacking the target, one had placed its bombs within *five miles* of the target. But "these figures relate only to aircraft recorded as attacking the target"—a third of the planes sent on bombing missions never attacked at all. Moreover,

> it must be observed also that by defining the target area for the purpose of this enquiry as having a radius of five miles, an area of over 75 square miles is taken. This must at least for any town but Berlin consist very largely of open country. The proportion of aircraft actually dropping their bombs on built-up areas must be very much less, but what this proportion is, however, cannot be indicated by the study of night photographs.[31]

In other words, a large proportion of the bombers counted in the Butt report as attacking the target city were actually bombing the countryside around the city. Sometimes bomber forces completely missed the targeted cities, leaving those on the ground unaware that an air raid on their city had even taken place. This happened in a raid on Essen on the night of June 1, 1942: The bombs fell so far off target that the Germans did not realize Essen was the target—their reports for the day just noted widespread bombing in the Ruhr countryside. In 1925 one authority had said that a bomber "can hit a town from ten thousand feet—if the town is big enough."[32] Not always.

Sometimes it was even worse. In daylight, crews not only missed the target city—they sometimes bombed the wrong country. On February 2, 1945, U.S. bombers struck the Swiss town of Schaffhausen—for the second time in the war. A month later crews of two flights of U.S. bombers looking down through holes in the clouds saw what they thought were their targets and released their bombs. One group was actually bombing Basel; the other hit Zurich. The target was Freiburg, which had been bombed by the Germans themselves on the day they launched their offensive in the west; they had mistaken it for Mulhouse. At the start of the war, on September 4, 1939, a British plane accidentally bombed a Danish town 110 miles from the intended target.

Once losses forced bombers into night missions, discriminatory attacks were virtually impossible. They could only have occurred if the target were miles from the nearest town, and even then the target would almost certainly be missed. Night bombers could not, unless they were extremely lucky, hit a target much smaller than a medium-sized city.

When in 1942 the U.S. Eighth Air Force became operational in Britain, it was with the expectation of putting into practice the doctrine exemplified by the B-17 Flying Fortress—precision daylight attacks by heavily armed "self-escorting bombers." The plan was viewed with suspicion by the British, and rightly so.

The initial attacks against coastal targets and targets in France seemed to go well. But as the Eighth Air Force reached into Germany in 1943, the situation changed. On March 4 a raid on the rail yards at Hamm resulted in the loss of 4 out of 14 Fortresses.[33] On April 17 in an attack on the Focke-Wulf plant at Bremen, the 1st Bombardment Wing had 16 planes lost and 46 damaged out of 107: "Never before had the Eighth encountered such heavy or well-coordinated defenses."[34] German fighter strength in the west was rising, and their tactics were improving. The climax came during "black week" in October. On October 8 in attacks on submarine and airframe plants at Bremen and Vegesack, losses were 30 out of 399. On the tenth, in a fifteen-minute attack on Münster, the 100th Bombardment Group (BG) lost all 12 of its planes, and its parent formation, the 3rd Bombardment Division, lost 29 of 119 planes, including 8 out of 17 in the 390th BG.[35] (According to Ronald Schaffer this was the first Eighth Air Force raid targeted against a city center—the official target was the Münster rail system.) As an adjunct to this raid, the 305th BG and 379th BG, attempting to attack the air base at Enschede in the Netherlands as a target of opportunity, hit the town, killing 155 people. The climax came with the October 14 raid on the ball-bearing plants at Schweinfurt: 291 planes were sent off, 60 were lost. In six days the Eighth had lost 148 heavy bombers—a rate of loss that would wipe it out in two weeks.

The Eighth Air Force pulled back to closer targets, which allowed friendly fighter cover and decreased the number of enemy fighters that could intercept. In 1944, with long-range fighter escorts becoming available, the Eighth resumed long-range penetrations, though not without serious losses. In April 1944, the Eighth Air Force lost 512 planes—577 if we include planes so badly damaged they had to be written off. Three hundred and sixty-one of the lost planes were heavy bombers. The Eighth Air Force remained, throughout the war, a daylight bombing force, but it too faced some of the problems that RAF Bomber Command faced.

First there was the problem of bomber accuracy. Daylight bombing was more accurate than night bombing, but it still fell far short of being precision bombing. The U.S. Strategic Bombing Survey estimated that in the first nine months of 1943, 80 percent of U.S. daylight bombers dropped their bombs a fifth of a mile or more off target. This inaccuracy occurred even where there were the strongest reasons, precautions, and incentives for accuracy. For example, despite Allied concern at the highest levels of government about Belgian and French civilian casualties during the attacks on the rail networks that preceded D day, 12,000 civilians were killed during such attacks. For the massive bombing of St. Lô that led to the U.S. breakout from Normandy, General Omar Bradley took extraordinary precautions to ensure that the high-altitude bombers would not hit U.S. lines. At the last minute, on July 24, bad weather forced most of the bombers to abort, but the ones that got through managed to bomb U.S. troops. As a consequence, the next day, when weather permitted the real attack, Bradley ordered more extreme precautions. U.S. troops pulled back from their advanced lines to the other side of a road; Bradley asked the air force to send in the bombers parallel to the road that would clearly mark the dividing point between the Americans and the Germans; orange smoke markers were ignited to indicate U.S. lines. All to no avail: The bombing of U.S. troops was worse than on the previous day. One company was virtually wiped out, and an entire battalion had to be withdrawn from the attack. The United States had suffered 800 casualties from friendly air action in two days, including General Leslie McNair, commanding general of Army Ground Forces, killed viewing the operation.

Two weeks later, on August 9, the Eighth Air Force, this time supporting Commonwealth troops, caused 300 friendly casualties among British, Canadian, and Polish troops. Five days after that, RAF Bomber Command accounted for 400 more. In three weeks, attacking in daylight and to the specifications of ground commanders, British and U.S. heavy bombers caused 1,500 Allied casualties—equivalent to destroying a regiment. When the heavies did not cause Allied casualties, the "solution" might be caution that negated the bombardment, as in Operation Charnwood on July 7: "So great was the fear of bombing short and causing British casualties that the bombline was fixed '6,000 yards ahead of the nearest troops. This meant that the bombs would fall on the enemy's rearward defences on the northern outskirts of Caen, some three miles behind the strongly defended forward area which the infantry and tanks would have to capture.'"[36] The air force simply was not able to hit factories without doing extensive damage to the surrounding areas.

Second, there was the problem of weather. Northern Europe has extensive periods of overcast skies during which precision bombing was impossible—flying at low altitude under the clouds, the bombers would be mauled by the flak. What was the United States to do with its bombers during those periods? It could keep the bombers on the ground, which would mean a reduction in the number of missions flown that would be equivalent to dismantling one out of every three bombers. Or the United States could do what it actually did: Stage the missions anyway, even though reduction in visibility caused by clouds meant that the raids would actually be area attacks. For bombing through clouds by radar was no more accurate than bombing at night by radar. In February 1945, General Henry H. ("Hap") Arnold would send a cable to Carl Spaatz "implying that he would like to know whether there was any significant distinction between morale bombing and radar attacks on transportation targets in urban areas."[37]

U.S. daylight raids were more accurate than night raids, but the bombers still could not attack railroad marshalling yards or industrial plants without doing heavy damage to the surrounding residential areas. And as the war moved toward its end, U.S. targeting policies drew closer to the British policies as the United States attempted, or so the claim went, to break German morale through bombing.

We are all familiar with the consequences. During the blitz, British cities were attacked by a German air force that had been designed to provide tactical support for the army: twin-engined bombers with relatively low payloads and short-range fighters unable to linger over Britain to protect the bombers. Besides the doctrinal origins for the lack of heavy bombers, we can also note that "Goering once told Field Marshall Kesselring that he was building twin-engined bombers rather than four-engine ones because Hitler would ask him how many bombers he had, not how many engines they carried."[38] The Luftwaffe had concentrated its resources on tactical support and failed to develop a serious strategic bombing force. Britain and the United States, by contrast, were building heavy four-engined bombers (the B-17, though only 50 percent heavier than the main German bomber, the Ju-88, carried four times the bomb load of the latter), and the United States was developing long-range escort fighters like the P-38 Lightning and the P-51 Mustang. By 1944 the RAF's Bomber Command, the U.S. Eighth Air Force in Britain, and the Fifteenth Air Force in Italy possessed extensive stocks of the right types of planes, and German cities suffered a fate worse than London or Coventry had experienced. In 1940, the year of the blitz, the Luftwaffe dropped less than 40,000 tons of bombs on Britain. In 1944 the U.S. and British bomber forces dropped almost 1.2 million tons of bombs on German-occupied territory.

The United States thus became, by virtue of the sheer power of its heavy bomber forces, a destroyer of cities on a grand scale—a lesson that Japan was about to learn in great pain. The same United States that at the start of the war in Europe had urged the belligerents to refrain from bombing civilian population centers had, by the end of the war, become the unrivaled champion of the art.

Large-scale war had undergone a major change: Civilian population centers far to the rear of the battle line had come under the gun. *Target Germany,* a 1943 U.S. Air Force book, explained: "The physical attrition of warfare is no longer limited to the fighting forces. Heretofore the home front has remained relatively secure; armies fought, civil populations worked and waited. . . . [But now] we have terror and devastation carried to the core of a warring nation."[39] The idea of civilian immunity seemed to many to have become a mockery. War, serious war, had acquired the feel that it has today in the nuclear age: No one is safe; all is threatened.

The Strategic Air War Against Japan

The chief disadvantage of a knowledge of the past, and particularly of a superficial knowledge of the past, is that in hindsight whatever has in fact happened may begin to appear inevitable. For the people who were there, though, the future was uncertain. Rarely in World War II was the issue more uncertain than in November 1944, when Brigadier General Haywood "Possum" Hansell's Twenty-first Bomber Command launched the first Marianas-based strike against the Japanese home islands.

Just thirteen months earlier, in October 1943, the Eighth Air Force had had its "black week" when in the skies over Germany the U.S. belief in the unescorted, self-defending bomber formation came crashing down in 100 wrecked B-17s. Hansell knew—he had been in Britain with the Eighth Air Force at the time. By 1944 when heavy bombers flew over Germany, they had fighter protection. Hansell's 100 B-29s were about to duplicate the effort that in 1943 had led to disaster over Germany. From Saipan in the Marianas, 1,500 miles from Japan, his shiny new planes would strike Tokyo, far beyond the range of friendly fighter cover. And they would attack in daylight. Hansell was an advocate of precision bombing. So was the Committee of Operations Analysts, which in November 1943 designated the Japanese aircraft industry as a primary target; the Joint Target Group, which gave first priority to the same industry, and the Joint Chiefs of Staff, whose first target directive to Hansell, two weeks before the mission, followed the recommendations of these committees. Hansell was ordered to attack Japanese plane production and repair facilities. The target Hansell picked for his first raid was the Nakajima aircraft engine factory complex in the Tokyo suburb of Musashino-Tama. This factory was estimated to produce a third of Japan's combat aircraft engines.

If past experience was a guide, the raid would not work, and Hansell's commander, General Arnold, had forwarded to Hansell a disapproving letter from a man with far more experience than Hansell in flying against the Japanese: General George C. Kenney, Douglas MacArthur's air commander, predicted complete disaster—the Japanese would destroy the B-29s.

From many points of view, the problems involved in attacking Japan were greater than they were in attacking Germany. There was initially only one airfield at Saipan that could handle the B-29s, which required the longest runways in the world at the time. Even then, the heavily laden planes required every foot of runway and sometimes used even more, and like the carrier planes that operated from the shortest runways in the world, the B-29s could only take off into the wind, whose boost was needed to get them aloft. To further complicate matters, Saipan's airfield was on a grade and the planes when fully loaded could not struggle uphill and get aloft safely: A wind shift that brought the prevailing breezes in across the high end of the field would scrub a mission. The first planes off the runway would have to circle overhead burning fuel as the others, one by one, took off and joined the formation. Then there would be the round trip between Saipan and Japan—at the B-29's cruising speed of 230 miles an hour, a fourteen-hour flight. During these fourteen hours any problem would be serious, for on the entire flight there was no emergency runway a plane in trouble could use—the nearest airfield to Saipan was at Kwajalein, a further 1,500 miles. The whole round trip was over the ocean, whose cold embrace would receive over 1,300 flyers before the war ended. In the movies calm waters provide planes with a soft pillow to land on. Anyone who has taken a belly flop off a high diving board knows differently, and a 130,000-pound plane does not ease itself into the water any more gently. Sailors on a convoy once watched a B-29 make a perfectly controlled landing in the ocean. The plane broke in half and within two minutes disappeared under the waves. Between Saipan and Japan the only landfall would be over Japan, and the Japanese were known to behead captured flyers.

All in all, from the time the first plane took off in the early dawn until the landing of the last returning plane, seventeen hours would elapse. At Saipan, planes would be returning at night, and the airfield, still without runway lights, would have to make do with smudge pots. The planes would be returning with their fuel gauges pointing toward empty: To make the flight at all, Hansell had to reduce the bomb load and increase the fuel load, authorizing the planes to fly with ten tons over their designed weight, which would strain the engines and increase the number of planes that had to be ditched. Whether they could make the trip at all was in doubt. To conserve fuel they would have to fly in formation on cruise control—a new and untried technique. Hansell had wanted the squadrons of his Seventy-third Wing to practice it while transferring from the United States to Saipan, but Air Transport Command, which had charge of the planes until they arrived in Saipan, refused. The command thought that even without bomb loads, the B-29s did not have the range for formation flying on the 2,400-mile leg from Sacramento to Hawaii. The round trip Saipan-to-Tokyo flight would be 3,200 miles, with the planes overloaded.

It was a great gamble, and one that history said would fail. And it did fail, but not for the reasons past experience predicted. On that score the past proved a poor teacher: Only two planes were lost on the first mission to Japan, as opposed to the sixty lost over Schweinfurt the previous August. It failed due to factors about which past experience had not given, and could not have given, a clue.

What made the gamble possible in Hansell's eyes was the incredible plane his crews flew. The sleek but heavily armed B-29 Superfortress was the first pressurized high-altitude bomber produced, and it would rely on that altitude for protection. The Superforts would come in between 27,000 and 35,000 feet, up to 6.5 miles up, where antiaircraft fire would be ineffective and where fighters that managed to gain the altitude would be able to get in only one pass. But as Brooklyn's General Rosey O'Donnell led his wing into their bomb run on the first mission, the planes started drifting, and in the run incredulous navigators clocked the planes careening along at 445 miles an hour. Propelled by a 150-mile-an-hour tail wind—well over hurricane force—they hurtled over their targets too quickly for the proper use of their bombsights and headed back out over the ocean. The air force had just discovered the jet stream, which dominated the air over Japan at the altitude the B-29s were relying on for protection. It would be one of the components of the meteorological quagmire that ruined Hansell's carefully laid plans.

Another component in the failure was a typhoon that unexpectedly appeared between Saipan and Tokyo. Weather fronts drifting southeast from Siberia and colliding with warm, moist Pacific air created unexpected, towering, and violent storms, with thunderclaps and lightning to 40,000 feet. The suddenness with which these storms could appear was compounded by the lack of cooperation on the part of the Soviets, who treated Siberian weather reports, like everything else, as a vital state secret.

Finally, the six miles between the jet stream and the targets below were frequently dense with clouds, so that the planes, bombing by radar, were no more accurate than they would have been at night. And stacked at different altitudes in those six miles there might be as many as five different wind patterns, the sum scattering the bombs and presenting the bombardiers with a calculation they could not work out.

After the war an examination of the Nakajima factory records showed that fewer than fifty bombs had landed in the general area of the plant, where they caused negligible damage. To deliver those fifty bombs the B-29s had used 80,000 gallons of gasoline. U.S. reconnaissance photos, hampered by clouds, showed only sixteen bomb craters in the target areas.

One might think perhaps that the winds and clouds had been a fluke. Three days later the bombers returned to Nakajima. This time, instead of winds at 150 miles an hour, they were at 220. The planes returned for a third raid on December 3 against another Nakajima plant near Tokyo. The wind was at 180 miles an hour, and Nakajima records showed that only twenty-six bombs fell in the target area. By now the raids did not take the Japanese by surprise, and those twenty-six bombs cost six B-29s—almost one bomber for every four bombs in the target area. On December 27 a fourth raid on Nakajima produced the same results. A fifth on January 9 cost six more B-29s for twenty-four bombs in the target area—exactly one B-29 for every four bombs. By then 5.7 percent of the B-29s that got airborne were not making it home. By March 4 the Nakajima plant had been attacked eight times from the Marianas. Eight hundred and thirty-five B-29 sorties had produced only 4 percent damage at the plant.

Other targets had been attacked as well, some with more success and some with less. A raid on the Mitsubishi engine plant at Nagoya on December 13 reduced production by 25 percent, though at the time the United States did not realize the raid had been that successful. Five days later a raid on the nearby aircraft assembly plant was less successful, causing a ten-day production loss, while a December 22 return attack with incendiary bombs on Nagoya's engine plant caused no production loss. An experimental incendiary raid on Nagoya on January 3 burned out an area no greater than three football fields; a January 14 return attack on Nagoya's Mitsubishi aircraft plant got only four bombs in the target area.

The one real success was a January 19 attack on a Kawasaki plant near Kobe that had been producing 15 percent of Japan's airframes. This time the planes flew around 26,000 feet to reduce the wind effect, and the weather was clear. The B-29s suffered no losses and were right on target. Reconnaissance indicated more than a third of the plant damaged, but postwar records showed the factory had lost 90 percent of its production. It was the most successful raid run by Hansell and his last. He had been told on January 6 that he would be replaced. On January 20, Curtis LeMay took over Hansell's command. Hansell, at his own request, was transferred to a minor training post.

By January 6, Hansell's Twenty-first Bomber Command had flown about ten missions against Japan, with very little to show for it. Most of these raids had caused insignificant damage to the Japanese aircraft industry, whereas, due to lost and damaged planes, Hansell's strength was shrinking from the 111 planes he launched on the first raid to an average of 75 for the two raids staged in the last ten days of December—a matter of great concern, given the B-29's $800,000 cost. Meanwhile LeMay's China-based Twentieth Bomber Command had used its B-29s to destroy the Japanese military depot area in Hangkow with an incendiary attack. On January 23 another attack against the Mitsubishi Nagoya plant, planned under Hansell's command but carried out under LeMay's, reverted to the familiar pattern. Nine bombers were lost; no significant damage to the target.

Under LeMay the Twenty-first Bomber Command would duplicate the evolution the RAF's Bomber Command had undergone five years earlier, from a precision daylight bombing force to a night bombing force. The targets would, of course, no longer be individual plants, but urban areas. Bomb loads would be mainly incendiaries, rather than high explosives, and protected by darkness, the planes would fly at lower altitudes, stripped of their defensive guns.

The test of the new strategy—new in the Pacific at least—came on an attack on Tokyo on the night of March 9/10. The Twenty-first had by then built up its strength, and more than 300 B-29s attacked, setting off a fire storm that destroyed 18 percent of the city's industrial area and 63 percent of the city's commercial center. The Japanese counted over 80,000 dead. It was and still is the most destructive air raid in history, almost equaling the toll taken in the great earthquake that struck Tokyo in 1923—the greatest natural disaster known.

In the following weeks and months LeMay's bombers would raid Japan over and over again. Until the atom bomb was used, none of the raids produced casualties on the scale of the Tokyo raid—at Kobe, Japan's sixth largest city, the Japanese counted 2,669 dead or missing after a raid on March 16; at Osaka, after Tokyo the largest city in Japan, 4,000 were killed on the thirteenth. But though the casualties were relatively few, the physical destruction was great, and one by one Japan's cities were being destroyed. After the war the Strategic Bombing Survey, comparing the output of undamaged plants with damaged plants, indicated that air attack had reduced Japanese industrial output by 20–25 percent. There had been a Japanese fighter attack for every three B-29 sorties. Though Japan had been attacked with only one-ninth the tonnage of bombs dropped on Germany, damage seemed equivalent in the two nations. Three hundred and thirty thousand civilians had been killed.

Japanese antiair defenses had forced the bombers either to fly daylight high-altitude missions or to fly night missions, and either way bomber accuracy was too poor for precision raids on strictly industrial or military targets. As had happened over Britain and the Continent, the defense made precision bombing costly and ineffective. Additionally, Japanese industry, unlike European industry, was fed by numerous small manufacturing shops scattered throughout residential neighborhoods—blurring the distinction between industrial and residential areas. The consequences were the same that we saw over Britain and Germany: Cities themselves, rather than the industrial and military facilities within them, became the targets. Area bombing became the norm. The city center, rather than the aircraft factory, became the aiming point, with damage assessed in numbers of acres burned out.

In the European theater, the Allies were moving away from area bombing. After the attack on Dresden on February 13, Churchill said that it was time to review "the question of bombing of German cities simply for the sake of increasing terror, though under other pretexts. . . . The destruction of Dresden remains a serious query against the conduct of Allied bombing." Dresden had been put on the target list on January 28, only a month after the Battle of the Bulge. At that time Germany still seemed to have a lot of fight left. A month later Germany may have looked much weaker, and targeting began shifting more heavily to grand tactical support. By the third week in March the Allied air forces, supporting the advancing ground troops, had effectively isolated the German army in the Ruhr from the rest of the Reich, destroying fourteen of the eighteen bridges and twenty of the twenty-five major rail yards that served the Ruhr. By April 9 the last oil production targets had been destroyed and RAF Bomber Command ceased area attacks.

In the Pacific the situation was different: No Allied armies were fighting in Japan—the Japanese home islands were being attacked solely by air power. The advocates of strategic air power thought that air power alone could win the war. They proved to be right.

The Legal Context

The directing of war against cities did not happen without some debate—debate within the armed forces and debate in the public arena, debate in the United States and debate in the international arena, debate in the 1920s and 1930s and debate during the war. Even as the strategic bombing campaign reached toward its peak in the European theater, a small but vocal minority of civilians in Britain and the United States argued against the morality of area (as opposed to "pinpoint") bombing. Father John C. Ford argued in a 1944 issue of *Theological Review* that if "modern war is necessarily total, and necessarily involves direct attack on the life of innocent civilians . . . so much the worse for modern war. . . . If it necessarily includes such means, it is necessarily immoral itself." Ford went on to ask whether the following categories of people could be treated as legitimate objects of attack:

> Farmers, fishermen, foresters, lumberjacks, dressmakers, milliners, bakers, printers, textile workers, millers, painters, paper hangers, piano tuners, plasterers, shoemakers, cobblers, tailors, upholsterers, furniture makers, cigar and cigarette makers, glove makers, hat makers, suit makers, food processors, dairymen, fish canners, fruit and vegetable canners, slaughterers and packers, sugar refiners, liquor and beverage workers, teamsters, garage help, telephone girls, advertising men, bankers, brokers, clerks in stores, commercial travelers, decorators, window dressers, deliverymen, inspectors, insurance agents, retail dealers, salesmen and saleswomen in all trades, undertakers, wholesale dealers, meatcutters, butchers, actors, architects, sculptors, artists, authors, editors, reporters, priests, laybrothers, nuns, seminarians, professors, school teachers, dentists, lawyers, judges, musicians, photographers, physicians, surgeons, trained nurses, librarians, social and welfare workers, Red Cross workers, religious workers, theatre owners, technicians, laboratory assistants, barbers, bootblacks, charwomen, cleaners and dyers, hotelmen, elevator tenders, housekeepers, janitors, sextons, domestic servants,

> cooks, maids, nurses, handymen, laundry operatives, porters, victuallers, bookkeepers, accountants, statisticians, cashiers, stenographers, secretaries, typists, all office help, mothers of families, patients in hospitals, prison inmates, prison guards, institutional inmates, old men and women, all children with the use of reason, i.e., from seven years up. (After all, these latter buy war stamps, write letters of encouragement to their brothers in the service, and even carry the dinner pail to the father who works in the aircraft factory. They all cooperate to some degree in the aggression.)

Though the voice of these critics never grew very strong, there was enough apprehension in the Allied governments and military leadership over the possibility of adverse public reaction that strategic bombing attacks were always described as attacks on military and industrial facilities—which, of course, they were, even when more damage was done to residential neighborhoods than to munitions plants, or even if the industrial damage was only a consequence of a certain sector of a city's being reduced to rubble.

The moral discussion that grew out of these events aroused strong feelings. Even at the linguistic level, people wore their affiliations on their sleeves: Father Ford consistently used *German* where Churchill would have said *Nazi.* At the one extreme there were those who claimed that the targets were military objectives, not civilians, even while bandying about statistics on the number of workers "dehoused." At the other extreme were those who claimed that the bombings were motivated by "villainous hatred,"[40] ignoring the fact that one of the most intensive air bombardments of the war was directed at a French town (St. Lô), not a German one.

And we must note the disingenuousness of saying that a major bombing campaign was aimed at breaking the enemy's morale. This might be an appropriate expression for psychological warfare—attack by leaflet and radio broadcast—or for a mere display of power. But it was not the morale of the enemy that the bombers struck, but their bodies and homes. It is not wrong to say that Hiroshima and Nagasaki broke the morale of the Japanese, but it is highly euphemistic. If one kills enough of the enemy, they may decide that they have lost, or that the game is not worth the candle, and at that point their morale may be broken. But to force a surrender by taking the death and destruction to an unbearable level is hardly to triumph through breaking the enemy's morale—a phrase better applied to victories gained through creating the threat of catastrophe, not the full reality. If one fools the enemy into thinking one has resources one lacks, and they consequently surrender, one has won by undermining their morale. If the enemy surrenders because they are crushed, they do not surrender because their morale is broken—their morale is broken because they are crushed.

We must also note the slippery slope that leads from the admitted legitimacy of attacks on certain industrial installations to the claimed legitimacy of attacks on the housing in which the industrial workers live. Would we then go on to countenance an attack on the workers themselves—on their Fourth of July picnic, for example? And would that be an attack on their morale?

The proponents of strategic bombing have sometimes put forward embarrassing defenses of the practice, trying to make virtues of its vices. But even if they have offered morally disreputable defenses of strategic bombing, it does not follow that what they did was wrong—it only follows that what they said when they argued for what they did was wrong.

In the most extensive treatment available of the attitudes of U.S. World War II commanders to the moral issues raised by strategic bombing, *Wings of Judgment,* Ronald Schaffer showed that U.S. military officers and government officials could insist that the United States, as a moral and humane power, does not conduct war against civilians, and yet release aerial photographs of bombed-out cities as proof of how well the air force was doing. In some cases this tendency could be seen in the same individual. Schaffer also noted that generally when the military and government people did raise the moral issue, they did so by discussing, not whether the bombing was immoral, but whether the public would think it immoral. He seemed to conclude that a group-psychology phenomenon prevented them from seriously examining the moral implications of the U.S. bombing policy: To do so would have threatened the cohesion of the group. There is, however, another possibility: They simply did not think that what they were doing was immoral. There would then be no reason for the "collective pattern of psychological defense through avoidance" that Schaffer postulated.[41]

There is something else for us to bear in mind. Most of these people believed in what they were doing, and they believed that it was very important that what they were doing got done. The world has long noted a tendency among such people to say whatever they think might help them get the support they need to get the job done—a phenomenon that is not totally unknown in the military, which in the 1930s sold the B-17 to Congress as a coastal defense plane to guard the country from enemy fleets. If some people had believed the United States could win the war by increasing the number of stray cats in Germany, a fair number of Army Air Corps officers would within a week or two have generated statistics on the number of stray cats the Eighth Air Force produced. But that activity would not have meant that that was why the bombing campaign took shape the way it did. And their producing the statistics would not have meant that the bombing was done in order to create stray cats. Deeds can have a logic of their own.

We might, for example, place great weight on the various directives for the strategic air war that were issued by or to the RAF Bomber Command and the U.S. bomber forces. We might then take the January 1945 Anglo-American directive, listing Berlin, Leipzig, Dresden, and other "associated cities" as second in priority only to oil targets, as ushering in a new U.S. acceptance of area bombing (as Schaffer did). But we might alternatively incline toward the more skeptical view expressed in the official U.S. history:

> These directives . . . were little more than formal memoranda for the record. The CCS [Combined Chiefs of Staff] could order the strategic air forces to attack any objective or target system it chose. Theater commands were authorized to call upon the heavy bombers for assistance whenever they needed it. Air force commanders actually enjoyed great latitude in waging the air war and sometimes paid scant attention to the official priority lists drafted with much care in higher echelons.[42]

In fact, despite the January directive, in the first four months of 1945 the effort (in tonnage) that Bomber Command directed against cities declined by 31 percent compared with the last four months of 1944.[43]

Therefore, rather than concentrating on what the proponents of strategic warfare said, I want to concentrate on what they did and why they did it. The answers are fairly clear. RAF Bomber Command resorted to night raids only because of the high losses sustained in daylight raids. Area bombing was not Bomber Command's preferred option but a consequence of the furious German defense. Bomber Command, rather than arguing that the Eighth Air Force's daylight raids were not preferable in principle to night attacks, argued that the Americans were underestimating the losses they would suffer in daylight raids.

From a military point of view, daylight raids and precision attacks were vastly preferable to area bombing: There was no military advantage to adopting a policy that reduced bombing accuracy. Bomber Command would have rather dropped its bombs on factories producing aircraft engines than have scattered them over a large area that included those factories. The bombs that fell in the surrounding neighborhood may have had some adverse effect on enemy aircraft engine production, but not nearly so much as they would have had, had they landed directly on the factory. There was not any advantage to a policy that made

Berlin and the rest of eastern Germany, because of their distance, immune from attack except during the long winter nights. Nor was there any advantage to a policy that required the crews of stricken planes to bail out in the dark. For the Eighth Air Force, flying by day, the mortality rate in planes that were brought down was 17 percent, whereas for night-flying Bomber Command, it was 83 percent.

The bomber losses that led to night bombing and area attacks were far more serious than most people realize. They were unbearable for long periods of time even after the change. They were so severe that it is hard to understand how the aircrews managed to summon up the courage to board their planes. If a person's goal was to survive World War II, and he or she was given the choice between standing in Hiroshima the day the atom bomb fell or serving in an RAF bomber as the air offensive against Germany got into high gear, the wise choice would be Hiroshima. At Hiroshima the odds of surviving would be two to one; in 1943 in Bomber Command they were one in five. The odds of surviving the war were hundreds of times greater in a German city being bombed than in the bombers overhead. In 1943 Bomber Command required its aircrews to do one tour of thirty missions, and then, after a respite, a second tour of twenty missions. The odds were two to one that a bomber would not survive the first tour. The odds were six to one that the plane would not survive the second tour. Given the average loss rate per mission (3.6 percent) for the year, and given the tendency for missions to be flown every three days, once assigned to a plane a person had a service life of about forty days. The U.S. Eighth Air Force's bombers at that time had an even higher loss rate per mission, but it required its crews to serve fewer missions. Their chance of finishing a tour was 34 percent. In 1942 the publisher and air power advocate, W. B. Ziff, claimed that the United States could win the war by air power alone if it had a force of 5,000 heavy bombers, "coupled with a readiness to write off 2,500 of the craft a month."[44] Ziff, a proponent of strategic bombing, was ready to accept a loss rate of 50 percent per month.

A nation that expressed serious concern in the 1980s over the loss of a single F-111 with its crew of 2 over Tripoli may find these figures hard to comprehend, but in the European theater, Britain and the United States lost more than 40,000 combat aircraft in World War II. More than half of these plane losses were bombers, and they took with them 165,000 airmen. RAF's Bomber Command had the highest casualty rate in World War II of any British service arm. In one month—April 1944—the U.S. Eighth Air Force had 512 planes missing in action, and 65 more landed completely wrecked.

There were legitimate military targets—steel plants, aircraft factories—but the enemy's defenses prevented accurate attacks on them. Had it not been for those defenses, bombing accuracy would have been impressive indeed. Planes could have afforded to make leisurely pass after pass until they got it just right, and only then would they have released their bombs. After the war J. M. Spaight wrote that area bombing

> was the natural and indeed inevitable reply to the intensification of the defence. Here was the situation: war factories turning out masses of lethal instruments for our undoing; the workers in the factories living all around them; the whole area bristling with anti-aircraft guns, predictors and searchlights. What were we to do? . . . "The German workers . . . tend to live in highly concentrated districts . . . close to the factories. Ideally it might be better to pick out the factories and destroy them. That would be the most humane kind of warfare possible. . . . What prevents us from doing so? The German defences. . . . Consequently, the German authorities, by trying to spare their factories, divert much of the attack on their own civilian population."[45]

During the war Spaight had written:

> It has come to pass, it seems, that the effective destruction of an enemy's sources of munitionment can . . . be accomplished only at the cost of incidental destruction . . . on a scale which was not formerly contemplated. One might almost say that it has been found necessary to reverse the process by which the Chinese arrived at the secret of roast pork. The cooking could be done, after all, only by . . . burning . . . the house down. . . . That development is deplorable, but modern war is full of terrible things.[46]

The question, therefore, is this: When the enemy, through a vigorous defense, degrades the accuracy of an attack on a legitimate target so much that the target can only be damaged through a general attack on its environs, does the target thereby become inviolable? If we seek an indisputable guide on this question from the legal point of view, we will be disappointed. The 1907 Hague rules, which we discussed in Chapter 2, cover land war and naval bombardments, but not air war. No agreement akin to the 1907 conventions, but covering air war, has ever been concluded by the nations of the world. In 1923 representatives of six nations met in The Hague and drew up rules for air war, the 1923 draft rules, but these rules were never ratified even by the participating nations, and thus never became part of international law.

Let us see what direction we can get from the 1907 rules that might apply to air war.

The Naval Rules

We saw in Chapter 2 that the land rules prohibit the bombardment of undefended localities. The naval rules initially seem to follow suit: Hague Convention IX (1907), "Bombardment by Naval Forces in Time of War," stated: "The bombardment by naval forces of undefended ports, towns, villages, dwellings, or buildings is forbidden (Article 1)." But the qualifications of Articles 2 and 3 of the same convention weaken this prohibition:

> 2. Military works, military or naval establishments, depots of arms or war materials, workshops or plant which could be utilized for the needs of the hostile fleet or army, and ships of war in the harbour, are not, however, included in this prohibition. The commander of a naval force may destroy them with artillery, after a summons followed by a reasonable interval of time, if all other means are impossible, and when the local authorities have not themselves destroyed them within the time fixed.
>
> He incurs no responsibility for any unavoidable damage which may be caused by a bombardment under such circumstances.
>
> If for military reasons, immediate action is necessary, and no delay can be allowed to the enemy, it is nevertheless understood that the prohibition to bombard the undefended town holds good, as in the case given in the first paragraph, and that the commander shall take all due measures in order that the town may suffer as little harm as possible.
>
> 3. After due notice has been given, the bombardment of undefended ports, towns, villages, dwellings, or buildings may be commenced, if the local authorities, on a formal summons being made to them, decline to comply with requisitions for provisions or supplies necessary for the immediate use of the naval force before the place in question.
>
> These requisitions shall be proportional to the resources of the place. They shall only be demanded in the name of the commander of the said naval force, and they shall, as far as possible, be paid for in ready money; if not, their receipt shall be acknowledged.[47]

The Ninth Hague Convention was formulated because of concerns that arose following the development of modern breech-loading naval guns. In an 1888 British fleet exercise, the "hostile" fleet threatened to bombard undefended British coastal cities—an eventuality discussed by a French admiral in an 1882 article and recommended by Prince de Joinville in 1844.[48] The 1907 Hague Rules of Naval Bombardment were substantially based on an 1896 draft by the Institute of International

Law, which itself had been the inspiration for an important section in the 1900 U.S. Naval War Code:

> The bombardment by a naval force, of unfortified and undefended towns, villages or buildings is forbidden, except when such bombardment is incidental to the destruction of military or naval establishments, public depots of munitions of war, or vessels of war in ports, or unless reasonable requisitions for provisions and supplies essential, at the same time, to such naval vessel or vessels are forcibly withheld, in which case due notice of bombardment shall be given (Article 4).

These naval bombardment rules anticipated two sorts of cases. First, fleets in immediate need of supplies—usually coal or water—were given the right to requisition those supplies for compensation. If the undefended town refused, a punitive and persuasive bombardment of the town was permissible. This provision is rather moot, as in modern times "no case has, it would appear, occurred in Europe of requisitions or contributions imposed by naval forces upon enemy coast towns," though there may have been an instance in South America in 1871.[49]

Second, and much more important, fleets are given the right to bombard targets of military significance in *undefended* towns, though they do not have the right of general bombardment of such towns. This deviation from the rule of land warfare stems from a crucial difference between naval and ground forces: Naval forces do not normally have the ability to capture and hold enemy ground. An army can march into an undefended town and take control of its military and industrial resources. Normally a fleet cannot land or maintain the shore party this would require. Nonetheless, the industrial or military facilities might be legitimate military targets, and the naval commander can order the local authorities to destroy these facilities. If the authorities refuse or if time is short, the commander can destroy the facilities himself with naval gunfire. In 1948, for example, a French Court of Cassation acquitted a German warship commander of the wartime destruction of an undefended lighthouse. The lighthouse, the court said, would have been used by the hostile navy.[50]

Legitimate Targets

What is included under "workshops or plant which could be utilized for the needs of the hostile fleet or army"? Naval bombardment of industrial facilities has not played a major role in twentieth century warfare, so this may not seem a vital question. But it is important because the moral and legal permissibility of air attacks is frequently understood on analogy with naval bombardments. The formulation of legitimate targets is extremely liberal if we allow a very broad interpretation of the needs of the army and fleet: If soldiers and sailors need recreation, that need could be interpreted to countenance deliberate attacks on baseball bat factories or motion picture production facilities. Or why not, as Father Ford asked, attacks on the wives and children whose emotional support boosts the morale of the combatants?

However, we do not want to insist on too narrow an interpretation. As one expert on the law of war, Morris Greenspan, has asked: "Is it logical to destroy men, weapons, and munitions on the field of battle, but leave intact the same munitions at the factory?"[51] The training camps that supply troops are legitimate objects of attack, and so must be the factories that supply their equipment. But how far through the industrial web does one go? "Under the category of factories," wrote Greenspan, "it is logical, in these days of total war, to include not only those which furnish the finished war products, but also the factories which supply the materials, such as steel, from which these finished products are made." And accordingly, the electrical generating plants that power these facilities? Is there any place, then, to draw the line? Or has the list already gotten too long? For as those who oppose such attacks point out, the product of the steel mill goes into baby carriages and scalpels, as well as weapons.

One of the most interesting and worthwhile suggestions has been made by the English philosopher Elizabeth Anscombe, whose proposal, with some modification, is that the line be drawn at what the normal life of the nation would require even if that nation had no military establishment. The idea is that troops require food, but those people would require food even if they were civilians. Food is a human need, not a particularly military one. Therefore a nation's food production is not a legitimate object of attack; it is not a properly military target. The properly military targets are, not those facilities necessary for the maintenance of a normal human existence even in an unarmed society, but those that specifically enable a nation to wage war. Interpreting this in a restrictive way, the tank factory could be a target, but not the steel mill. Interpreted less restrictively, the steel mill might be attacked, but not the grain storage facility. A large gray area still remains, but Anscombe's suggestion seems in principle a step in the right direction.

We must note, however, that by deciding that a lighthouse was a proper target in the case of *In re Dross-Branckmann,* the French Court of Cassation took a less restrictive view, for lighthouses are useful to all ships, not just to ships of war. The intention of the Hague rules for naval bombardment goes beyond Anscombe's proposal:

> The first Article having laid down the rule of non-bombardment of undefended coastal towns, the second and third Articles proceed to make exceptions. These exceptions were considered necessary owing to the special character of naval warfare. Military works, military or naval establishments, depots of arms or war material, work-shops or plant which can be utilized for the needs of the hostile fleet or army, as well as ships of war in the harbour, are not included in the prohibition against bombardment. Considerable difficulty was experienced in framing the first paragraph. The word "installations" was adopted to cover such works as are not solely for warlike purposes. An undefended coastal town may be an important railway centre, or have floating-docks of great value for the repair of vessels; these are intended to be included under "installations." The word "provisions" was inserted in one of the drafts but "*materiel de guerre,*" an extremely wide term, was ultimately substituted. This Article might, and probably will, be held to confer a right on a commander to destroy by bombardment railway stations, bridges, entrepots, coal stacks, whether belonging to public authorities or private persons.[52]

Application to Air War

At any rate, the naval rules allow the bombardment of targets of military value in undefended towns and absolve the naval commander from responsibility for any collateral damage this might cause, whereas the land rules prohibit this. If we are to extend the Hague conventions to apply to air war, we must pick one or the other. The obvious candidate is the naval rules. The air fleet, like the naval fleet, can destroy military targets in undefended towns, but, unlike ground troops, the air fleet cannot capture those facilities or take prisoners. Because the inability of naval fleets to hold ground is the source of the difference between the naval and ground rules, and because that inability holds equally for air fleets, the extension of the Hague rules to air war should be by analogy with the naval rules. And those who have tried to derive air rules by analogy based on the 1907 conventions have generally taken this approach.

The most widely used reference work in international law, Sir Hersch Lauterpacht's, argued against this tendency. It claimed that the impermissibility of indiscriminate air bombardment does not follow by analogy from the naval laws but derives directly from a fundamental principle of the law of war—the prohibition against indiscriminate attacks on civililans. This dispute, however, seems unnecessary. The relevant naval rules themselves follow from fundamental principles of the law of war; thus there is no substantive difference between the two approaches. But it remains true that air war is best conceptualized by analogy with naval war. In both air and naval war there are justifications for bombarding targets in undefended towns—justifications that are usually absent in ground war, where these objectives can be seized.

The analogy with the law of naval war would allow the general bombardment of defended towns. When is a town defended? The U.S. Air Force's current official view on this question is incompatible with the naval analogy. The air force takes a town to be defended if it is behind enemy lines. That view was supported by a post–World War I British General Staff memorandum that "pointed out that with trench lines stretching from Switzerland to the sea, in some sense every German town was defended."[53] In *some* sense every German town *was* defended. But the question remains whether the sense in which they were defended is pertinent.

The naval rules do not count a town as defended so long as it is behind enemy lines: If the rules did, there would hardly have been any reason for distinguishing between defended and undefended towns. And what, then, would have been the point of claiming that many British coastal towns were undefended? They were defended, in a sense, by the Royal Navy. But if the Royal Navy were far to the north at Scapa Flow when an enemy bombardment force showed up at Manchester, and if Manchester were unprotected by coastal defense batteries, Manchester would have been undefended from that force. In such a case the naval rules counted Manchester as undefended and allowed only bombardment of military installations, not general bombardment. Similarly, the presence of a czarist fleet in the White Sea would not have made Leningrad, on the Baltic, defended. The enemy navy would have to be in a position to engage, or at least threaten immediately to engage, the attacker's fleet. The principle we should expect to invoke in this case ought to be a cousin of the one invoked in a different context by Daniel Webster—in the famous *Caroline* case: "necessity of self-defence, instant, overwhelming, leaving no choice of means, and no moment for deliberation."

By analogy, then, the existence of an enemy air force does not by itself make every enemy town defended, just as the existence of an enemy navy does not make every enemy coastal town defended. The analogy from naval to air rules would count a town as defended if enemy fighters were based within range of the target, or if the town were defended by antiaircraft guns, or perhaps if the attacker could reasonably believe this to be so.

While the Hague naval conventions were being drafted, a dispute arose over whether a harbor protected solely by mines counted as defended. The mines of the time were contact mines, which exploded automatically when they bumped against a ship. Therefore, a harbor could be protected by mines without any combatants being stationed there. This early example of automated warfare gained a majority of votes at the Hague for not by itself making a place count as defended—a position to which a number of nations, including Britain, formally objected. Their official reservations made them not bound by this particular provision. The British naval representative at the Hague, Captain Charles L. Ottley, argued:

> Mines . . . being a general danger to navigation, and far more destructive than guns, it was illogical to render inviolable a town defended by mines and to refuse inviolability to one defended by guns. Moreover, if undefended towns are free from bombardment, what is the need of laying mines on the sea front? A belligerent who has undertaken not to bombard an undefended coast town is entitled to make use of the coast without expecting to run the danger of destruction on approaching it.[54]

Higgens, who paraphrased Ottley, sided with him: "This argument is sound and unanswerable. A town which has mines moored before its harbour has taken the most effective steps to defend itself against occupation."[55] And as John Westlake had said: "A place cannot be considered undefended if means are taken with an eye to preventing the enemy from occupying it. *The price of immunity from bombardment is that the place must be open for the enemy to enter.*"[56] This is the principle that supports the air force's interpretation of a defended place: If enemy troops block the way to an otherwise undefended city, the city is not open to occupation.

But as we noted, if we interpret the laws this way, every German coastal town during World War I would have counted as defended. Westlake's principle must get a narrower interpretation: The place must be undefended from the enemy forces that manage to arrive there. That enemy ground forces are unable to approach the town overland does not make it defended from naval or air attack. German coastal cities were defended by the Wehrmacht (German army) from the Anglo-French armies in France. But the Wehrmacht forces in France were not defending those coastal towns from amphibious or airborne assault. Forces attacking by sea or air would have been unopposed, and thus a general bombardment by such forces would have been gratuitous violence.

This seems the reasonable standard. Against an undefended town the attacker is in no peril and can concentrate on maximizing accuracy against military targets. He is then held to the accuracy his weapons permit. If the defender places the attacker in danger, however—if the attacker is dodging surface-to-air missiles or antiaircraft guns or maneuvering at high speed to avoid coastal batteries—the attacker is free to conduct the attack in the manner he thinks produces the most desirable combination of safety to himself and damage to the target. For allowing general bombardment against a defended locality has only two justifications: (1) The presence of defenders makes the locality a battle field, where general bombardment is permissible, or (2) the need to evade the defenders, or to subdue them, reduces the accuracy we can expect of the attackers. Neither of these justifications applies unless the forces that make the place defended are a threat to the attacking planes or ships.

A similar dispute arose over whether the attacking fleet had an obligation to warn the enemy of an impending bombardment. The final version of Article 6 of Convention IX held that the attacking commander should do so "unless military exigencies render it impossible":

> The original draft laid down that previous warning of a bombardment should be given to the authorities, but Captain Ottley pointed out that it was frequently of the greatest importance to attack and destroy as speedily as possible a fortress or arsenal of the enemy or warships in port. Notice would in many cases be fatal to the attack. A fleet, for instance, arrives before a fortress or naval port without having been observed by the enemy; to give warning of the bombardment would nullify the effect of the manoeuvre.[57]

The standard interpretation also counts a place as defended if enemy combat forces are stationed there or passing through. These forces might not have the ability to harm warships or airplanes, but they can kill friendly soldiers, and the rules of war do not require military units to restrict their attacks to enemy units that are capable of harming them. Thus a place that has no defense against air attack may still be subject to strategic bombing. It might, for example, harbor an armored brigade.

This is, however, irrelevant for our question, for we have seen not only that enemy targets in World War II were defended from air attack but also that it was the problem of dealing with that defense that led to area attacks. On these grounds, the strategic bombing attacks of World War II were, by and large, attacks on defended places. I said "by and large" because, though every attack was not on a defended locality, whether targets could be treated as defended was a function, not of whether each individual target was defended on given occasions, but of whether for a given campaign targets had to be treated as defended. Air tactics and target selection were not instantly revisable:

A mission planned a certain way to meet the threat from enemy fighters could not be changed in midair if the fighter opposition did not materialize. And there is a longer-term "inertia" in the planning of any campaign. If fighter opposition was dwindling, that fact would not be instantly noticeable. The enemy might be holding fighters in reserve, as sometimes happened, or might have had a stretch of bad luck in intercepting the bombers.

By the end of the war in Europe, U.S. planes were operating over enemy territory with a fair degree of impunity compared with earlier days. The last major interception of U.S. bombers took place on January 1, 1945, if we look at things from a large, strategic point of view. On a more elemental level however, the war in the air continued, with bomber flights occasionally intercepted by as many as 50 of the new German jet fighters—an April 10 mission lost 10 bombers to the jets—and bomber missions continued to be heavily escorted by fighters until the end of the war. Even when no interceptors rose, German antiaircraft guns continued to exact a heavy toll. In a February attack on Berlin, flak brought down 21 bombers. In the Pacific, B-29 losses in January 1945 were running at the heavy rate of 5.7 percent per mission, and in March there were still 500 fighters in Japan.

The Moral Context

From a legal point of view, then, area bombing in World War II was permissible. The practice did not constitute a war crime. For many people, that may be sufficient to justify area bombing. They can argue that it was the job of the military commanders to bring the war to a successful conclusion and to do so at minimal cost to the nation. If that is so, perhaps commanders have an obligation to use all effective legal means to that end. Perhaps that is the way commanders instinctively dealt with these questions; perhaps they thought that if area bombing was not a violation of the laws of war, and if it would help the cause of victory, then it would be either derelict or foolish not to area bomb.

And as the area bombing of defended places was not criminal, the only question left would be about the effectiveness of area bombing. Was it the most effective way to use the strategic bombing forces? This is not a view to be casually dismissed, for commanders have a grave responsibility to those under their command and to the nation. But there is another side to the story.

Proportionality and Military Targets

It is a fundamental principle implicit in the law of war that gratuitous harm ought not to be inflicted. This principle can be seen in several of the provisions of the Hague conventions. Article 25 declares that it is forbidden "to kill or wound an enemy who, having laid down his arms, or having no longer means of defense, has surrendered." The same article forbids the employment of weapons that will cause superfluous injury—a reference to the 1868 St. Petersburg declaration that said that the military purpose is accomplished when enemy troops are disabled and that this would be exceeded by the use of weapons that "needlessly aggravate the sufferings of disabled men, or render their death inevitable." And the same principle lies behind the bombardment of undefended places being restricted to installations of military value.

But if a town is defended, the law allows a general bombardment. The bombardment cannot be gratuitous because the destruction of the defenders is a legitimate military objective. What is missing from the law in this case is a principle of proportionality. The law forbids gratuitous harm, but that only means that there must be some military gain to be attained by the harm. It does not mean that the military gain must be proportional to the harm.

From the moral point of view, however, we want some principle of proportionality. It would not be morally justifiable to level a city, however large, to destroy a military target, however minor—a single jeep, for example. (Nor would this be the way any sane commander would want to allocate his finite resources.) So though the law allows attacks on defended places, we want those attacks to meet some further test of proportionality and not merely of military gain.

For attacks against enemy military forces, the principle of proportionality has very limited scope, a situation that has not always been noticed. Richard A. Falk has written that the principle requires "that the military means used bear a proportional relationship to the military end pursued."[58] But the destruction of enemy forces is itself a legitimate military end, and we would not be imposing any restrictions if we said that the harm done to enemy military forces must be proportional to the military gain if the destruction of enemy forces is itself a military gain: We would then have the completely empty principle that the destruction of enemy forces should be proportional to the destruction of enemy forces. That the military means be proportional to the military end is a maxim of strategy, not of morality.

Nonetheless, there is some room for proportionality even here, for it is not the destruction of enemy forces, but the imposition of the nation's will on the enemy that is the ultimate goal in warfare, and this can sometimes be accomplished by neutralizing enemy forces without destroying them. Under certain circumstances it may be possible to capture them, or to isolate them, or even to ignore them, at no significant military cost. In these cases to harm them may be gratuitous or completely out of proportion to the military gain.

The law of war does not require this gentility. The law forbids cases of gratuitous harm in quite specific situations where it is obvious that the harm would be gratuitous—the enemy is surrendering, for example. It would not serve the law's juridical purpose to forbid harm in situations as ill defined as those I am now discussing. But forbearance in those circumstances is in keeping with the principle behind the specific injunctions of the law.

However, where there is a military gain, it is not morally incumbent upon the attacker to pursue these alternatives (and it is never legally incumbent on the attacker to do so). The enemy's position in the town may at the moment be hopeless, so that if the town is rushed it will certainly fall. But perhaps, in the time it would take to get a response to a parlementaire's request for surrender,[59] the town can be reinforced, or perhaps it is vital that the objective be secured in short order. It is not morally incumbent on the attacker to offer terms to the defender, even if the defender's position is hopeless.

Proportionality and Civilian Casualties

The case is different when we turn to civilian casualties, for the destruction of civilian population, unlike the destruction of the enemy's military forces, is not a legitimate goal in war. But large-scale destruction of civilian population is justifiable in some circumstances, and here the principle of proportionality looms larger. The United States would, I believe, have been justified in destroying Oslo during World War II if in Oslo the Germans were building a plant for manufacturing atomic bombs and if the destruction of the city were the only way to destroy the plant. But the United States would not have been justified in destroying Oslo to take out a regimental command post.

It is important to this example that Oslo was not an enemy city, but an enemy-held city. Military necessity may require a nation to destroy one of its own cities if that city is enemy occupied, contains a target of overriding military importance, and if there is no other way to neutralize the target. Indeed, in Chapter 2, I used as an acid test of military necessity as opposed to military exigency the following rule: If it really is imperative to destroy the target, a belligerent will attack it even if the collateral casualties are its own. Everything I have said so far bears on the question of civilian casualties, regardless of whether they are friendly, neutral, or enemy.

That is not to say that one must treat one's own civilian casualties on a par with enemy civilian casualties. In Operation Pointblank there were operational restrictions placed on U.S. bombers in order to lower French and Belgian civilian casualties, but U.S. airmen were pointedly told that those restrictions would not be in effect over Germany. Combatant nations must give enemy civilian casualties some weight, but they are under no obligation to weigh them so heavily as their own.

John Finnis, Joseph M. Boyle, Jr., and Germain Grisez have disagreed: "The magnitude of damage caused to civilians by Allied air attacks on targets in Germany greatly exceeded that caused by more careful attacks on enemy targets in occupied France and thus evidenced the unfairness with which military actions were chosen when they destroyed non-combatant citizens of the enemy rather than of an ally."[60]

In reply one can argue that (1) the more careful attacks were less costly over France, as Germany's flak and fighter defenses were concentrated to defend the Reich. The air force would not have required that degree of care had the antiaircraft defenses of the occupied countries been as strong as those of Germany herself. And (2), the care taken in these attacks was in any case unnecessary, so there is no question of unfairness. To save French lives, Allied aircrews were willing to take risks beyond what morality required. They were not morally required to assume the same risks in all cases.

As evidence for both of these claims, some of these attacks were so dangerous that volunteer Free French aircrews were used: Allied commanders felt that they could not ask U.S. or Commonwealth crews to take such great risks to reduce French civilian casualties. Had those French airmen not been available, the attacks would have been carried out in a manner less dangerous to the bombers, but likely to produce more civilian casualties.

Weighing the harm inflicted against the military gain is not a matter of counting heads, and the principle of proportionality is harder to apply in practice than it is to introduce in theory. Consider, for example, Operation Pointblank—the Allied bombing campaign to destroy or interdict the rail lines leading into Normandy in preparation and support of D day and the subsequent fighting. Pointblank required attacks on rail marshalling yards in France and Belgium that were generally located in the center of cities. As we have seen, the United States could not bomb the rail yards without inflicting heavy damage on the surrounding areas. Allied leaders were concerned about French and Belgian casualties, but the attacks went through anyway, costing, as it subsequently became known, 12,000 civilian casualties. Some estimates had placed the anticipated civilian casualties much higher. How was it decided that the benefits outweighed the costs?

Let us first see how it was not decided. No one sat down and tried to calculate that Pointblank would save 5,000, or 15,000, or 50,000 Allied troops and that therefore Pointblank should be staged. No one tried to make these calculations because no one could have made them. It was possible, for example, that the Germans would choose not to defend Normandy. General Karl Von Rundstedt favored a mobile battle in the interior of France, where he thought his Panzer and Panzergrenadier divisions could be used to better effect. If the Germans had fought the battle that way, much of Pointblank would have been for naught. Pointblank would have severed rail links over which the Germans would have had no intention of rushing reinforcements.

No one knew or could have known at the time just what contribution Pointblank would make to the Allied cause. Pointblank would certainly reduce the German's ability to reinforce their forces in Normandy. Whether that reduction would be a significant constraint on the enemy would depend on how the Germans fought the battle. No one knew just how effective Pointblank would be in its stated aim, or whether attaining that aim would be crucial, or even whether circumstances would make it a gain or a loss: Had the Germans quickly withdrawn from Normandy, a good deal of the rail yard and rail bridge destruction would have hurt the Allies more than the Germans.

Why, then, was Pointblank carried out? It was because the worst fear of the Allied commanders was that the invasion would be repulsed or contained. If it were repulsed there would be another Dunkirk, and it would be at least a year before the Allies could try again. And in the course of that year who knew what might happen? Perhaps the Germans would throw their western front troops at the Russians; perhaps the Russians would suffer a horrible defeat and withdraw from the war as they did in World War I. Perhaps the war would go on for decades. Even if the invasion were only contained, as the invasion at Salerno had been, the result would be disaster. If the beachhead did not expand rapidly to permit the Allied buildup that was required for success, the invasion would have been defeated another way.

The Allied commanders knew what their worst fears were, and they knew that Pointblank would help to some undeterminable extent to prevent those fears from being realized. In an operation as crucial as Overlord that was enough. Pointblank was on. It was one more factor—and as it turned out a quite significant one—helping avert an Allied disaster. The loss of 12,000 or 25,000 civilians would be regrettable. A defeat of the invasion would have been the worst disaster of the war.

There can be cases in which a commander can roughly calculate the number of civilian casualties a course of action might create and the number of friendly casualties it might reduce. But the uncertainties of war make these calculations highly unreliable, and in any case the results of these calculations may not be decisive. How many casualties it is worth to take a given objective depends on the value of the objective, which is not easily quantifiable.

Therefore, the consideration of proportionality is, not a simple comparison of expected casualties, but a comparison in our case of civilian casualties caused by strategic bombing with the military benefits that were derived from that bombing. And if there is some morally justifiable reason for distinguishing friendly and enemy civilian casualties (and I suspect there is), we have not yet reached the point where that is necessary. Proportionality requires the weighing of military gain in view of civilian casualties whether the civilian casualties are German, as in Operation Thunderclap, or French, as in Pointblank. On these grounds was area bombing immoral?

The Case for Area Bombing

The principle of proportionality requires us to ask whether the civilian casualties were justified by the military gain. In Germany the bombings killed between 300,000 and 600,000 civilians, though by no means were all of these people killed in area attacks. But then proportionality does not require that we distinguish between area attacks and precision attacks. A precision attack might fail proportionality by killing a fair number of workers even though the facility was only of minor military importance. And an area attack might cause major damage to military-industrial facilities, while harming very few civilians. On the whole, did the military gain brought about by strategic bombing justify the civilian casualties?

That is hard to say. According to Hitler's minister for armaments, Albert Speer, in *Spandau: The Secret Diaries*:

> Defense against air attacks required the production of thousands of anti-aircraft guns, the stockpiling of tremendous quantities of ammunition all over the country, and holding in readiness hundreds of thousands of soldiers, who in addition had to stay in position by their guns, often totally inactive, for months at a time.
>
> As far as I can judge from the accounts I have read, no one has yet seen that this was the greatest lost battle on the German side. The losses from the retreats in Russia or from the surrender of Stalingrad were considerably less. Moreover, the nearly 20,000 anti-aircraft guns stationed in the homeland could almost have doubled the anti-tank defenses on the Eastern Front. (pp. 375–376)

Speer was talking here about military forces diverted because of the strategic air campaign, and to his figures we can add the hundreds of German fighter planes that fought against the bombers. On D day there were only a handful of Luftwaffe combat planes in France, but there were as many fighters defending Germany from British and U.S. air power as there were deployed against the Russians on the eastern front. And we have not yet taken account of the loss of industrial and armaments production due to bombing, the deprivation of oil and gasoline, the damage to the transportation network, or the diversion of effort required to constantly repair bombed facilities. So perhaps the civilian deaths were justified by proportionality. And that is probably enough to justify the bombing campaign. For if we can be unsure whether the civilian losses were justified by the military benefits, then those losses were not wildly out of proportion to the military gain. And how can we hold a belligerent accountable to a more stringent standard (for example, to proving beyond a shadow of a doubt) if the civilian casualties are largely a function of the enemy's defense of legitimate military targets—targets that, if they had been left alone, would undoubtedly have significantly increased the enemy's ability to wage war?

This is not to say that every individual attack could be justified on the principle of proportionality: The 1945 attack on Dresden is the most well-known case that has been questioned. The attack has been justified on the grounds that Dresden was an important transportation center and legally on the quite different grounds that an SS Panzer Division was railing through the city. The presence of the SS division, even in transit, made Dresden technically a defended city, allowing the attack. But this *legal* justification is, from a moral point of view, disingenuous. That the division was in Dresden was viewed not as an unfortunate circumstance but as an opportunity. Otherwise the division's trains would have been attacked outside the city, as they would have been had the city been U.S., British, or French.

Sometimes the military gain did not justify the civilian losses. As often it was the other way around: The bomber losses did not justify the military gain. War is not an exact science. To say that the civilian casualties at Dresden were not justified by the military gain is not to say that the U.S. command ought to have known better, or that it could have known that those casualties would be so high. The fire storm that started there—a rare and unpredictable occurrence—was only the second seen in Europe, and the last: The awful destruction Dresden suffered led the United States to end the massive bombing attacks.

One sometimes hears that the attack on Dresden was wrong for another reason: that when Dresden was bombed, the war in Europe was "more or less over." Those who find this persuasive should reflect on the 304,000 casualties the Russians admit to taking in the months after Dresden. To say that the war was more or less over when so many were yet to fall is not just absurd—it is worse. There are positions that can be defended only by those who confuse studying history with suffering it.

The civilian casualties at Dresden were out of proportion to the military gain. It does not follow that Allied commanders should have known that would be so. To say that some of the bombings were not justified is not to condemn those who ordered or executed those attacks. It is a philosophical commonplace that we need to distinguish between the morality of an act and the moral assessment of the agent. As John Stuart Mill pointed out in *Utilitarianism,* a man may save a drowning child simply for the reward and with no concern for the child. His act, the act of saving a drowning child, is morally praiseworthy, but we will not praise the agent's morality, for his motives were base. The right thing can be done for heinous reasons, and the wrong thing can be done for admirable reasons. To judge the morality of a bombing raid—particularly in light of information that was available only subsequently—is not to rule on the morality of the commander who ordered the raid.

Paradoxically, the initial case is even stronger for the bombing campaign against Japan. U.S. estimates were that an invasion of Japan's main island, Honshu, would cost 1 million U.S. casualties. Fighting on Japanese home soil, the enemy would not be cut off from resupply and reinforcement as it had been in the recent battle of Okinawa. Yet on Okinawa, the United States had suffered 12,000 battle deaths, and the Japanese, 150,000. Iwo Jima, too, had been bloody:

> On the first day at Iwo Jima, the 4th and 5th Marine Divisions lost over 2,400 men, 600 of them killed. Five weeks later they and the 3rd Marine Division had lost a total of 6,821 men dead and 18,000 wounded in subduing the island. To put it another way, out of 3 divisions 1 and 1/3 had become casualties. . . . On Okinawa, four divisions, the 1st and 6th Marine and 7th and 96th Infantry, suffered over 30% casualties.[61]

On June 8, 1945, the Joint Chiefs of Staff met with President Harry Truman to present their recommendation for a November invasion of the Kyushu, the southernmost of Japan's home islands: "Admiral Leahy recalled that troops on Okinawa had suffered about 35 percent casualties, and that this was a reasonable estimate for Kyushu. With 767,000 men scheduled to participate in the campaign, this would mean around 268,000 dead and wounded."[62] If the lessons of past experience held up this would mean at least 1 million Japanese casualties for the invasion of Kyushu. The invasion of the main island, Honshu, would produce greater casualties. Even restricting the discussion to Kyushu, though, the balance looks defensible: Invasion would have meant far more deaths than the 300,000 Japan suffered through bombing. And without the strategic bombing campaign, invasion would almost certainly have been necessary.[63] Therefore, the bombings can be defended on the grounds of proportionality.

Military Targets and Enemy Morale

But this is only an initial assessment, and there are considerations that count against it. In late summer 1945 the United States controlled the skies over Japan: By August 14 the Fifth Fighter Command, which had been flying over Japan since early July, had suffered only nineteen losses—one to enemy fighters, four to antiaircraft fire, and the rest to unknown causes. At that point it was no longer the defense that forced the United States into area attacks—it was habit, as Twenty-first Bomber Command climbed toward 1,000 planes. The accuracy of the final nuclear attacks on Hiroshima and Nagasaki showed that the precision daylight bombing that the air force could not attain in January was by the end of the summer within its ability. At Nagasaki the bomb fell only 500 yards north of the targeted Mitsubishi Steel and Arms Works.

The principle of proportionality requires us to consider not just whether a place is defended, but how well defended it is, as well as to consider the ratio between harm and gain. We might find that we can destroy an aircraft factory in a lightly defended town either with a precision attack involving very few bomber losses or with an area attack involving none. We would then have to decide whether the additional civilian casualties the area attack would cause would be justified by the reduction in plane losses. For Bomber Command throughout most of the war this calculation was unnecessary: aircraft losses in precision attacks exceeded Bomber Command's replacement rate—the air war could not be sustained in daylight precision attacks without heavy fighter escort. Over Japan the U.S. Twentieth Air Force had had the same experience.

As summer 1945 approached, though, the formula was changing. Daylight precision raids against industrial targets—mainly aircraft plants—in April proved quite successful when they were flown at 20,000 feet, though at lower altitudes losses mounted: An April 24 raid at 12,000 feet wrecked an aircraft factory, but 70 percent of the 100 B-29s were damaged. In good weather, precision bombing was working, though cloud cover would still make precision bombing unwise. Flying beneath the clouds, the bombers were too close to the antiaircraft guns. So on precision missions, bombers were given secondary, radar targets to attack if the weather over the visual target was dense. The success of these precision missions, and the decreasing U.S. loss rate in the closing months of the war, showed that the original moral justification for area bombing had lost much of its validity by midsummer. But the area attacks continued, culminating in the atomic attacks on Hiroshima and Nagasaki. They had perhaps proven too successful to abandon.

The legal justification remained. If the Japanese defenses were becoming feeble, at least for high-altitude attacks, Japanese cities nonetheless were defended by antiaircraft guns and fighter planes. From the legal point of view, General LeMay was acting properly. From a moral point of view, though, the bombings became more dubious as the war drew toward its close. For we cannot adopt the moral position that the defense, however paltry, justifies civilian casualties, however heavy. As long as the defense has forced area attacks as the only way of damaging military and industrial targets, those attacks can be morally justified, subject to proportionality. Once the defense no longer is forcing area attacks—once they are adopted as the technique of choice—our principles no longer justify them.

By summer 1945 the proponents of strategic air power were hoping that the bombing campaign would by itself lead the Japanese to surrender—a hope that the U.S. experience in Germany seemed to mock, but that proved to be justified. That is where the great temptation arose. If area attacks could induce the Japanese government to surrender, an invasion would be unnecessary, and many lives, Japanese as well as American, would be saved. Does proportionality justify area attacks in that case?

Our interpretation of proportionality allows civilian casualties if they are incidental to a military gain but does not countenance civilian casualties as a means in itself to victory—the civilian casualties that are accepted are collateral; they are not the chosen path to victory. We do not allow deliberate and intentional attacks on civilians as a morally justifiable means of waging war, and a voluntary campaign of area bombing to induce surrender takes the destruction of civilian lives and property as a major part of the means to the end.

However, an invasion of Japan's home islands would undoubtedly have led to more deaths, Japanese as well as U.S., and civilian as well as military, than the bombings did. So our moral principles would have forced us to conduct the war in a way that was more costly in human life. How did this dilemma arise?

Earlier I said that a military commander would prefer the accurate bombing of military targets to the wastage of area bombing. That is true, but another factor has now been introduced—the possibility that the less accurate bombing might produce the enemy's surrender, whereas the more accurate bombing might not. At this point the effect of the bombing on the enemy's properly military capabilities becomes secondary; the bombing campaign is now being determined by political considerations. From a strictly military viewpoint, area bombing remains wasteful, for the destruction is not pinpointed on enemy combat capacity. But if we are seeking victory through inflicting great numbers of casualties, regardless of whether they are civilian or military, the strictly military point of view has been abandoned. Political considerations, not military ones, now determine policy.

General Devastation

In the traditional law of war that antedated the Hague conventions, there was a category under which area bombing as a matter of choice might seem justified. In Chapter 2 we saw that the Hague conventions, Article 23, Section (g), forbid the destruction or seizure of enemy property "unless such destruction or seizure be imperatively demanded by the necessities of war." What the necessities of war demand has always been a matter of dispute, but it was not so long ago that they were taken to demand, from time to time, "general devastation."

Devastation, William Edward Hall wrote, can be thought of either

> independently as one of the permitted kinds of violence used in order to bring an enemy to terms, or as incidental to certain military operations, and permissible only for the purpose of carrying them out.
>
> Formerly it presented itself in the first of these aspects. Grotius held that "devastation is to be tolerated which reduces an enemy in a short time to beg for peace," and in the practice of his time it was constantly used independently of any military advantage accruing from it. But during the seventeenth century opinion seems to have struggled, not altogether in vain, to prevent its being so used in more than a certain degree; and though the devastation of Belgium in 1683 and of Piedmont in 1693 do not appear to have excited general reprobation, Louis XIV was driven to justify the more savage destruction of the Palatinate by alleging its necessity as a defensive measure for the protection of his frontiers. In the eighteenth century the alliance of devastation with strategical objectives became more close. It was either employed to deny the use of a tract of country to the enemy by rendering subsistence difficult, as when the Duke of Marlborough wasted the neighborhood of Munich in 1704, and the Prussians devastated part of Bohemia in 1757; or it was an essential part of a military operation, as when the Duc of

> Vendôme cut the dykes and laid the country under water from the neighbourhood of Ostend to Ghent, while endeavouring to sever the communications with the former place of the English engaged in the siege of Lille. At the time devastation was still theoretically regarded as an independent means of attack. Wolff declares it to be lawful both as a punishment and as lessening the strength of the enemy; Vattel not only allows a country to be "rendered uninhabitable, that it may serve as a barrier against forces which cannot otherwise be arrested," but treats devastation as a proper mode of chastising a barbarous people; and Moser in like manner permits it both in order to "deprive an enemy of subsistence which a territory affords to him," and "to constrain him to make peace."[64]

Theoreticians still claimed the legitimacy of devastation as an independent means of attack, but increasingly the trend was to limit it to the support of normal military operations and hence to interpret military necessity as limited to such cases.

In Hall's own time devastation was regarded as permissible in the extreme case "when really necessary for the preservation of the force committing it from destruction or surrender." That still was the case at the time of the post–World War II war crimes trials. In *U.S. v. List* and *U.S. v. von Leeb* German generals were charged with devastation beyond what military necessity allows, in the course of retreating from the Red Army in Norway and the Soviet Union. In both cases there was a thorough destruction of food and houses after the local population had been forcibly evacuated. The eight generals charged were all found not guilty: In the opinion of the tribunal: "Defendants . . . were . . . in retreat under arduous conditions wherein their commands were in serious danger of being cut off. Under such circumstances, a commander must necessarily make quick decisions. . . . A great deal of latitude must be accorded to him."[65]

Otherwise, devastation was permissible only as "a necessary concomitant of ordinary military action, as when houses are razed or trees cut down to strengthen a defensive position . . . or when a village is fired to cover the retreat of an army."[66] This sort of tactical devastation was justified in the Middle Ages by the philosopher and theologian Moses Maimonides, who wrote that the king "may break through (private property) to make a road for himself, and none may protest it. No limit can be prescribed for the king's road; he expropriates as much as is needed. He does not have to make detours because someone's vineyard or field (is in his way). He takes the straight route and attacks the enemy."[67] Devastation is never permissible, Hall wrote, "when no military end is served," for example, if a church or museum, not used by the defenders, is deliberately shelled.

The strategic bombing in World War II certainly did not fall into Hall's first category—it was not necessary to prevent the Allied military forces from surrendering to the Axis. Did it fall into the second, as "a necessary concomitant of ordinary military action"? If we want to stretch military necessity, we might argue that the destruction of the enemy's material ability to wage war is a valid military objective, and thus the destruction of an industrial city is quite different from an attack on a Buddhist shrine. Unlike the destruction of churches and museums, strategic bombing reduces the enemy's ability to produce the instruments of war.

Hall considered this type of case while discussing naval strategists who were advocating general bombardment:

> In 1882 Admiral Aube, in an article on naval warfare of the future, expressed his opinion that "armoured fleets in possession of the sea will turn their powers of attack and destruction against the coastal towns of the enemy, irrespectively of whether these are fortified or not, or whether they are commercial or military, and will burn them and lay them in ruins . . . and he pointed out that to adopt this course would be the true policy of France, in the event of a war with England. There is no reason to believe that either the political or naval opinion in France dissented from these views; very shortly after their publication Admiral Aube was appointed Minister of Marine; and he was allowed to change the shipbuilding programme of the country, and to furnish it with precisely the class of ships needed to carry them out.[68]

The strategy, Hall said, was offered "on the plea, it would appear, that every means is legitimate which drives an enemy to submission . . . a plea which would cover every barbarity that disgraced the wars of the seventeenth century." Similarly, "the bombardment, during the siege of a fortified town, of the houses of the town itself in order to put an indirect pressure on the commandant inducing him to surrender on account of the misery suffered by the inhabitants" is a measure "of peculiar cruelty" that "cannot be excused," though "for the present . . . it is sanctioned by usage."[69]

The phrase "indirect pressure" gets at the heart of the issue. Hall was envisioning a town whose the defenders are in fortifications. The shelling of the town's adjacent residential areas makes no contribution to the reduction of the defenses, though concern for civilian casualties might induce the enemy to surrender. Civilian casualties are not incidental in that case—they are the means to the end. But the destruction of purely residential areas serves no direct military purpose. The rounds that land in the residential area leave the defenders unharmed.

Though it may ultimately and indirectly serve a military end, destroying a city is not even a *normal* concomitant of ordinary military operations (the way razing a house to clear a field of fire is), let alone a *necessary* concomitant. It is simply another course of action: One can attack the civilian population instead of attacking the enemy's military forces or in addition to attacking them. An attack on a civilian population indirectly supports military operations against the enemy's military forces only because anything that harms the enemy supports such military operations. An earthquake, flood, or epidemic can indirectly support military operations the same way. But none of these directly support military operations.

To countenance such indirect attacks on the enemy's military forces through direct attacks on the enemy's civilian population is to radically transform the nature of war. War at that point ceases to be a contest between military forces fighting each other; it becomes a contest between military forces attacking the other side's population and material civilization.

That in turn can be understood two ways. If the idea is to punish the civilian population so heavily that the enemy surrenders, the principle of proportionality would mean only that any harm beyond what is needed to obtain the surrender is excessive. The alternative would be that we are not trying to induce surrender through civilian casualties—we countenance attacks on the civilian population only if those attacks can be justified by their effect on the enemy's military forces. But this middle ground is illusory. We would at that point be trying to distinguish: (1) attacks on legitimate military targets, even though by area bombing; (2) attacks on cities as such, with the aim of directly bringing about the enemy's capitulation through such attacks; and (3) attacks on cities as such, with the aim of harming the enemy's military capacities.

The last, (3), though, will collapse into (1) or (2) depending on how we understand it. If we take "with the aim of harming the enemy's military capacities" as referring to the legitimate military targets in (1), then deliberately to attack the larger area when a more precise attack on the military target is feasible amounts to adopting (2): "The enemy's military capacity" is then understood to be legitimately diminished with every dead enemy person. In contrast, if we read (3) to forbid this, (3) involves the same restrictions as (1).

Proportionality can play its role because a nation's military forces and capacities are only a part of the nation—the "nation in arms" is a myth. If the nation itself, rather than its military forces, becomes the target, proportionality becomes an idle restraint. The destruction proportionality would then forbid would only be destruction beyond what is necessary to bring about the other side's surrender, and the prohibition against disproportionate harm shrinks into a prohibition against gratuitous harm. It is a restraint if we ask that the harm that is incidental to the means not be out of proportion to the contribution the means makes to the end. That restraint vanishes if that harm is itself the means: In that case, the greater that harm, the greater the contribution to the end.

Today towns are no longer defended with forts, and because artillery and air power have made dispersion a better technique than concentration, the defenders—particularly if the town's buildings are of sturdy construction—are likely to be scattered throughout the town. But there can be no doubt that during World War II proponents of strategic air power hoped to induce the other side to surrender "on account of the misery suffered by the inhabitants." This is what lay behind the Allies' hopes that they could win the war by breaking the morale of the civilian population. Indeed, the reason given by Emperor Hirohito when he announced his decision to end the war was that he could not allow the Japanese people to suffer any further.

I have argued that area bombing was morally justifiable when, because of the enemy's defenses, it was the only way to attack legitimate military and industrial targets. But it seems that it cannot be justified as a policy of choice. To do so is to justify killing civilians to force the enemy into submission.

A Final Consideration

But what if the abandonment of the strictly military view will produce fewer casualties? What if by attacking the civilian population we can bring a war to a quicker end, with a reduction in civilian casualties—the enemy's, as well as our own? According to some writers, targeting the civilian population can then be morally justified.[70]

One can argue that if the United States had not used the atom bomb against Japan, the war would have gone on, and an even greater number of Japanese civilians would have died. At the time of Hiroshima, Japan was facing starvation. A gradually increasing number of deaths due to starvation might have caused less shock than the sudden bombings, and Japan might have held out while those deaths surpassed the bombing fatalities. And we have seen that if Japanese civilian deaths, primarily through suicide, in an invasion of their home islands were in proportion to their deaths at Okinawa, civilian casualties would have been greater.

One might then argue that at Hiroshima and Nagasaki the United States was doing a kindness to the Japanese—indeed, that argument has been made. But if, as I believe, we do not have the moral right to reduce our own civilian casualties by attacking the enemy's civilian population, much less do we have the right to reduce their civilian casualties by this means. Nations can make great sacrifices if the circumstances warrant it. Other nations cannot commit murder to save them from those sacrifices.[71]

This last claim, though, takes me beyond the boundaries I have set for myself. Perhaps it is morally permissible to kill intentionally one child to end a horrible war. If so, murder is sometimes morally permissible. But this does not directly bear on the ethics of war, for murder is not a legitimate act of war. As the Belgian representative to the Brussels conference said, One cannot attack those who cannot defend themselves. One can harm or kill them, but war presupposes a less passive enemy. Military units have been ordered to massacre defenseless civilians—the German *Einsatzgruppen* in World War II, for example—but those activities are not military actions, no more than it is a military action if a platoon cleans up its barracks. Battles require that both sides be armed.

There are acts of violence so uninhibited that they fall outside the scope of the immunities of war. The question whether it is morally permissible to engage in such acts as a means of promoting some presumably greater good is then a question for general ethics, not a question for war and morality: Whether or not such acts are morally permissible, the war code does not permit them. Whether a surgeon might be morally justified in murdering an evil patient is similarly a question for general ethics, not a question for medical ethics. If a surgeon were ever so justified, however, so would the evil person's plumber or waitress. It is not in virtue of being a surgeon, or of the moral principles pertinent to medicine, that a surgeon could have such a right. It is not in virtue of being a soldier that a soldier could have the analogous right. The law of war absolutely forbids certain practices, regardless of the objections that might be made in the name of effectiveness, utility, military necessity, or the greater good. It rejects the view that the end always justifies the means.

The art of war differs from the art of destruction—even destruction in the service of a comprehensible goal. Whatever is the final truth about the morality of attacking civilians to bring about a greater good, deliberate attacks on them undermine the framework whereby we distinguish soldiers from killers in the service of the state.

This raises another question: Do we want commanders to do whatever is legal to save friendly lives, or do we want them to do what is moral, even if legality does not require it, and even if that would increase friendly casualties? Civil law allows businesses to act in ways that are legal though morally questionable, but in business the stakes are not so high as in war. If life and death were routinely at issue in these transactions, we would be strongly inclined to modify the law. We do not expect law to mandate that all our behavior be moral, but we do expect it to outlaw the most extreme forms of immorality. We would not want our laws to permit immoral killing.

International law, however, allows immoral acts that can kill thousands and now millions. If we want to prevent such acts, we can modify the law—either international law or our own law—to make them illegal. The blame for the adoption of these practices attaches to our failure to do so, rather than to the willingness of commanders to exploit all the legally permissible means of waging war we have afforded them. Our instructions to those commanders cannot be: We have neglected to make certain immoral practices illegal, but we wish you to identify and refrain from them, even at the cost of increasing your casualties. To do so would be to place on the commanders a burden that would be far more lightly borne on our shoulders, but that we nonetheless find too heavy to assume.

By 1945 the prewar prophecies of the advocates of air power had, in a way, come true. Air power alone in 1945 was capable of winning wars—not by destroying civilian morale, but by inflicting damage so great that governments would sue for peace. But at the very moment that air power's new strength was changing the old rules by making attacks on urban centers the shorter road to victory, a more basic premise was dissolving. Weapons were becoming so destructive that as the atomic age dawned our ability to use them in the national interest would come into question. What victory could military force attain if the enemy could destroy five hundred of our cities? What would there be for the loser to surrender? What would there be for the victor to gain?

Appendixes

The 1923 Hague Draft Rules

Michael Walzer has argued that though some area bombing in World War II was justified by what he called "supreme emergency," the bulk of it was not.[72] His position is that the democracies faced, in Nazi Germany, an evil so heinous that in the early stages of the war area bombing was justified as the only way to avert defeat but that once that emergency was over, area bombing ceased to be justified. If he was right, then (except in the case of "supreme emergency") it is immoral to attack legitimate targets with area attacks if the enemy's defensive efforts make precision attacks impractical. My view is that such attacks *are* morally justifiable, subject to proportionality.

A set of rules proposed in the 1920s, but never adopted, captured Walzer's stricter restraints. Article 24 of the 1923 Hague Air Warfare Draft Rules stated that

> (1) Aerial bombardment is legitimate only when directed at a military objective—that is to say, an object of which the destruction or injury would constitute a distinct military advantage to the belligerent.
>
> (2) Such bombardment is legitimate only when directed exclusively at the following objectives: military forces; military works; military establishments or depots; factories constituting important and well-known centers engaged in the manufacture of arms, ammunition, or distinctively military supplies; lines of communication or transportation used for military purposes.
>
> (3) The bombardment of cities, towns, villages, dwellings, or buildings not in the immediate neighborhood of the operations of land forces is prohibited. In cases where the objectives specified in paragraph (2) are so situated that they cannot be bombarded without the indiscriminate bombardment of the civilian population, the aircraft must abstain from the bombardment.
>
> (4) In the immediate neighborhood of the operations of land forces, the bombardment of cities, towns, villages, dwellings, or buildings is legitimate provided that there exists a reasonable presumption that the military concentration is sufficiently important to justify such bombardment, having regard to the danger thus caused to the civilian population.

Section (3) of the draft rules forbids strategic area attacks—and would encourage nations to place their war industries in the protected city centers. We will turn to its principle in Chapter 6.

Unconditional Surrender

In *Just and Unjust Wars* Walzer argued that it was the U.S. insistence on Japan's unconditional surrender that would have necessitated the U.S. invasion of Japan, and hence it is illegitimate from the start for Americans to defend area bombing on the grounds that it saved lives. As Walzer saw it, Americans argue that area bombing was necessary to save them from the consequences of their own policy of seeking unconditional surrender—a policy he took to have been unjust: "People . . . have a right not to be forced to continue fighting beyond the point when the war might justly be concluded. Beyond that point, there can be no . . . cost-accounting in human lives. To press the war further than that is to recommit the crime of aggression" (p. 268).

It is certainly true that if U.S. terms had been more generous the war might have been concluded earlier. That depends, of course, on just how generous the United States was willing to be. However, I cannot see why the United States was under a moral obligation not to insist on unconditional surrender. At the very least, the knowledge of widespread Japanese war crimes—the beheading of prisoners of war, their use as targets during bayonet practice, and the wholesale slaughter of nurses, doctors, and patients in captured hospitals—demanded that the surrender give the United States the right to conduct war crimes trials, a right that would by itself be tantamount to unconditional surrender. Even with unconditional surrender, U.S. adherence to the Hague and Geneva conventions gave the Japanese a great measure of protection. They would not, for example, be forced to march into the sea to die by drowning, as they had forced thousands of ethnic Chinese in Singapore. U.S. occupation of Japan would be benign and enlightened as these things go.

As always we must resist the temptation to attribute to the historical protagonists the knowledge we have and to project the actual result into counterfactual situations. The actual, in hindsight, takes on the appearance of inevitability, which is bad enough; then, worse, the consequence, now regarded as inevitable, is assumed even in the absence of the events that actually caused it. A defeatist Japanese quotation can be cited and we are told the Japanese would have surrendered anyway, even without the final bombings. But there were defeatist Japanese views after Okinawa, after the U.S. recapture of the Philippines, after the first B-29 raids, after the capture of the Marianas, after the Battle of Midway, and for that matter, before the strike on Pearl Harbor. And for every defeatist statement, we can find nondefeatist ones: Right after Hiroshima "some Japanese leaders were already speculating that perhaps the Americans had but one bomb or that a defense could be quickly improvised."[73]

The only defeatist statement that finally counted was the emperor's—the one that led to the surrender. And it came after Hiroshima and Nagasaki. If the Japanese were going to surrender even without those horrible final bombings, they would have. This is not to deny that the Japanese *might* have eventually surrendered even without those bombings. As autumn 1945 approached, the Japanese were facing starvation.

A nation at war is not obligated to ensure the food supply of the enemy—it was for the Japanese to decide when their sacrifice had grown too great. Had the United States continued the naval blockade of Japan without area bombing, more Japanese might have died, but the United States would have been less open to criticism. We cannot condone attacks on the civilian population as a policy of choice rather than as a by-product of military reality, but we also cannot take responsibility for the consequences of the enemy's determination.

Double Effect

According to the doctrine of double effect, which has long been a standard in Catholic moral theology, it is wrong to kill innocent people intentionally. On the best interpretation, this does not mean that it is permissible to kill the innocent as long as one does so regretfully. It means that attacks on the innocent cannot be the *means* to the end, for as Elizabeth Anscombe has said, "It is nonsense to pretend that you do not intend to do what is the means you take to your chosen end."[74] Her conclusion was that area bombing was immoral, for however the end was specified (destruction of the enemy's military capacity, civilian morale, and so on) the means was wholesale attack on cities and hence on their inhabitants.

I disagree with her conclusion because if she were right, it would follow that bombardments in support of ground assaults would also be immoral. In that case, too, the means is a wholesale attack on defended towns—and hence on their inhabitants. From that point of view it hardly matters whether the bombardment is by plane or artillery, or whether it is in conjunction with a ground attack. We only ask whether the bombardment is chosen as a means to the end.

I defended tactical bombardments on the grounds of military necessity. If a town's defenders stay in forts, the shelling of the town's dwellings would be unjustifiable. By dispersing throughout a town, rather than staying in fortifications, defenders on the ground pose a problem: Shell the whole town or not at all. In that case, I claim, military necessity—*military reality* is a better phrase—justifies the general bombardment.

Strategic bombardments get a more complex, but similar, defense. The dislocation of the enemy's war industry is a legitimate goal in war. If the enemy's defense of such targets makes it unfeasible to attack them except through an area attack, the attack is not immoral. The means chosen is in these cases displaced by the defender, who gives the attacker the choice: Adopt area attacks or cease the strategic air war.

Judith Jarvis Thompson has posed a problem for the double effect theory.[75] Suppose a runaway trolley is bearing down on four people, and the only way to save them is to switch the trolley to another track that has one person on it. Most of us would say that switching the trolley is permissible—that it is permissible to kill the one to save the four. But now suppose that the track with the one person loops around and puts the trolley back on the same course, but that the impact with the one person will stop the trolley. In that case the trolley's hitting that person is the means to saving the others, violating the principle of double effect. Yet most of us think it would be morally permissible to switch the trolley.

Thompson's example seems persuasive, and if she is right, double effect cannot be an absolute principle of morality. But it still is defensible as a limited principle. It might, in other words, be an appropriate principle for bombardment and civilian casualties, without being a binding moral principle in all contexts.

Suggestions for Further Reading

The official British and U.S. histories of the air war in World War II—Wesley Frank Craven and James Lea Cate, eds., *The Army Air Forces in World War II* (University of Chicago Press, Chicago), and Sir Charles Webster and Noble Frankland, *The Strategic Air Offensive Against Germany* (Her Majesty's Stationery Office, London, 1961)—are still the best sources for the historical background, but they should be balanced by later, more critical sources such as Anthony Verrier's *The Bomber Offensive* (Macmillan, London, 1968) and Ronald Schaffer's *Wings of Judgment* (Oxford University Press, Oxford, 1985).

The relevant law has been discussed in many texts. William Edward Hall, *A Treatise on International Law,* 8th ed., ed. A. Pearce Higgins (Oxford University Press, Oxford, 1924); A. Pearce Higgins, *The Hague Peace Conferences and Other International Conferences Concerning the Laws and Usages of War: Texts of Conventions with Commentaries* (Cambridge University Press, Cambridge, 1909); Sir Hersch Lauterpacht, *Lassa Oppenheim's International Law: A Treatise,* 7th ed., vol. 2 (Longmans, Green, London, 1952); and John Westlake, *Traité de Droit International,* tr. A. de Lapradelle (Oxford University Press, Oxford, 1924), are the ones I find most incisive, but these older authors need to be balanced by more modern sources: Morris Greenspan, *The Modern Law of Land Warfare* (University of California Press, Berkeley, 1959), and Hans Blix, "Area Bombardment: Rules and Reasons," *British Yearbook of International Law* 49 (1978), are quite useful.

The moral issues raised by area bombardment are discussed by Elizabeth Anscombe, "War and Murder," in *Nuclear Weapons: A Catholic Response,* ed. Walter Stein (Sheed & Ward, New York, 1961), and John C. Ford, "The Morality of Obliteration Bombing," *Theological Studies* 5 (1944), both reprinted in *War and Morality,* ed. Richard Wasserstrom (Wadsworth, Belmont, Calif., 1970).

There are also discussions by George I. Mavrodes, "Conventions and the Morality of War," *Philosophy and Public Affairs* 4 (1975); Jeffrie G. Murphy, "The Killing of the Innocent," *Monist* 57 (1973); Thomas Nagel, "War and

Massacre," *Philosophy and Public Affairs* 1 (1972); Richard Wasserstrom, "The Laws of War," *The Monist* 56 (1972); Richard B. Brandt, "Utilitarianism and the Laws of War," *Philosophy and Public Affairs* 4 (1975)—all reprinted in Malham Wakin, ed., *War, Morality, and the Military Profession* (Westview Press, Boulder, Colo., 1981).

5

Little Wars

The course of nature does not adjust itself to our merit.

—Immanuel Kant
"Fragments of a Moral Catechism"

The Historical Context

In *Platoon Leader,* James McDonough recounted a night patrol in Vietnam. A short while after his platoon had repulsed an intense attack, McDonough took a squad out to flank the now disorganized attackers. Moving cautiously in an area that was supposed to contain only combatants, they heard whispering ahead. McDonough could make out nine figures in the darkness.

> I was in no mood to take any chances. Already many men had died that night, and I was not about to let the tally rise any higher if I could help it. But before I could follow through on my intentions, [Sgt.] Killigan tugged at my arm and motioned for me to stay. Apparently he had read my thoughts and disapproved of the plan. . . . In one of his rare moments of speech he hissed at me, "Let me check it out first."
>
> I could not deny him. He was not asking anybody else to take a chance. He would go forward on his own. I knew he was no stranger to combat. He was not reluctant to close with and destroy the enemy, yet he was virtually pleading with me to hesitate. . . . I gave him a nod. Silently, he crept forward into the darkness.[1]

The whispers turned out to come from a family that had ignored the government's orders to spend the night in the village and came close to dying for it.

On another patrol the squad made out two figures, a man and a boy, bending over a mound of dirt. They looked as if they were setting a mine, but McDonough could not be sure: "I would not allow the squad to fire. I did not see any weapons, and regardless of the political leanings of the older man, the boy, to my way of thinking, deserved a little more consideration." As the squad moved forward, the two Vietnamese darted into the brush, and the Americans pursued. McDonough was thinking that he was glad they had not killed the boy when a deafening explosion threw him into the air. He had stepped on a mine. When he landed, he tried to look at his legs: "Oh, be there! Please be there!"[2]

Like most armies today, ancient Roman armies were composed of fairly equivalent large units (legions), which were in turn composed of subunits (maniples), composed of subunits (centuries), and so on down the line. Roman soldiers were drilled and trained to fight and maneuver as members of these units. Each unit had its officers, and the soldiers were recognizable by their uniforms.

In contrast, the Goths, whom the Romans fought, were bands of men who went to war in their own clothes, fought as they had learned to fight at home, and owed their primary loyalty directly to the chiefs who led them. This sort of army is called an irregular army. A Gothic army would resemble an American Indian army more than it would a Roman army—a Gothic army would have the appearance of an informal horde of armed men. This appearance, of course, is compatible with a well-developed system of strategy and tactics—the Huns and the Zulu, for example, were known for their use of envelopment. The military world today is dominated by regular armies, but some of the great armies of the past have been irregular: the Huns and the Vikings, the Crusaders and the Scythians. The Afghan *mujahadeen* are irregulars; the Russian and Afghan army troops they fought are regular troops. American militia in the Revolutionary War were irregulars; the Continental Army was a regular army.

In the Middle Ages, the Byzantines, carrying on Roman tradition, continued to field regular armies, but the feudal armies of western Europe were irregular. Then, in the fifteenth century, regular national armies started to reappear. In 1471, Charles the Bold of Burgundy copied the new French institution of the professional officer, paid by rank rather than by hereditary title. In 1473 Charles ordained colored ensigns for his army, "having various devices painted upon them," to facilitate recognition between soldiers and their officers. The cornets and helmet plumes of commanders of subordinate units were color coded to match the ensigns of the parent units, with the lesser units differentiated from each other numerically.[3] Since then European military history has increasingly been the history of clashes between regular armies, with irregulars playing a role mainly in civil wars and in wars on the fringes of empire: the Revolutionary War in North

America, the Boer War in South Africa, and the colonial wars on India's northwestern frontier.

The distinction between regular and irregular troops is, thus, a distinction between two types of army organization or military unit. The distinction between guerrilla and conventional warfare, however, is a distinction between two different methods of waging war. In conventional warfare the opposing armies face one another and engage. Guerrilla warfare consists of the use of hit-and-run tactics to harass the enemy and engage weak enemy units while avoiding stronger ones (particularly behind enemy lines). Guerrilla actions are essentially raids, with the guerrillas attempting to disengage when the enemy brings up stronger forces: The guerrillas consider themselves to be too weak to fight the enemy if the enemy has had the opportunity to bring his strength to bear. They rely on evasion in order to survive, in a way in which conventional forces do not. Guerrilla warfare has consequently been practical only in areas where the terrain makes evasion practical: in mountains and forests. In 1927 Mao Tse-tung, ordered by the Chinese Communist party to continue disastrous attacks on cities in Hupei Province, instead took his troops to the mountains of Ching Kang Shan and developed a base. There he taught his men: "When the enemy advances, we retreat. When the enemy halts, we trouble them. When the enemy seeks to avoid battle, we attack. When the enemy retreats, we pursue."[4]

We tend to associate guerrilla warfare with irregulars, but it is not their exclusive province. Guerrilla warfare was used by Confederate cavalry under Colonel John Mosby in the U.S. Civil War. Cavalry units of the Red Army operated behind German lines in the Pripet marshes in World War II, and regular units of the U.S. and British armies fought a guerrilla war against the Japanese in Burma. In Vietnam regular units of the North Vietnamese Army used guerrilla tactics against the U.S. and South Vietnamese troops, and South Vietnamese Rangers and U.S. Special Forces units replied in kind.

Just as regular troops can engage in guerrilla warfare, irregular troops can fight pitched conventional battles. The irregular Scythian horse archers of the ancient world tried to avoid pitched battles. They were nomads who withdrew with their tents and flocks when a superior force confronted them; they would engage only at long range with their bows. Hence the canny advice given to the Greeks by one who knew the Scythian ways: You cannot defeat them, for they carry their towns with them. But the equally nomadic Huns went straight into pitched battles, as did the Crusaders. Irregular troops sometimes fight on a battlefield alongside regular troops, as did Montagnard tribesmen at Khe San in Vietnam, colonial militia at Yorktown, and Thracian cavalry at Gaugamela.

Guerrillas played an important role in Spain during the Napoleonic Wars and were at the center of a heated controversy in the Franco-Prussian War, when French volunteer civilians, often in civilian clothes, sniped at German soldiers in areas the Germans had already occupied and thought under their control: At one point there were about 60,000 of these *francs-tireurs* (snipers).[5] Some of these characters were quite extraordinary, like the *Garibaldiennes,* women in military dress, some of them dressed as officers, "whose appearance at Dijon 'stupified' the inhabitants."[6] Some were criminals using the war as a pretext. Others were true volunteer militia, following the customs of war. Many fell into a mixed group somewhere between these two and to which a standard objection applies:

> A large part . . . of the case against popular private military enterprise is that those undertaking it cannot normally be aware of the obligations resting on lawful combatants. Properly officered and disciplined soldiers at any rate are supposed to do what they are told; and if they are told to restrain their passions and forget about their prejudices, they may do so. But what were civilians likely to do when encouraged in such styles as were employed by some Frenchmen with access to paper and ink? The Préfet of Côte d'Or was at least tactless in causing this bill to be posted all around his department:
>
> "Your fatherland does not ask you to gather in large numbers and oppose the enemy openly; it only expects that each morning three or four resolute men will leave their village and go where nature has prepared a place suitable for hiding and for firing without danger on the Prussians."[7]

The Prussians, as might be expected, responded with some of the same lack of discrimination: Innocent civilians and law-abiding combatants were shot by way of error, retribution, anger, and deterrence.

In the twentieth century the Boer War was largely a guerrilla war, pitting Afrikaner *kommandos* (the origin of "commando") against British regulars. The war had begun in October 1899 as a conventional war fought between Boer irregulars and British regulars. The Boers won a few victories, but the British reinforced and quickly defeated the Boers, and in June 1900 occupied Pretoria. When, at that point, Boer President Paul Kruger announced "that the war would begin only now, the British generals were inclined to dismiss this as idle talk on the part of an old man, a civilian who lacked understanding of military realities."[8] But begin in earnest it did, with Boer commandos attacking British garrisons, convoys, railways, and strategic targets.

By the end of the war in 1902, the British presence had increased from 12,000 troops to 448,000 and the British, fighting during most of the war against fewer than 20,000 Boers, had suffered 46,000 dead and wounded. To deny the guerrillas the support of the noncombatant population, the British adopted a technique the Spanish had used in Cuba, gathering the civilian population into camps—100,000 women and children were interned. The British also burned farms, practicing a "scorched earth" policy designed to deprive the guerrillas of provisions. This policy worked: By the end of the war the Boers were too low on food, clothes, and ammunition to continue. One Boer leader, Denys Reitz, said that "he had exactly four bullets left when he joined Smut's raid into Cape Colony."[9]

In World War II guerrillas played the major role in Yugoslavia, where they operated in brigade strength and controlled large portions of the mountainous countryside. By the end of 1943 they were about a quarter of a million strong, "one of the few cases in history in which a partisan movement liberated a country and seized power largely without outside help."[10] Elsewhere regular and irregular guerrillas provided a significant auxiliary force, harassing the occupying troops and making transportation networks unsafe.

After World War II, guerrilla fighting, negligible or nonexistent in the French and Russian revolutions, became an important element in revolutionary movements. In Greece, the Philippines, and Malaya, guerrillas were defeated by conventional forces. In French Indochina and Cuba the guerrillas won. In the opening stages of the Korean War, North Korea used bands of infiltrators to confuse and harass the South Korean army, but thereafter both sides fought the war conventionally.

In the early years of the war in Vietnam, irregular Communist South Vietnamese forces, the Vietcong, played the major role in the fighting, operating both as guerrillas and in regular units up to division size. But in the Tet offensive of early 1968 the Vietcong took such heavy casualties that they were never again a serious military force and never again capable of threatening to topple the government of South Vietnam.

As early as spring 1965, however, a regiment of the 325th North Vietnamese Army (NVA) Division had been identified in the Central Highlands of South Vietnam.[11] After the Tet offensive, regular, uniformed NVA troops did the bulk of the fighting on the Communist side. They operated in small units, using guerrilla tactics, but also, as at Khe San, in division- and corps-sized units, and they frequently fought to defend bases and fortified areas. The war had acquired a mixed character combining elements of guerrilla and conventional warfare. The U.S.

public, perhaps confusing jungle warfare with guerrilla warfare, seemed to fail to realize this.

In 1975, three years after U.S. troops had been withdrawn, the North Vietnamese, fielding the fourth largest army in the world, attacked South Vietnam with sixteen divisions and defeated the South Vietnamese army in a conventional military campaign. In the 1980s there was guerrilla fighting in Afghanistan, Latin America, North Africa, and the Philippines.

Irregulars can fight conventional wars, and regulars can fight guerrilla wars. None of this poses any particular moral problems. The moral problems arise when we introduce another development: guerrillas practicing evasion by posing as civilians, rather than by retreating into concealing terrain. The legal issue involved here is expressed by the dress code.

The Legal Context

In December 1944, small teams of German commandos parachuted down through the wintry clouds and landed in the snow-covered Ardennes behind U.S. lines. The teams had been gathered together weeks before, after a call had gone out in the German army for volunteers who could speak English with an American accent—a call that had been answered by several German soldiers who had grown up in the United States.

On the ground the scattered teams assembled as best they could. U.S. Army boots and overcoats concealed the German uniforms the men wore underneath. Each team had an English-speaking member who was to do the talking. Their mission was to disrupt the flow of Allied reinforcements driving into the Ardennes in response to the German attack. They had been told not to open fire on anyone unless they first removed their overcoats. Otto Skorzeny, the commando leader who organized this operation, had been told by a German expert on the law of war that as long as the commandos removed their deceptive outer clothing before opening fire, their operation would be legal. The Americans who captured the commandos took a different view: They sent them before firing squads.[12]

The law of war recognizes the legitimacy of irregular armies, but it places restrictions on all combatants. In Chapter 2 we examined two of the requirements for lawful belligerents: They must obey the law of war and have responsible commanders. The other two requirements, applicable equally to regular and irregular troops, constitute a sort of dress code. Lawful belligerents must: (1) *bear arms openly,* and (2) wear *distinctive dress,* or a fixed badge or emblem recognizable at a distance.

In only one case—the *levée en masse*—does international law allow combatants to violate these rules. A population may spontaneously rise against an approaching invading army, with no time to distribute armbands or organize a chain of command. In that case it is excused from the first three requirements. But the *levée en masse* is legitimate only as the spontaneous response of a population to the approach of an advancing enemy army. Once the enemy has occupied a place and things settle down, the opposition has the time to organize itself and make armbands, and the *levée* no longer applies.

These requirements forbid soldiers from hiding their hostile and belligerent status. Members of regular armed forces are expected to wear uniforms. Members of guerrilla groups and other irregular forces or volunteer forces, who may not have uniforms, must wear distinctive emblems—prominent armbands, for example. The emblem should be "something which cannot be instantly taken off or assumed at will, thus enabling a combatant to appear a peaceful citizen one moment and a soldier the next."[13] All must carry their weapons openly. They cannot dress as civilians or hide their weapons in suitcases. They cannot, in short, attempt to pass for noncombatants or for troops of the other side.[14] This requirement expresses "the impossibility of sanctioning the most enthusiastic demands, that the citizen's right to fight should extend to a right to insurgency against an established occupier. The lawmakers could never say more to that than they could to the spy—that he might be heroic and what he did might be useful, but it was incapable of legitimization."[15]

Or at least, they cannot hide their status, within certain limits. The Hague conventions do not absolutely prohibit the use of enemy flags, emblems, or uniforms—the conventions prohibit their *improper* use.[16] In former times it was an accepted ruse of war to display the enemy's banners during a maneuver, in the hope of confusing the enemy into thinking the marching unit was friendly, just as it was an accepted ruse to trick the enemy by using their bugle calls. A modern equivalent is in the use of false radio messages to confuse the other side. But even in former times combatants had to show their true colors before opening fire. The deception is limited to the maneuvering that takes place before combat.[17]

In the nineteenth century a firmer requirement began to evolve. Instead of merely requiring the enemy to show his true colors in combat, he was required to show them as soon as he came close enough for combat (the naval equivalent would be requiring a warship to show its true colors not just before it opened fire, but as soon as it was in gunnery range). Thus in the Franco-Prussian War, the Prussians and the French Garde Nationale required a distinctive sign visible at the range of a fusil—the musket from which we get the word *fusilier.* A few decades later, Westlake declared that criterion outdated: Technological advances had increased the effective range of small arms far beyond the reach of the fusil, and at a thousand yards a recognizable sign would be too large to be practical—soldiers could not walk around carrying billboards.[18] In the twentieth century the distance at which one can recognize an emblem is less than the effective distance of the weaponry, and no one tries anymore to specify a distance at which the emblem must be recognizable. The requirement is simply that the sign must be visible *at a distance.*

In response to the increased effective range of small arms fire, regular troops adopted modern uniforms.[19] Bright uniforms had not, until then, been a liability: At the short ranges and in the close orders in which battles had previously been fought, enemy soldiers were clearly visible—having them wear red coats did not make them significantly more vulnerable. And before the advent of smokeless powder, the enemy's fire would in any case have given their positions away. Now that soldiers could deliver rapid, long-range fire from cover, those who had to advance against them sought some measure of protection themselves: "The old terror of a visible foe had given way to the paralysing sensation of advancing on an invisible one."[20] Khaki, field gray, pale blue, and yellow-green replaced the brilliant hues of former days, and soldiers could no longer be readily spotted at great distances.

The Moral Context

Camouflage, Concealment, and the Dress Code

But is it really true that soldiers must bear their arms openly and wear distinctive dress? When I was discussing the Paris Pact (Chapter 3), I cited von Glahn's argument that in international law a law that is consistently ignored is not really a law. It is a mere "moral preachment." In recent years several authors have argued that the dress code has at best a similar status.

Michael Walzer claimed that because it is an accepted custom for soldiers to fight from ambush, and because hiding themselves, they can hardly be expected to make a display of their weapons, the law is in practice not taken seriously even by regular troops.[21] What sense does it make, he asked, to talk of "distinctive dress visible at a distance" if woodland camouflage is an acceptable uniform pattern for fighting in forests, or if white parkas are standard issue for troops fighting in snow? Instead of making combatants visible at a distance, these uniforms make combatants difficult to detect and therefore seem contrary to the law's requirement. Why say you are openly displaying your arms if your artillery park is placed in a grove and covered with camouflage netting?

Keith Suter cited two other academic observers in support of the claim that the dress code is outmoded:

> The unreality of determinations which permit life and death to hinge upon a man's garb is accentuated when one considers that military uniforms today are deliberately designed to enhance invisibility by visual integration into the immediate environment. Uniforms or dressmarks might have been a meaningful test of belligerent qualifications in days when each knight had his own crest and colours, or when military dress was more spectacularly cut and coloured. In modern war where insignia or dress afford little, if any, protection against surprise, the rationality of this rule-of-thumb on permissible combatants must be regarded as open to serious doubt.[22]

This assumes that the purpose of the "distinctive dress" requirement is to make soldiers stand out from the background—to make them readily observable. Uniforms would then serve the way Ambrose Bierce claimed flags serve: to indicate that "rubbish may be shot here."

But there is no reason to think that the dress requirement is meant to mark soldiers for easy targets—that to keep within the bounds of the law, troops must wear the bright scarlet, blues, and grays of former wars. The acceptance of camouflage, cover, and concealment shows, rather, that the customary law of war does not require that soldiers make a blatant display of themselves. It only requires that they display their belligerent status.

There is an important difference between these two. The soldier can hide, but he cannot hide the fact that he is a soldier. He must, if seen , be readily identifiable as a belligerent, but he need not dress to facilitate being readily seen. Camouflage uniforms make it difficult to detect soldiers, but they still identify soldiers as soldiers. Ski troops in snow parkas are hard to see, but they cannot be confused with high school students on an outing. Such practices as concealment, camouflage, and ambush do not compromise the requirement to display one's belligerent status and affiliations. They are in keeping with it. The requirements of distinctive dress and bearing arms openly are meant to enable soldiers to distinguish combatants from passersby, not to make it easier for them to detect one another.

This, however, is too simple. For though the written laws of war specifically require that combatant personnel not be disguised as noncombatants, the less well-defined customs of war do not work the same way for equipment. A soldier fighting in civilian clothes violates the laws of war, but coastal guns have been disguised to look like beach cottages, and tanks have been concealed inside houses, without anyone complaining that the laws of war have been violated. The customs surrounding the camouflage and concealment of the machinery of war, as opposed to the people who operate the machinery, allow civilian disguises.

But there is a common strand that accounts for this discrepancy in a more basic principle. Whether for people or equipment, military custom allows concealment and camouflage if what is being hidden is concealed by or disguised as something that is itself a lawful target. Soldiers, vehicles, and guns may hide in woods, but it is permissible to shell woods. They may be disguised to look like snow, but you can fire at snow. They may be done out to look like hotels and cottages—the law of war allows soldiers to call in fire on a hotel or cottage suspected of harboring the enemy.

Soldiers may *not* be disguised as "mere civilians," for the mere civilian is not a legitimate target. Similarly, a tank may be camouflaged to look like a house, but not like an ambulance—ambulances are not permissible targets—and a coastal gun can be disguised as a seaside inn, but not as a church.

Soldiers, through camouflage and concealment, attempt to hide themselves and their equipment. When they violate the dress code they are not attempting to hide themselves—they are attempting to hide their status. They can do this by attempting to pass as soldiers of the other side or by attempting to pass as *civilians* who are members of neither side. There is an important difference between these deceptions—between disguising oneself to look like a combatant of the other side and disguising oneself to look like a noncombatant.

The German commandos in the Ardennes dressed as U.S. soldiers, not as Belgian civilians. Once some of them were found out, the inevitable result was to make U.S. soldiers suspicious of other U.S. soldiers, who might, after all, also be Germans in disguise. This can lead to tragic results and did so during the Boer War. Boer militia whose clothes had worn out put on British uniforms—not as a ruse, they claimed, but because they had nothing else to wear. Soon British soldiers were being fired on by Boers in British uniforms. The troops understandably became jumpy, and as a result several British soldiers were shot by their own comrades. The British then began shooting

Boers captured in British uniforms. The Boers seemed to have understood that the British had little alternative.

It is distasteful enough to the normal person to have to shoot an enemy soldier. It is far worse to shoot one of your own, and soldiers look with peculiar horror on a practice that encourages them to do so. They also do not like having to worry, in addition to all their other fears, about being shot by their friends. If they have to worry about this, they will have very few circumstances in which they are able not to worry. The practice of wearing the other side's uniform has therefore been made an illegal ruse. It is too conducive to insecurity, and it would make an already unpleasant situation even more unpleasant. In the interests of all, it is forbidden.

When combatants disguise themselves as *civilians* they raise a different problem. The threat this poses is not just to military cohesion or the soldier's peace of mind but to fundamental moral principles of the law of war. Combatants so disguised do not place enemy soldiers at risk from their compatriots; they place innocent civilians at risk. For just as the Boer adoption of British uniforms led British soldiers to shoot British soldiers, combatant adoption of civilian clothes will cause soldiers to shoot civilians. This makes it a worse offense. The combatant who dresses in an enemy uniform increases the chances that other combatants will die in particularly tragic circumstances; the combatant who dresses as a civilian increases the chances that noncombatants will die. The measure of security he obtains is taken from them. As Michael Walzer observed, "it is not the case, as Mao once suggested, that guerrillas are to civilians as fish to the ocean. The actual relation is rather of fish to other fish."[23]

We have seen that though soldiers are allowed to do things that place civilian lives at higher risk, they are not allowed to target civilians. The dress requirements enable combatants to obey this principle, by enabling them to distinguish one another readily from noncombatants. The breach of these requirements when a combatant disguises himself as a civilian therefore strikes at the roots of the modern law of war, for it undermines the practice of noncombatant immunity.

This may seem an odd claim in a century in which planes, not soldiers out of uniform, have caused the really massive civilian casualties, and undoubtedly the widespread harm that came to civilians from airpower in World War II has lessened the world's indignation at forms of warfare that put civilians at risk. Whether the oddity is more than superficial is another question.[24]

As far as the law of war is concerned,[25] it is not criminal to bombard a resisting town, even if schoolchildren may be killed. But it is a crime to direct fire at schoolchildren, and it is a crime for combatants to try to pass as schoolchildren.

The Dress Code and Guerrilla Warfare

In 1949 the Geneva conventions made it clear that if irregular troops meet the normal criteria, they are lawful belligerents, even when they operate behind the lines, in enemy-occupied territory.[26] This is sensible—regular troops have the same right. But guerrillas may fail to carry their weapons openly or to wear uniforms and thereby hide their combatant status. From the guerrilla's point of view this deception offers distinct advantages. By making it impossible for the enemy to tell who is a noncombatant, who a mere civilian, the guerrilla poses a dilemma for his enemy, who can wait for the guerrilla to show his hand at a moment of the guerrilla's choice, or who can treat all civilians as enemies, with dire consequences for the real civilians.

Some writers on guerrilla warfare, perhaps inured to the violation of law this involves, have not even mentioned the dress code. They characterize guerrilla warfare as a war of evasion and have let it go at that, as though a soldier's hiding in the bushes were morally equivalent to his dressing as a parcel delivery man.[27] Guerrilla warfare, even when conducted by regular troops, is certainly a war of evasion—guerrillas cannot avoid strong enemy units if they cannot evade them, but this does not mean they cannot obey the dress code. Guerrillas can evade the enemy by dressing as noncombatants, but they can also evade the enemy by hiding in mountains, forests, marshes, or jungles, as uniformed guerrillas did in World War II. At that time tens of thousands of Yugoslavian partisans fought in the mountains. One of Tito's aides described a meeting of their commanders: "They were all dressed as Partisans, in half-military, half-civilian clothes, furnished with chest straps and belts from which hung submachine guns and revolvers."[28] Fidel Castro's forces living in the Sierra Madre range wore combat fatigues; French partisans in the *massif centrale* wore identifying armbands.

Others have defended violations of the dress code. According to Richard Falk, the requirements of "being commanded by a person responsible for his subordinates, having a fixed, distinctive sign recognizable at a distance, carrying arms openly, and conducting . . . operations in accordance with the laws and customs of war . . . seem to be weighted heavily in favor of the constituted power of governments and to carry over into the laws of war the statist bias of the overall system of the world order."[29] According to Nicholas Fotion and G. Elfstrom, the deception involved in dressing as a civilian "is not in itself immoral":

> It is only a deception relative to standards established by establishment powers. For a variety of military and perhaps a few moral, reasons, governments follow a practice concerning uniforms. Following such a practice, there is a degree of immorality (and illegality) involved when some of their military people do not fight in their uniforms or switch uniforms for the purpose of deceiving the enemy. But being obligated to wear a uniform as a result of a standard practice is not the same as being obligated to accept the practice. There is no obligation that every side fighting in war must accept any practice pertaining to wearing uniforms. If there were, and if the obligation were strong enough to apply to guerrilla fighters, then morality would be serving the interests of the establishment powers. In many cases at least, for the guerrillas to put on and continue to wear uniforms would be tantamount to making themselves easy targets for attack. . . . There is nothing immoral about not wearing a uniform.[30]

In general the argument is quite simple. It would be a serious military liability to guerrillas to wear uniforms, so it is not immoral for them not to. Falk, Fotion, and Elfstrom viewed the dress requirement as favoring the regular troops of the state and hence as unfair to guerrillas. Fotion and Elfstrom went further: Morality, they held, cannot serve the interests of "the establishment powers."

That is a peculiar claim. It implies that acceptable moral principles cannot in fact favor one side—that they must be impartial or, at least, not to the disadvantage of either side. This is not the way the laws of *jus in bello* work. These laws are not a distillation that imposes equal burdens on everyone *regardless* of how one chooses to fight. They forbid certain ways of fighting, even if the forbidden ways are preferred and advantageous for some groups in certain circumstances.

Indeed, we have gone over this ground before, for what we have here is an appeal to military necessity: The claim is that guerrillas are not bound by the dress code because that would make their military operations unfeasible. It is one of the striking oddities of contemporary politics and values that military necessity, so indignantly and unanimously rejected when it is brought in to justify the behavior of regular troops, should be so timidly readmitted through the back door when it is guerrillas who have come to call. Similar suggestions have been raised about other guerrilla indiscretions. Myres McDougal and Florentino Feliciano, for example, wrote: "While observance of the laws of war would seem a reasonable requirement, the conditions under which guerrilla operations are carried out are not commonly propitious for adherence to some of these rules. For instance, the need for high mobility . . . as well as shortage of food and other supplies, are not calculated to encourage guerrilla troops to encumber themselves by taking prisoners."[31]

We saw in Chapter 2 that military necessity, legally, is no excuse: The law of war explains when military necessity is a valid excuse, and the dress code and the granting of quarter are not included in those exemptions. Regular soldiers in conventional wars often need to be mobile and sometimes are low on food, but even so, for them to refuse quarter is a war crime. If they cannot take prisoners with them, they are expected to disarm and release them, not kill them. No matter how dire their situation, the law does not allow them to kill prisoners out of military necessity. Similarly, the law does not allow military necessity to overide the dress code: The war crimes tribunals that sat after World War II consistently held that the executions of those who violated the requirements for lawful belligerency were not war crimes.[32]

One might argue, however, that though military necessity is not a legal excuse, it is a moral one in this case—that the dress code favors government troops over rebels and hence is unjust or unfair. Fotion and Elfstrom went further. They saw in this provision of international law nothing more than a "standard practice" affecting only those who accept it—a form of promise keeping. If the guerrillas choose not to accept the practice, if they do not accept the relevant international law, they are simply not (morally) bound by it. Fotion and Elfstrom view the dress code as having the same sort of status I claimed in Chapter 1 for the prohibition against attacking military medical personnel. But the cases are different. If we allow attacks on medical personnel, the persons who come to harm are military personnel. But the dress code has a moral aspect apart from the effect it has on the relation between military personnel. By providing a clear means of distinguishing civilians from combatants, it protects civilians. The guerrilla who violates the dress code "becomes a threat to noncombatants because he undermines the principle which protects them."[33] Shall we say that the guerrillas' rights override this protection for civilians?

Michael Walzer, more sensitive than Fotion and Elfstrom to the problems posed by combatants disguised as innocents, wrote that guerrillas' violation of the dress code ought to deprive them of the rights of lawful belligerents: "They violate the implicit trust upon which the war convention rests: soldiers must feel safe among civilians if civilians are ever to be safe from soldiers."[34] He concluded that guerrillas in civilian clothes are more properly treated as assassins than as soldiers and hence are not entitled to the rights accorded lawful belligerents. They can be compared with spies, who also lack lawful belligerent status.

We can go further: If the guerrilla's situation makes it moral for them to violate the dress code on the grounds of military necessity, then the situation of regular troops must sometimes make it moral for them to violate central provisions of the law of war on the same grounds. Military necessity cannot be a justification available to guerrillas, but no one else.

There is some merit in the claim that the laws of war have "a statist bias." This is not accidental: They were formulated to govern conflicts between states. If the guerrillas cannot hold any terrain and the government can hunt them down at will, then the guerrillas cannot fight the government *and* obey the dress code. But in that case they are not the armed forces of a state but an insurrectionary movement, and the laws of war do not apply to insurrections or revolutions. If, in other words, it really would be suicide, and not just disadvantageous, for guerrillas to wear uniforms, there is no war.[35]

But if we are dealing with a war, the guerrillas will have a relatively secure base (and hence can claim to be agents of a state). Whether it would then be suicidal for them to obey the dress code depends on the circumstances. The three guerrilla armies I just mentioned wore uniforms or identifying armbands, so obviously it is not always suicidal. Guerrillas want to evade large enemy units or at least pitched and prolonged battles where the enemy could eventually bring superior force to play. For that reason they frequently do not hold terrain—the enemy will eventually overwhelm them. But that is not because they are guerrillas, but because guerrillas frequently are weaker than their opposition.[36] Attempts by any troops, regular or irregular, to hold positions in the face of a superior foe are unwise. It does not follow that it is suicidal for guerrillas (or any weak force) to wear uniforms: Castro's uniformed guerrillas took Havana. Guerrillas avoid the battles they do not want, but when they do fight—usually at a time of their choice and against a relatively weak force—to identify themselves as combatants places them at no greater risk than soldiers always are under in combat: The other side, seeing that the guerrillas are out to kill them, will fire at them. Quite often the guerrilla's risks are less: If the battle is not going well they can dissolve into the hills or forests; regular troops are more often expected to hold their position.

In short, the claim that it would be suicidal for guerrillas to identify themselves as combatants is misleading. It is suicidal only in two cases. In the first they control no territory, and the laws of war do not apply. In the second the would-be attackers are so outnumbered or outgunned that they can successfully attack only by hiding their combatant status. But this is not a peculiarity of guerrilla warfare; it happens just as often with regular troops. Regular troops, competently led, do not attack if the enemy is so strong that attacking is suicidal unless the enemy can be deceived into thinking the attackers are clerics, housewives, and farmers. They dig in and defend, or they withdraw. In the same circumstances some people are willing to allow the guerrillas to hide their combatant status and go ahead with the attack and the deception. It does not occur to them that all combatants have the same problem, and that any unit might plead the same excuse: It would have been suicide for us to obey the laws of war. The answer is obvious: Build your strength, pick a weaker target, attack anyway, or go home and think it over.

To this we can add that if the rebel cause is sufficiently popular it will either not be necessary to fight the government's regular troops, or the fighting will be minimal. In the French Revolution of 1789 and the Russian Revolution of February 1917 the regular army largely refused to fire on the revolutionaries. As Bonar Law told the House of Commons in 1914: "If it is a question only of disorder, the army I am sure will obey you, and I am sure that it ought to obey you, but if it is really a question of civil war, soldiers are citizens like the rest of us."[37]

We cannot hold that military necessity makes it morally permissible for combatants to gain an equalizing tactical advantage by passing for civilians when they are fighting the armed forces of a state, but never makes it morally permissible for the armed forces of a state to do the same, or to violate some other similarly central component of *jus in bello,* when such armed forces are in an equally awkward position. The situation of insurgents is not more desperate than was that of the regular armed forces of Finland attacked by Russia, Holland by Germany, or Ethiopia by Italy. If the right is granted at all, it should be granted to all combatants who struggle in extremis. In that case noncombatants would have moral rights only when violating those rights could not snatch victory from the jaws of defeat. Most wars end in defeat for one side. The rights of noncombatants would mean very little if whenever that were imminent, those rights were forfeited.

The circumstances of troops who find themselves fighting enemy disguised as civilians were described by a division commander of the Royal Irish Constabulary during the Sein Fein insurrection of 1916–1921:

> Shut up in their barracks, watching nightly for attacks, murdered if they go out singly, ambushed if they go in parties, liable to be shot in the back any time by an innocent civilian, unable to get exercise or recreation except at the risk of their lives. . . . [The enemy] is conducting warlike operations against us and we are not permitted to do so against him. He also enjoys the usual advantages of guerrilla warfare

> without suffering any of the penalties attached to it. We have to act largely on the defensive, for we have no-one to take the offensive against. As far as we possibly can we take the offensive but our blows fall on empty air, as the enemy forces at once take up the role of innocent peasants whom we must not touch.[38]

Under these circumstances, troops can no longer tell who is neutral and who is the enemy, and it is their ability to do that that enables them to attack only the latter. An assumption of noncombatant immunity has been violated: "If civilians must be protected from soldiers, then it follows that soldiers must also be protected from civilians. We require, that is, a principle of 'combatant immunity.' Soldiers must be guaranteed against attack from the civilian quarter if they are to respect the immunity of civilians. Soldiers *and* civilians can be murdered."[39]

The violation of this principle, though, does not mean that soldiers can shoot at every civilian they see on the grounds that any civilian *might* be a combatant. It is not the innocent civilian's fault that the enemy violates the dress code, and that this practice is known to be followed by the enemy does not justify attacking everyone—everyone is not a guerrilla. Yet we cannot ask troops to pretend that they do not know the enemy dresses as civilians, and we cannot demand that this knowledge not influence their behavior. The practice puts their lives at risk.

The behavior of McDonough's platoon illustrates the solution that has been adopted by better troops. If the enemy obeys the dress code, as the Germans did in World War II, disciplined troops with Western moral values will not fire at apparent civilians. If the enemy does not obey the dress code, disciplined troops will not fire at every civilian, but they will sometimes fire at suspicious civilians. In the first incident McDonough recounted, this was not a factor: That night he did not see civilians and assume they were enemy soldiers—he heard noises and thought they were made by enemy soldiers. This can happen in any war, and the enemy troops that McDonough's platoon was routinely encountering were in fact regular and uniformed. His problem was that it is dark at night, not that the people he saw seemed to be civilians.

His second incident, though, does fit the bill. The boy and the old man, bending over a mound in an area the Vietcong were known to mine, *were* suspicious: They seemed to be placing a mine. McDonough had his platoon hold their fire only because of the boy—not because of the behavior of the two Vietnamese—and there is a strong suggestion in McDonough's account that if the boy had been twenty years older, the platoon would have opened fire.

There is no exact rule in these cases. Was the behavior of the old man and the boy sufficiently suspicious to justify firing at them? That is a question it is difficult to answer without knowing more about the incident, and perhaps even so it would not be answerable. The odds of killing innocent civilians must be balanced against the casualties the mines, if the civilians are not innocent, will produce if the civilians live to plant more another day, and it is fortunate that it was McDonough himself who stepped on the mine: Had it been one of his soldiers, he may have regretted his decision. And we cannot say that the Vietnamese were innocent until proven guilty. Combat does not operate under such domestic juridical principles (neither would domestic laws under the circumstances of war zones, mines, and the constant threat of ambush): The soldier firing on what he takes to be an enemy is not executing a judicial sentence—he is fighting a war. The decision he makes when confronted with suspicious civilians in a war in which the dress code is commonly violated is not in principle different from the decision he makes when he hears unexpected whispers in the night. The less frightened he is, the less prone he will be to open fire. Sometimes his fright will lead him to shoot the innocent; sometimes his courage will get his friends killed.

McDonough was justified in holding his platoon's fire, but he also would have been justified if he had allowed his platoon to fire. If the enemy persistently violates the dress code, soldiers are justified in attacking *suspicious* civilians, and there simply are no exact standards for how suspicious the civilians must be to justify attack. At one level of clandestine guerrilla activity, soldiers may not be justified in shooting at a man bending over a mound in his garden but may be justified if the man is bending over a mound on a trail or road. At a higher level, they might be justified in either case; at a lower level, in neither. In reality, where the soldiers draw the line will depend on a variety of extraneous factors: whether they have recently taken casualties from mines or been ambushed by people in civilian clothes; how much sleep they have had and how hungry, frightened, nervous, experienced, exhausted, or benevolent they are. Sometimes they will kill the innocent, and sometimes they will spare the guilty. The guerrillas have drawn the darkness of night over the whole population.

If the other side abides by the dress code, no one has to make these guesses. That is why there is a dress code. Its violation is such a serious offense precisely because it forces soldiers to make these decisions.

Appendix: Terrorism

In Algeria and Lebanon a new phenomenon became prominent: terrorism directed against civilians. Any violent and hostile act can have the effect of terrorizing those at the receiving end, but that is not what I mean by terrorism. Even when the military end relies, in part or whole, on that terror, that is not what I mean by terrorism: The World War II Stuka dive-bomber was deliberately fitted with a whistle that for psychological effect gave off a frightening shriek as the plane went into its dive, but that hardly means that dive-bombing in a Stuka was an act of terrorism.

The acts I think of as terrorist involve two features beyond the fact that they are intended to cause terror. First, they tend to have a clandestine nature, and unlike the clandestine activities of the spy, they are the sorts of acts forbidden by the war code as acts of treachery or assassination. The terrorist disguises his hostile intention, passing for a civilian, and then strikes. I dealt with the moral issue this raises in the previous section.

The second feature of contemporary terrorism is the intentional attack on the innocent in order to attain the terrorist's goals. According to George Habash, leader of the Popular Front for the Liberation of Palestine: "In the age of the revolution of peoples oppressed by the world imperialist system there can be no geographical or political boundaries or moral limits to the operations of the people's camp. In today's world no one is 'innocent,' and no one is a 'neutral.'"[40] In war the innocent are often killed. What distinguishes the terrorist is that he deliberately aims at the innocent in conditions that allow the greatest discrimination. The bomber or artillery crew can say that they do not deliberately attack supermarkets, though their bombs and shells may fall on them. The terrorist sets out to attack the supermarket, precisely because there are large numbers of shoppers there. He likes to point out that what he does is no worse. But of course it is. He gets a child in his sights and pulls the trigger.

This special characteristic of terrorism appears in many ways. William O'Brien commented on the difficulty of applying the principles of *jus in bello* to insurgency: The principle of military necessity permits only the use of force necessary for military success, but "purely military success may not be congruent with the political, economic, and social successes that are equally, if not more important in such conflicts."[41] Even such restraint as military necessity might impose is absent, if *military* goals and operations are not in question.

Michael Walzer pointed out that this second feature of contemporary terrorism distinguishes it from the anticzarist assassinations of prerevolutionary Russia or the assassination of Archduke Ferdinand. Late nineteenth- and early twentieth-century revolutionary terrorists aimed at high public officials of the regime in power. Whatever we think of this, it is qualitatively different from contemporary terrorism. Their late twentieth-century descendants aim at whoever happens to be in reach, as long as the nationality of the victim fits their "enemies' profile." Sometimes even that is unnecessary, as occurred in the bombing of a train outside Bologna a few years ago.

There is nothing I can see about this that requires serious moral discussion. The terrorist, if George Habash can be taken as a spokesman, disavows moral limits and claims that no one is innocent—everyone is rightly killed. This is not a moral position but the disavowal of morality in the name of some presumed higher value. What value that might be has not, so far, been articulated, but we can assume that it presupposes a group so abused that it has acquired the right to do anything to anyone who stands in its way. There is no such right, and we can take comfort from the fact that groups subjected to far worse abuse than Habash's constituency has been have not claimed one.

Suggestions for Further Reading

Walter Laqueur's *Guerrilla: A Historical and Critical Study* (Little, Brown, Boston, 1976; reprinted by Westview Press, 1984), provides a good introduction to its subject. Guy Hartcup's *Camouflage: A History of Concealment and Deception in War* (Scribner's, New York, 1980), gives a detailed account of the use of camouflage in the twentieth century. The moral issues raised by the concealment of combatant status are discussed by Michael Walzer, *Just and Unjust Wars* (Basic Books, New York, 1977), and Nicholas Fotion and G. Elfstrom, *Military Ethics* (Routledge & Kegan Paul, London, 1986). The view from the guerrilla's side is given in Gérard Chaliand, ed., *Guerrilla Strategies: An Historical Anthology from the Long March to Afghanistan* (University of California Press, Berkeley, 1982).

6

Nuclear War and Nuclear Deterrence

Deep under ground, materials dark and crude,
Of spiritous and fiery spume, till toucht
With Heav'n's ray, and temper'd they shoot forth
. . . op'ning to the ambient light.
These in thir dark Nativity the Deep
Shall yield us, pregnant with infernal flame,
Which into hollow Engines long and round
Thick ramm'd, at th' other bore with touch of fire
Dilated and infuriate shall send forth
From far with thund'ring noise among our foes
Such implements of mischief as shall dash
To pieces, and o'erwhelm whatever stands adverse
. . . .
In future days, if Malice should abound,
Some one intent on mischief, or inspir'd
with dev'lish machination might devise
Like instrument to plague the Sons of men
For sin, on war and mutual slaughter bent.

—John Milton, *Paradise Lost*

It is already known to us all that a war with atomic bombs would be immeasurably more destructive and horrible than any the world has yet known. That fact is indeed portentous, and to many it is overwhelming. But as a datum for the formulation of policy it is in itself of strictly limited utility. It underlies the urgency of our reaching correct decisions, but it does not help us to discover which decisions are in fact correct.[1]

The Historical Context

In December 1938 German physicists discovered nuclear fission. A few months later President Roosevelt received a letter written by Leo Szilard and signed by Albert Einstein. It said that nuclear fission might be used to build "extremely powerful bombs" and concluded: "I understand Germany has actually stopped the sale of uranium from the Czechoslovakian mines which she has taken over."[2]

On July 16, 1945, the first atomic bomb in history was tested at Alamogordo Air Force Base in New Mexico. Three weeks later the United States dropped the second one on Hiroshima. The next morning Bernard Brodie, a new member of the Yale Political Science Department, stopped with his wife at a drugstore and bought a newspaper. Brodie, an expert on military strategy, looked over the lead story and said to his wife, "Everything that I have written is obsolete."[3] The new weapon, the U.S. Strategic Bombing Survey's *Summary Report* (*Pacific War*) said in 1946, raised "the destructive power of a single bomber by a factor of between 50 and 250 times, depending upon the nature and size of the target."[4]

Brodie quickly came to a novel conclusion: "Thus far the chief purpose of our military establishment has been to win wars. From now on its chief purpose must be to avert them."[5] The destructive force of the new weapons was so great that nuclear powers could not achieve a victory. Numerical nuclear superiority was pointless because 2,000 nuclear weapons would bring any enemy to ruin. Surprise attacks were pointless because the enemy would retain a devastating counterstrike capacity. Deterrence, based on a "reciprocal ability to retaliate in kind if the bomb is used," would be the purpose of nuclear weapons: "No victory . . . would be worth the price."[6] The point of having them would be to keep others from using theirs.

In 1946, when the United States was the only nuclear power, this analysis was visionary. The nuclear monopoly meant that the United States could deter its enemies from attacks on its allies without its having to worry about nuclear retaliation. But it was only a matter of time before the Soviet Union would develop its own nuclear weapons—the requisite theoretical physics was in the public domain. Once that happened, "deterrence" would become ambiguous. It might mean the threat of nuclear attack to deter an enemy from launching a nuclear strike against the United States. In that case, the aim of the policy of deterrence was to prevent nuclear attacks. Or it might mean the threat of using nuclear weapons to deter an enemy from launching a conventional attack. In that case the threat was that the United States would launch a nuclear attack.

These two uses of deterrence were not always clearly distinguished. Brodie had in mind the first: deterring nuclear attack. But after the Japanese surrender the United States quickly demobilized, whereas the Soviet Union did not, and the resulting disparity in conventional forces led the United States to rely on nuclear deterrence as a counter to a Soviet conventional attack. From the Soviet point of view, U.S. disarmament may not have been persuasive, because it did not involve nuclear disarmament. The United States was building its nuclear arsenal, and at the end of the 1940s had almost 300 atomic bombs.[7] But even when the Soviets did acquire their own nuclear arsenal, they retained their large wartime army.[8]

The policy of nuclear deterrence, as it emerged in the postwar years, was aimed at enemy cities. Brodie had written that "the primary targets for the atomic bomb will be cities. One does not shoot rabbits with elephant guns."[9] But Brodie also realized that the intent was not to destroy those cities but to deter the other side. In a 1948 speech in Chicago he said that there was "more strategic leverage to be gained in holding cities hostage than in making corpses."[10]

Brodie's analysis ceased being visionary in the early 1950s when the United States and the USSR started building hydrogen bombs. The atomic bomb dropped on Nagasaki was a 20,000-ton weapon; the new hydrogen bombs could range up to 20,000,000 tons.[11] A RAND Corporation study indicated that fifty H-bombs could destroy as many Russian cities, killing thirty-five million Russians. Even if such an attack were planned to minimize civilian casualties, ten or eleven million would still die:

> Brodie had decided that the atomic bomb was "not so absolute a weapon that we can disregard the limits of its destructive power," and that, therefore, the "problem of target selection, for example, [was] still important." The hydrogen bomb, however, "makes strategic bombing very efficient, perhaps all too efficient. We no longer need to argue whether the conduct of war is an art or a science—it is neither. The art or science comes in only in finding out, if you're interested, what *not* to hit. . . ."
>
> Brodie concluded that there could no longer be anything rational about the strategic bombing of any target that lies inside the Soviet Union. That would only spark Soviet retaliation. . . . "National objectives cannot be consonant with national suicide."[12]

Yet after the Korean War the United States seemed wedded to a policy of massive retaliation. In a speech on January 12, 1954, President Dwight Eisenhower's secretary of state, John Foster Dulles, said that the United States would exhaust and bankrupt itself if it had to respond conventionally to the ground forces the Communists could commit in numerous trouble spots around the world. The nation would meet these threats, not by deploying U.S. soldiers to these hot spots, but by deterring aggression through the threat of massive retaliation. The United States would, Dulles said (with the semantic awkwardness of the Eisenhower era), place "more reliance on deterrent power and less dependence on local defensive power."[13] The United States would use its nuclear arsenal not only to deter nuclear attack against it but to inhibit Communist expansion as well. The threat of nuclear attack would prevent another Korean War, without the expense of maintaining a large standing army.

To many foreign policy analysts, this was madness. Bernard Brodie, Paul Nitze, William Kaufman, and George Kennan argued that the threat of massive retaliation as a response to a small, local war was irrational and therefore not credible. The policy required the nation, in conflicts not vital to it, nonetheless to put its life on the line—the policy backed the United States into a corner it was not in its interest to be in. If the other side called the U.S. dare, the nation would have to decide whether to back down, with a devastating loss of credibility and prestige, or go ahead with the threat, at the cost of national ruin. Instead, these critics urged, the United States should build up its conventional military forces and have a flexible nuclear policy that allowed various levels of response to crises.

These critics were supported in these claims by the army, which was left a secondary role under the policy of massive retaliation, by important elements in the Democratic party, and by a 1956 RAND Corporation game about North Atlantic Treaty Organization (NATO) defense policy. The game asked which forms of deterrence were rational responses, likely to be credible, and hence effective.[14] It concluded that if the United States wanted to deter the Soviet Union from attacking Western Europe, the U.S. NATO allies should have their own nuclear arsenals. Under massive retaliation, the deterrent was that if the Soviets invaded Western Europe, the United States would strike the Soviets' homeland. Of course they would retaliate by striking the U.S. homeland. So to deter aggression, the United States was offering to sacrifice itself. But if push came to shove, could the NATO allies count on a U.S. sacrifice? Would it really sacrifice "New York for Paris, Chicago for Bonn"?[15] Or would it back down at the last moment?

If the French and Germans had their own nuclear weapons, the threat would be credible. The United States might not be willing to sacrifice New York for Paris, but the French would defend Paris by threatening Moscow. U.S. allies meanwhile were reaching the same conclusion. Great Britain was developing its own strategic nuclear force, while Charles de Gaulle announced in 1960 that France was building its own *force de frappe*.

Short of this, there was an alternative. Massive retaliation had targeted Soviet cities. But if the United States was unwilling to trade U.S. cities for Soviet cities, it could still defend Europe by using nuclear weapons against Soviet military targets (counterforce), rather than against Soviet cities (countercity). And just as it would not be in the U.S. interest to attack Soviet cities, thereby placing its own in danger, it would not be in the Soviet interest to retaliate by striking at U.S. cities, putting theirs in harm's way. The RAND study

> talked about targeting the enemy's military forces, whereas virtually all previous RAND efforts in this field concentrated on economic targets; second, through Brodie's insight, it attached the whole question of targeting to the broader questions of war objectives and strategy—connecting the intensity with which the war is waged to the task of bringing the war to a successful conclusion with minimal damage done, in the process, to American cities.[16]

(The suggestion of targeting the enemy's military forces had been made in 1946 by William Borden, who had asked why the United States should attack cities when it would be the enemy's air force that would be the threat.[17])

In 1960 John F. Kennedy became the president, and under Secretary of Defense Robert McNamara the U.S. posture switched to flexible response and counterforce targeting. On May 5, 1962, at a meeting of NATO ministers in Athens, McNamara said: "Our principal military objectives, in the event of a nuclear war stemming from a major attack on the Alliance, should be the destruction of the enemy's military forces. . . . Our studies indicate that a strategy which targets nuclear forces only against cities or a mixture of civil and military targets has serious limitations for the purpose of deterrence and for the conduct of general nuclear war."[18] Thus, the United States renounced massive retaliation.

There were, however, a few problems. First, counterforce strategy required "a measure of connivance with the Soviet Union. . . . The adversary . . . needed to understand how, by co-operating with the United States, the arms race could be stabilized and wars prevented from getting completely out of hand."[19] But the Soviets were uncooperative. They denounced counterforce: Nuclear war, they insisted, could not be fought by Marquis of Queensberry Rules. Because their large and inaccurate rockets lacked the technological ability to be used in a counterforce role, they may have felt that the U.S. doctrine was one they could not join, and that therefore it was best for them to insist on standing by the countercity strategy their forces were designed for.

Second, with countercity targeting there was a limit to the number of nuclear weapons needed: Once the enemy's large and medium cities had been struck, there would be diminishing returns in striking lesser targets. Counterforce, in contrast, led naturally to a proliferation of nuclear weapons. For although the Soviet Union had a few score or hundred cities worth targeting, it had thousands of military targets. And whereas a counterforce strategy assumes enough nuclear weapons are kept in reserve to deter a countercity strike, counterforce strikes would attack those weapons. So the strategy requires building still more weapons so that even after a nuclear exchange, there is still a missile park adequate to deter a countercity strike: Counterforce targeting requires a "second-strike" capability. This means building more missiles and hardening missile silos to protect the missiles from attack. This in turn increases the number of military targets, calling for still more nuclear weapons. Counterforce, in other words, seemed to involve an endless nuclear build-up and a bottomless money pit.

Finally, there was a fear that the Soviets might think that the U.S. counterforce strategy involved an attempt to build a first-strike capability: an ability, if the United States struck first, to inflict so much damage on the Soviet strategic forces that the damage from their counterstrike would be acceptable.

The air force had, in fact, embraced counterforce, hoping to build a first-strike capability that would be credible to the Soviets. This would mean a capability to win a nuclear war if the United States struck first. Both Kennedy and McNamara rejected this notion. According to Alain Enthoven, one of McNamara's advisers, "the no-cities doctrine . . . was being erroneously interpreted as a theory whereby thermonuclear war could be made tolerable, and therefore fought and won."[20]

In 1963 McNamara told President Kennedy, as he had the previous year, that what the air force was really seeking in its budget requests was a first-strike capability.[21] He then told the air force that it was no longer to base its strategic plans on counterforce.[22] The new U.S. policy was "assured destruction."

Assured destruction limited the U.S. nuclear arsenal to a force that after a Soviet attack would still be able to retaliate with a 400-megaton strike. A computer study by Enthoven had indicated that a 400-megaton strike aimed at Soviet cities would destroy the Soviet military and governmental command structure, half its industrial capacity, and kill 30 percent of its population. Doubling the figure to 800 megatons would increase the damage only by a few percent—at 400 megatons the curve flattened out. With a countercity strategy, then, there was little incentive to build missiles armed beyond that level.

It is odd that McNamara said that these figures calculated "the destructive capacity of our force on the hypothetical assumption that all of it is targeted on cities, *even though we would not use our forces in that manner if deterrence failed.*"[23] Assured destruction was the declared policy, but McNamara controlled the targeting of U.S. nuclear forces, and 82 percent of that targeting remained counterforce. Assured destruction was a policy aimed at the Pentagon, not the Soviet Union. It was McNamara's way of blocking endless requests for more money.

Counterforce itself was now coming under attack. RAND's James Schlesinger wondered how confident the United States could be that the Soviets would recognize a limited counterforce strike for what it was. As both sides hardened their missile silos, counterforce strikes become more unlikely to knock out the enemy missiles. And as nuclear arsenals grew and launching systems proliferated, more and more missiles would be required for a counterforce attack. At what point would the counterforce attack be indistinguishable from a general attack?

By 1970, however, counterforce was saved by the MIRV—multiple, independently targetable reentry vehicle. The MIRV meant that instead of carrying a single massive warhead, a ballistic missile could now carry several smaller warheads, each of which could be targeted at a different objective. This, in combination with the dramatic increases in missile accuracy that had been attained, meant that hardened silos could be attacked, and more military targets could be hit with less damage to surrounding civilian areas. "We do not, in our strategic planning, target civilian population *per se,*" Secretary of Defense Elliot Richardson told the House Armed Services Committee in 1973.[24] (Just before the outbreak of World War II, the British and French staffs had said the same: "We have no intention of attacking the civil population as such."[25]

This debate was conducted within government circles. But in 1974 James Schlesinger, the new secretary of defense, told the world that he was changing targeting strategy to allow for alternatives to "a suicidal strike against the cities of the other side." The rejection of assured destruction, which had taken place ten years earlier, was now public knowledge. The United States had adopted a policy of flexible response built up out of limited counterforce strikes. Two years later the chairman of the Joint Chiefs reaffirmed Richardson's testimony: "We do not target population *per se* any longer. We used to."[26] Yet because many military targets are located in heavily populated areas, a major counterforce exchange might result in civilian casualties far in excess of those that were produced by the countercity attacks of World War II. A 1988 study estimates that such an exchange would produce twelve to twenty-seven million U.S. deaths and fifteen to thirty-two million Soviet deaths.[27]

In World War II a 200-plane raid on an aircraft plant or an oil refinery was a better use of resources than a 400-plane raid against the city where the plant or refinery was located. Economy and concentration of force spoke for precision bombing; area bombing was adopted only when precision bombing failed.

The atomic bomb changed those calculations. Its development meant that the precision attack became more costly: Fifty B-29s with conventional bombs would do less damage than one B-29 with a nuclear bomb. But the B-29 with the nuclear bomb was incapable of a precision attack in the traditional sense: It might put its bomb right on target, but the attack would still devastate a large area. The old prudent calculations no longer were valid. It had become easier to destroy a city than to destroy a barracks or factory within it. Until then the interests of morality and military effectiveness had roughly coincided. The atomic bomb ended that.

A second development had even more momentous implications. The development of the intercontinental ballistic missile (ICBM), and subsequently of the multiple warhead, meant that the destructive force of the strategic nuclear arsenal could be used in a single massive attack.

World War II had seen strategic bombing *campaigns* that lasted months or years. These campaigns were elements in a wider war that took place over years. In the course of those months and years, enemy governments contacted one another and discussed terms for ending the war. They considered prospects for negotiating favorable or at least acceptable terms. Would those chances improve if they continued the war? Would the other side grow weary? Was the loss of life and wealth worth the struggle?

The point is not that the bombing campaigns were important elements in these calculations—though of course they were—but rather that there could be and were such calculations. The strategic bombing of World War II had a place in a wider system of rational deliberation of national interest. Clausewitz's dictum still held: War was a continuation of foreign policy by other means.

The development of the atom bomb did not change that. But the development of the ICBM meant that in World War III the entire strategic destructive capacity of a nation could be expended in a few brief attacks. Negotiations would have to take place before a war. Once an *all-out* war began, there would be nothing left to negotiate and no time in which to negotiate. The maximal destructive force would have already been unleashed. At a minimum, the protagonists would be in ruins, and their ability to inflict further harm on each other would be, in comparison with the destruction that had already been suffered, minimal. The traditional motive for surrendering—to avoid further suffering and destruction—would have lost a good deal of its force. What greater harm could the enemy inflict?

Jan Lodal, an adviser to Henry Kissinger in 1970, had concluded that

> there was no conceivable circumstance under which using nuclear weapons would create an advantage. . . . The more engrossed he became in nuclear strategy, the more he agreed with Brodie's fundamental conclusion: that there would be no winners. But Lodal also felt that a nation had to behave as if it really would use nuclear weapons, or else the credibility of its power to deter aggression against allies might erode in a crisis. And so the analysts had to keep going back to the problem over and over again, even if the problem could never be solved. Besides, Lodal knew that nobody wanted to be the man to step forward in the middle of a ghastly conflict with the Russians and say to the President of the United States, "I'm sorry, sir, but there are no good options in a nuclear war, and there is nothing you can do about it."[28]

We frequently hear that in a nuclear war between the United States and the USSR neither side would emerge victorious. Anyone who has any doubts about that should ponder whether a Soviet nuclear exchange with France, or a U.S. exchange with Great Britain, would benefit either superpower. The smaller nation would be destroyed, but the superpower would be devastated. In the case of missile-armed nuclear powers, the gain that might result from a nuclear exchange even with a weaker enemy is offset by the damage the enemy can inflict. Though a smaller nation can inflict less damage than a larger nation, the damage it can inflict remains disproportionate to the benefit of conquering it. In conventional wars a great prize can sometimes be obtained at small cost. In nuclear war modest prizes can be obtained only at exorbitant costs.

War is an attempt to attain goals that are in the national interest. The destructiveness of nuclear weapons means, however, that an all-out war could not serve the national interest. So an extraordinary change took place in military thinking. Strategic nuclear forces, it was said, will have failed their purpose if they are ever used. Their sole purpose is deterrence—they exist only as a threat. If the threat ever has to be made good, deterrence will have failed and the nation will be in ruins. The paradoxical nature of this policy is the source of most of the philosophical literature on the subject and a good deal of the military perplexity. For thousands of years we have told soldiers to win wars. Now we tell them that this is a war they can only lose, and our security depends on convincing the other side that if we are pressed, we will act in a way we know is self-destructive anyway.

The Legal Context

Legality and Technology: Raising the Issue

Our legal account of strategic air warfare (Chapter 4) derived from the Hague rules for naval bombardment, which allow general bombardments only against defended towns. That account can be extended to cover the ballistic missile developed by Germany in World War II—the V-2. The defenses against air attack had already forced a shift from precision bombing to area attacks. Because precision attacks on strategic targets were prohibitive and area attacks by plane were already common, what legal objection could there be against area attacks by rocket? If area attacks by plane could be justified, so could area attacks by rocket.

But whether by plane or rocket, area attacks are not justifiable as a matter of *choice*. Even though antiaircraft defenses justified the bomber's resort to area attacks, if the rocket's accuracy had made it capable of precision attacks, it would not have been justifiable to use it in area attacks. The bomber's resort to area attacks was justified by antiaircraft fire and enemy fighters, and these were ineffective against the V-2.

Our principle cannot be that if we are justified in resorting to area attacks with one weapons system because of the defenses against it, then we are justified in using any weapons system in an area attack. That would be akin to conducting area attacks by plane against targets that lack antiaircraft defenses but that are protected by submarine mines. Naval forces may invoke the mines to justify a general bombardment; air forces cannot.

In strict law this may not be so. In strict law the right of general bombardment obtains when the locale is defended, and a place that has an antiaircraft battery or an infantry company posted there may count as defended: The naval rules do not require that the place be defended against *naval attack*—merely that it be defended. This could be justified on the grounds that enemy troops and weapons are always legitimate targets, and that towns containing them can be subjected to a general bombardment.

Strict law, though, is not our concern. We are concerned with the rational point behind the law. Even if the placement of mines in a channel leading into a harbor means, in strict law, that the port city is defended and hence legally justifies an aerial bombardment of the city, the mines would be no more than a legal pretext for the bombing. The city is not defended against air attack, and the air attack is not directed at the mines. The *only* role the mines would play in the operation would be in providing a legal excuse for a general bombardment.

In World War II Germany did not have the choice of using the V-2 in precision attacks—the V-2 was too inaccurate. "Aimed at a target the size of London . . . [it] might come down anywhere in southeastern England."[29] Only the manned bomber was capable of precision attacks, and the enemy's defenses precluded precision bomber attacks.

In the 1970s and 1980s, however, missile accuracy has increased dramatically. The most accurate ballistic missiles in the early 1980s were claimed to have had a 50 percent chance of hitting within 90 to 180 yards of the target point, as opposed to the Titan missile's figure of roughly 1,350 yards.[30] And as the missile's accuracy has gone up, the size of the nuclear weapon it carries has gone down: the Titan II carries a 5,000-kiloton warhead; an MX warhead, with a claimed 82-yard circular error of probability (CEP), is 335 kilotons.[31] Nuclear weapons are becoming smaller and more accurate.

So the legal defense we used for World War II area attacks is increasingly less applicable to the legality of attacks by missiles. When only the manned bomber was capable of precision attacks and the enemy could defend against the manned bomber, the missile's area attack could be legally justified. But now that the accuracy of ballistic missiles allows them to be used in precision attacks, this legal argument no longer applies. There is at the moment no effective defense against attacks by ballistic missiles, and thus there is no legal justification for using them for a general bombardment if their accuracy permits more precise targeting. Area attacks are not justifiable, I said, as a matter of choice. Therefore, the primary consideration in my legal and moral justification of area bombing in World War II is inapplicable to nuclear war—not because of the nature of nuclear weapons, but because of the nature of the delivery systems. If strategic nuclear war can be given a legal foundation, we will have to look for new grounds.[32]

Legal and moral issues are now intertwined with technological issues in an historically unprecedented way. Accuracy in the missile and miniaturization in the weapon are expensive: It is cheaper to destroy a city than to attack a few targets within the city selectively. One must now pay a higher price if one wants to do less damage.

We sometimes hear that the development of nuclear weapons has made restrictions on general bombardment outdated. Technological developments can affect legal notions—that much is true. But what sorts of effects do they have? The most frequently cited instance of the law of war's changing under the influence of technological developments is the legal response to the rise of the submarine. When the twentieth century began, maritime law and custom decreed that naval forces, before sinking merchantmen or passenger vessels, had an obligation to provide for the safety of their crew and passengers. This obligation was frequently fulfilled by the naval force's taking them aboard. Submarines, their quarters always cramped, could not do this, but they could at least warn ships of their impending doom, allowing them time to launch their lifeboats. Even this, though, proved so dangerous to submarines, which are vulnerable to ramming once they surface, that it was almost never done. In World War I, submarines attacked without warning. Even if they could not warn their prey, they could at least (and in World War I frequently did) surface after torpedoing isolated ships, and make certain the lifeboats had adequate provisions. And they could radio for other vessels to rescue the people in the lifeboats.

In World War II, however, even this practice declined, and in one notable case, it was deliberately eschewed. When a German submarine torpedoed the liner *Laconia,* carrying Italian prisoners of war, Admiral Karl Doenitz ordered submarines to assist the survivors. But the submarines attempting the rescue were attacked by enemy planes, and Doenitz subsequently issued a new order: "All attempts to rescue the crews of sunken ships should cease, including picking up men from the sea, righting capsized lifeboats, and supplying food and water."[33]

At the Nuremberg trials, there was an attempt to prosecute Doenitz. But the charges were dropped when Allied admirals, including Nimitz, stated that their own submarines attacked without warning and rarely assisted survivors. The technology of the submarine and the conditions under which submarines are at great risk had made the old rules, civilized as they were, impractical, and the former customs had fallen into disuse.

This shows that humanitarian legal requirements can be diminished by the rise of a weapons system that makes their observance impractical or dangerous in ways the original requirement had not foreseen. It does nothing, however, to support the point in contention. The submarine received, we might say, an exemption precisely because it could follow the humanitarian practice only by placing itself at grave risk. Had the submariner a choice of two modes of attacking the enemy vessel, neither of which would place him in greater danger, but one of which would spare civilian lives, we would not think it permissible for him to choose the more wanton attack, and the law would not be so prone to change. That a new weapon makes a wanton form of attack possible is no reason for the law to accommodate that attack.

Legality and Technology: Bad Weather Bombing

A more pointed case involves the use of strategic air power in World War II and an issue I avoided in Chapter 4. The effectiveness of antiair defenses was only one factor inclining strategic air forces toward area attacks. A second factor was more purely technological: weather and visibility.

Precision attacks were possible in World War II only in clear weather. Even the radar with which bombers were eventually equipped was not accurate enough for pinpoint bombing. Attacks in cloudy weather were no more accurate than night attacks, and in northern Europe the skies are often overcast. So even if Germany had had no defenses against air attack, technological limitations would have required a decision. Should the United States attack only in clear weather, when precision attacks were possible, or should it attack in overcast weather, though that would mean area attacks? Given the probability of bad weather, to attack only in good weather would have meant flying only about 65 percent of the sorties the air force could otherwise launch—equivalent to not using every third plane. The United States attacked in bad weather.

The U.S. Eighth Air Force was willing to accept heavy losses in daylight attacks in order to achieve higher accuracy in bombing. But the strength of the defenses justified night attacks, so Eighth Air Force's daylight attacks were not legally obligatory. It chose, in the belief that the military benefits outweighed the disadvantages, to conduct operations in a manner that would increase its own casualties. It had a legal right to general bombardment that justified night attacks, but it chose not to exercise that right.

Its bad weather attacks were not meant to reduce its own bomber losses. They were force multipliers: 65 planes flying in all weather were equivalent to 100 planes flying only in clear skies. But as it already had the right to conduct area attacks, that was irrelevant. Its willingness to persist in daylight precision attacks despite high losses did not cost it its right to conduct area attacks. The right it did not exercise when it thought it not advantageous was not forfeited.

Suppose, however, that there had been no effective defense against air attack in the 1940s, and that daylight precision bombing was subject only to normal operational losses. Would bad weather attacks, strictly as force multipliers, have been justified? This question brings us very close to the moral issues surrounding nuclear targeting.

My justification of area bombing invoked costs the defender exacted on precision bombing, forcing the attacker either to face unacceptable losses or to abandon attacks on valid military targets like submarine pens, armament factories, dry docks, and aircraft plants. Now I am asking whether area bombing can be justified on the grounds of cost per se—not a cost exacted by the defender.

If World War II cases do not raise this question very clearly, that is because the capacity of the weapons of the time meant that in general, were it not for the defense, precision attack would be the most economical form of air attack. But as the switch from Hansell's bombing program to LeMay's showed, the question could arise.[34] The dissatisfaction with Hansell's program stemmed from a perceived lack of results due to the inaccuracies of precision bombing from high altitudes over Japan. Given the fact that bomber safety required daylight raids to be at high altitude, LeMay's solution, we saw, was night incendiary attacks. This still could be justified by our legal account, for it was the defense that forced daylight bombers to attack at high altitude. But the final air attacks against Japan—the two atomic attacks—were essentially *daylight, low altitude,* incendiary attacks. The incendiary attack had become the method of choice. And incendiary attacks are, by their very nature, area attacks: self-spreading area attacks, whose area of destruction is controlled by the wind as much as by the bombardier's skills or the target committee's priorities.

To assess the legality of such attacks let us again turn to the naval rules. They allow bombardment of military targets in undefended localities. Such a bombardment must be directed against proper military targets, but the naval force need not guarantee that every round will fall in the target area. (Collateral damage does not make the bombardment illegal.) The bombarding force must direct its attack specifically against the military target, but the commander "incurs no responsibility for any unavoidable damage which may be caused by a bombardment under such circumstances."[35] "Unavoidable" is a slippery word, meaning that the commander should exercise due care. When a child pours herself a glass of orange juice, she may get a few drops on the counter, but that is not the same as pouring the juice onto the counter. Some spillage is inevitable, but we teach her to aim for the glass. The naval rules allow for spillage, but they do not allow the general bombardment of an undefended town. They require that the naval force aim its fire at military targets. Some rounds will inevitably fall off target, but when the naval force fires, its accuracy is limited only by technological restrictions: It is not allowed to fire with less accuracy than it can effect in order to produce collateral damage.

We can now construct our analogy with bad weather bombing. Suppose that undefended enemy coastal towns containing valid targets are covered by fog a third of the year, and the fog rules out the accuracy needed to bombard those targets directly. Would the naval law allow fleets to conduct general bombardments in fog? One might argue that it would, on the grounds that it holds the bombarding force only to the accuracy technologically feasible, which depends in part on the weather. But this is not quite what the law says. It does allow for spillage, and that spillage is due to technological reasons. But the spillage it permits occurs in the course of attacks on military targets. One has to be trying to pour the juice in the glass for the spills to be excused. If one just aims in the general direction of the table, the inaccuracy the law takes account of is not in question. The law does not allow the spillage to constitute the attack.

We might reasonably want to amend this. Suppose an important military target were almost always shrouded in fog and thus could be attacked only by a general bombardment. Perhaps it was built in that valley because of the fog. We might think that in this case a general bombardment is justified even though the target is undefended. But this is a special case. Necessity is not the same as convenience or advantage.

Another difficult question arises about the accuracy of the weapons system itself and the responsibility of nations for that accuracy. The smaller and more accurate ballistic missile is more expensive to build than the larger, less accurate one. A nation with moderate resources might build the less accurate missiles and then claim that as it is bound only to the accuracy technologically feasible, and as its missiles are by nature area weapons, it is legally justified in conducting area attacks against undefended targets. The obvious reply is that this is no excuse because the situation it is in is its own doing—rather like the man who claims no responsibility for what he did because he was drunk, though he got himself into that condition.[36]

The Moral Context

"Nuclear war" is not a well-defined phrase. It might be taken to cover a war in which small, accurate nuclear weapons were used for strictly military purposes: nuclear armed torpedoes fire at enemy warships on the high seas or nuclear artillery shells fired at tank parks secluded in a desert. Such temperate uses of nuclear weapons need not violate proportionality or discrimination.

Against this it is frequently said that any attempt to use nuclear weapons temperately would be likely to lead to their intemperate use. Even if that were so, it would still remain true that a limited use of nuclear weapons need not by itself raise any moral questions. And in any case that claim is misleading.

It is certainly trivially true that a limited use of nuclear weapons is more likely to lead to an unlimited use than will no use, because no use is no use: If nuclear weapons are not used at all, they cannot be used intemperately. But one can argue as well that forbidding the temperate use of nuclear weapons will increase the chances, should conventional weapons fail, that nuclear weapons will be used intemperately: If limited use is forbidden, the only possible use is massive use. We are left with the rather uninformative and obvious truth that forbidding the limited use of nuclear weapons ensures that either there will be no use or there will be a massive use. Nothing about probable consequences in the real world follows from this tautology.

At any rate, there are environments in which the risk would be minimized: A torpedo armed with a miniature nuclear warhead (.01 kiloton) would have an explosive yield equivalent to half the bombload of a single conventionally armed A-6 Intruder carrier attack plane.[37] It is hard to see why the use of such a small nuclear device against an enemy warship on the high seas would be likely to provoke a massive response. At a certain point a small nuclear weapon is just a small (nuclear) weapon. These uses of nuclear weapons need not violate either proportionality or discrimination. But some uses would.

We have seen that massive retaliation and a countercity strategy are no longer the U.S. policy. It might therefore seem odd that philosophers who write on nuclear deterrence concentrate on them. It certainly seems odd to defense theorists. But massive retaliation and countercity strikes, even if U.S. and Soviet defense analysts agree that it is in no one's interest to create the situation in which they might be invoked, are still the final deterrent threat: Attack our cities and we will attack yours. This has led some philosophers to treat it as though, as the final threat, it is the *real* threat.[38] That is a mistake. But however much a strategy aimed at cities has receded into the background, and however much everyone is agreed that the point of nuclear strategy is to avoid massive retaliation, it remains as the background theme against which limited nuclear strategies are played. Its ominous tones called them forth, and they raise the most serious moral questions.

Ethicists have asked three questions about nuclear deterrence, understood as a policy threatening massive attack against enemy cities. Would it be immoral: (1) to *launch* such a strike, (2) to *intend to launch* such a strike, (3) and to *threaten to launch* such a strike?

Launching the Strike

Those who argue that it would be immoral to wage nuclear war usually are thinking of a nuclear war in which civilians suffer heavily or of a nuclear war directed against civilians. Thus Richard Wasserstrom has argued that nuclear war is immoral on the grounds that it would involve the "intentional or knowing" killing of innocents.[39] (Obviously, he did not have in mind a nuclear-armed torpedo fired at a warship.)

But if the argument of Chapters 2 and 4 was correct, to take actions knowing that they will cause the deaths of innocents is not in itself immoral. An act of war causing civilian casualties is immoral: (1) if the civilian casualties are the direct purpose of the attack (I take it that this is what Wasserstrom meant by "intentional" killing of civilians); or (2) if those casualties, while not the object of the attack, are disproportionate to the military gain. On these grounds, a nuclear attack directed against a city is not necessarily wrong.[40] The example in Chapter 4 supposed that during World War II Germany was building nuclear bombs in Oslo, and that destroying the city was the only way of destroying the facility. The Norwegian casualties would not be a goal in the attack, so the attack would pass (1), and if proportionality allowed the attack, it would pass (2).

We derived these moral principles by modifying the law of war, supplementing it in two ways. First, even if a place is defended (and therefore *legally* subject to area attack), a general bombardment is *morally* permissible only if it can be justified by proportionality. Even against a defended town, an attacker is not morally justified in inflicting massive civilian casualties to destroy an installation that is of minor military significance.

Second, the care a unit should take to minimize incidental destruction and casualties is maximal if the bombardment force is in no danger and decreases to the extent to which it is in harm's way. The law of war draws a simple distinction between defended and undefended places. For moral purposes we replace this distinction with a graduated scale. We must take into account, not just *whether* a place is defended, but *how effective* the defenses are. We cannot morally justify a general attack on a major city on the grounds that it is defended by a single rifleman.[41]

Area attacks are morally unjustified against ineffectively defended major targets and effectively defended minor targets. This leads us to the following principles for strategic warfare:

1. Precision attacks are legitimate to destroy a valid military target even if civilian casualties are likely (subject to proportionality).[42]
2. Area attacks are morally wrong if precision attacks can destroy the valid military target while producing fewer civilian casualties.
3. Area attacks, when they are the only way to destroy valid targets, are morally permissible even against undefended targets (subject to proportionality).

And as a special case of this principle:

4. In spite of the civilian casualties they cause (but still subject to proportionality), area attacks are morally permissible to destroy valid military targets if the effectiveness of the defense makes precision attacks against those targets inordinately expensive.

In all these cases the principle of proportionality holds. But the principle of proportionality cannot be used to justify *targeting* the civilian population; it can only be used to justify collateral civilian casualties.

These principles are the furthest I am inclined to go in justifying strategic warfare. But there is one more extension that might be reasonable, and I want to revise my model to accommodate it. My strategy is to lay out the most permissive account of strategic warfare that might plausibly be offered and then see whether a massive countercity strike would be allowed by it.

To restrict World War II attacks to clear weather would have been to mount a third fewer attacks over a given time span—attacks in bad weather were the only way to destroy that third within a given period of time. Precision attacks were, plane for plane and bomb for bomb, more effective, but any attack is more effective than none. So assuming that fuel and munitions were plentiful and did not have to be utilized in the most efficient way, one harms the enemy more over a given period of time by adding the three area attacks to the six or seven precision attacks.

Let us suppose that, in that case, bad weather attacks against undefended or lightly defended targets are morally justified. Such attacks fail my second principle—precision attacks on clear days could destroy the targets with fewer civilian casualties—and do not come under my third principle: Area attacks are not the only way to destroy the targets. But to create the most permissive model that still rejects targeting the civilian population, I shall modify my criteria. This gives us:

1′. Precision attacks are legitimate to destroy a valid military target even if civilian casualties are likely (subject to proportionality).
2′. Area attacks are morally wrong if precision attacks can destroy the valid military target while producing fewer civilian casualties, unless the area attacks possess a distinct military advantage over precision attacks (subject to proportionality).

The fourth principle now becomes unnecessary, being merely an instance of 2′.

I have argued that we cannot justify shortening a war through intentional attacks on civilians or through massacres.[43] But in the circumstances I am envisioning, area attacks are not intended as attacks on civilians: The desired effect (the destruction of valid targets) could be as readily achieved if all civilians were evacuated from the town under attack.

This condones attacks that increase civilian casualties if the attacks produce a military gain that is not disproportionately small in comparison with those increased casualties. This brings the justification of strategic attacks in line with the justification in Chapter 2 of general bombardments in support of ground combat: Civilians do not draw fire, and they deflect it only because of proportionality.

It gives us the least restrictive principles for bombardment consistent with forbidding attacks directed against civilians. Does it allow countercity nuclear war? We have gone as far as we can go without contenancing the deliberate assault on civilians that is the hallmark of terrorist attacks. If those terrorist attacks are morally wrong, as I have argued, then if countercity targeting can be morally justified, that will be by principle 2′. This allows area attacks if they possess a distinct military advantage over precision attacks (subject to proportionality). It cannot, however, be used to justify countercity strikes. There is *no* proper military advantage to destroying a city if one can already destroy the valid military targets within the city. There is a military advantage to destroying the city, but it is just the advantage any destruction that befalls the enemy would bring—killing their firstborn children or afflicting them with a plague.

Second, even if that were not the case, a countercity strategy fails the test of proportionality embedded in principle 2′. Consider the following (admittedly simplistic) way of calculating proportionality: Suppose countercity targeting amounted to a ×2 force multiplier. Strategic nuclear weapons account for about 10 percent of the 1988 U.S. military budget of $333 billion, so maintaining strategic capabilities at no cost by adopting a countercity strategy would produce a 5 percent reduction in the defense budget—a savings of $16 billion. That $16 billion is within the boundaries of normal debate over the defense budget. It is an amount equal to approximately 0.5 percent of current Social Security payments. I said in Chapter 2 that the acid test of whether civilian casualties are justified is whether the United States would be willing to accept them among its own population for the military gain. If, in other words, a certain military gain is justifiable even at the cost of 20,000 civilian casualties, then it is justifiable regardless of whether those casualties are U.S. or the enemy's. But it is inconceivable that the U.S. government would accept the loss of 30 million U.S. lives to reduce Social Security payments by 0.5 percent. Proportionality as a test can be difficult to apply, but for comparative purposes we can note that the force multiplier of bad weather bombing in World War II may have cost Germany 0.06 percent of its 80 million population in casualties;[44] the figure we are considering would have yielded 40 percent.

If countercity targeting offered a ×10 force multiplier, the conclusion would be the same. The United States would not trade $30 billion for thirty million lives. At some point a trade of lives for dollars may become defensible, but, at $1,000 a head, developed nations are nowhere near that point.

The sort of calculation involved here is simplistic because it ignores the broader context. The government would not trade millions of lives to save a few billion dollars under normal circumstances, but in exceptional circumstances it might. It might, for example, if those few billions were the total U.S. resources available at the moment, and if failure to make the trade meant capitulation to a thoroughly evil power. There are circumstances in which we can justify trades that from a humanitarian accountant's point of view are bad bargains: Military operations in general are rarely cost effective in any strict sense. But this is not one of those circumstances.

This failure of countercity strategy to pass the test of proportionality is not an accident. It is by design. The idea of massive deterrence is, after all, to make the punishment so terrible that the offense that calls it forth will be omitted. "The essential thing," John Foster Dulles said, "is that a potential aggressor should know in advance that he can and will be made to suffer for his aggression more than he can possibly gain by it."[45] This establishes a situation in which the principle of proportionality works against war as an instrument of national policy: The cost in destruction to the belligerents would be so great that it could not be in their national interest to go to war.

Mutual assured destruction (MAD—assured destruction with the knowledge that the other side will reply in kind) can deter because it is *meant* to cause the failure of proportionality. It deters by ensuring that military gains will be outweighed by civilian losses.

Intending to Launch

The launching of a massive countercity strike seems in itself to be morally inadmissible. But one can argue that even though it is in itself inadmissible, it is not inadmissible as a part of a strategy of deterrence. Consider the following argument. There is an evil event that will occur with a 90 percent probability. But if one intends to do something twice as evil in response to that event, one deters it, and the probability of the first evil event's occurring reduces to 1 percent. There is then only a minuscule chance that one will have to carry out the threat and an excellent chance that by intending the greater evil one averts the original evil and therefore both evils. Under these circumstances it might be rational and morally justifiable to intend the second evil.

It is possible, in other words, that even if it would be wrong to launch the strike apart from a strategy of deterrence, it might not be wrong to form a conditional intention to launch it—to intend to launch it if certain eventualities occur: "It can sometimes be legitimate to intend to do X if A, when it would not be legitimate to intend to do X *simpliciter:* it is all right to intend to imprison someone if *duly convicted* when it would not be all right to intend to imprison him come what may."[46] This is the view defended by Gregory Kavka, who argued that even if the massive strike, considered in isolation, is not justifiable, as a component of a policy of deterrence it might be justifiable.[47] For the intention to retaliate with such a strike might deter an aggressor, thereby preventing a great evil, and it might do this while involving "only a small risk of performing an inherently evil act." A repudiation of deterrence would, on this view, ensure that the repudiator would never commit one particular great evil, although making it much more likely that other great evils would be committed. Weighing the probability of deterrence's preventing those evils against the probability of having to carry out the retaliation threat, the scale might tip in favor of deterrence. The policy of deterrence could be justified, for example, as a means of preventing the evils of war, including nuclear war: "The sole end is to prevent a war from coming into existence in the first place."[48]

It is the threat that deters, not the execution of the threat: If the threat has to be carried out, the deterrent has failed. So it might seem that at best this would justify threatening the strike—not carrying it out and not even intending to carry it out. If so, what is justified is a bluff (see below, "Threatening to Launch," for a discussion of this option). But the view we are now considering is that what is justified is not just the threat but the intention to carry it out. It might be justifiable to threaten the strike as a deterrent and to do so while one has no intention to carry the threat out. But it might just also be justifiable, in order to deter the enemy, to form the intention actually to launch the strike under certain conditions. That is what we are now considering.

David Gauthier has formulated an argument that addresses the connection between the intended threat and its execution.[49] Suppose that Mr. A, in midlife crisis, is threatening to buy a Ferrari, and Mrs. A, to deter her husband from this foolish act, threatens to leave him if he does. Actually, even if he goes ahead and buys the Ferrari, she would prefer to stay with him. But she calculates the likelihood of her threat's working and finds that it is so likely to work that even if she must go through with her threat, she is better off making it. The odds that it will deter her husband are so great that even if she must act on her threat, the wise thing is to go ahead with her announcement. She makes the threat, intending to carry it out if her husband does not yield. He buys the Ferrari anyway. Is it rational for her to carry out the threat?

Gauthier answered that it is. When Mrs. A. made the threat, she calculated the price of failure and decided that in view of the chances of success it was a wise gamble. She then lost the die roll. But that the improbable won out does not make her bet irrational. She gambled well, but lost. And it was part of her gamble that she would carry out her threat if she lost.

> If it is rational to form this conditional, deterrent intention, then, should deterrence fail and the condition be realized, it is rational to act on it. The utility cost of acting on the deterrent intention enters, with appropriate probability weighing, into determining whether it is rational to form the intention. But once this is decided, the cost of acting on the intention does not enter again into determining whether, if deterrence fails, it is rational to act on it. Acting on it is part of a deterrent policy, and if expected utility is maximized by forming the conditional, deterrent intention, then deterrence is a rational policy.[50]

As Gerald Dworkin put it:

> It is possible that one comes to the conclusion that one ought not to have formed the conditional intention in the first place, that it was not rational to be prepared to risk these costs for these benefits. But . . . it cannot be the mere failure of one's strategy that one relies on to make this recalculation. For there was always the possibility of failure. . . .

> The justification for the initial intention . . . carries over to the carrying out of the intention. We do not need additional moral reasons for being justified in carrying out the intention.[51]

Of course, it might be that Mrs. A can achieve the same level of deterrence simply by threatening to leave, even though she has no intention of ever carrying out her threat. As she does not really want to leave, that might seem the better policy. She attains the benefits of deterrence by threatening to leave, but if her bluff fails, she does not have to pay the price. If so, this is the wise policy.

But the threat without the intention might have a lesser deterrent value. Mrs. A's husband might be very perceptive and likely to surmise that she is bluffing. Or perhaps she cannot pull off the bluff without taking others into her confidence, and the truth will leak out. Her threat is effective only insofar as her husband thinks she means it, and if she does not intend to carry it out, it may be difficult to impress him. This is the basis for Herman Kahn's conceptual device of the doomsday machine—a machine that automatically retaliates if the United States is victim of nuclear attack and thereby guarantees the credibility of the deterrent threat.

Mrs. A then has two choices. She can acquiesce to her husband's desire. She should do this if she prefers the 80 percent chance that her unthreatened husband will buy the Ferrari to the 5 percent chance of divorce. Alternatively, she might decide the 5 percent chance of divorce is preferable to the 80 percent chance of a Ferrari (the percentages are hypothetical). In that case she should decide to leave him if he buys it.

If she is set on preventing the purchase and doing so is worth the 5 percent chance of divorce, it is rational for her to steel herself and intend to leave if her threat fails, and not just to bluff: Anything less would not have the desired deterrent value. And if her threat fails, it must then be rational (or so the argument went) for her to carry out the intention. For she already factored in the 5 percent chance of divorce in her calculations. If it was rational for her to intend to carry out the threat if the deterrent failed, then if it fails, it is rational for her to carry it out.

If it seems irrational for her to carry out her threat, I suspect that is because we see no reason why she should. She has already lost her gamble; why should she compound things by leaving her husband? Suppose I enter into a rational wager, given the odds, in which I intend to burn $1,000 in the unlikely event that I fail to win $100. I lose. Why should I burn the $1,000? I would have nothing to gain at that point.

But in that case bluffing carries no penalty, and the rational thing *would* be to bluff. We are assuming, however, that bluffing will not work, and one enters into the wager anyway. Why burn the $1,000 if one loses? Because the wager was rational, and it was part of the wager's analysis that it would be rational to accept the consequence that one would burn the $1,000 if one lost.

We might be tempted to say that if bluffing will not work, the rational policy for Mrs. A would be to intend to leave her husband if he buys the Ferrari, as long as he does not buy the Ferrari, but to stay with him if he does buy it. Now she certainly can abandon her intention to leave him should he buy it, and she can abandon it the moment that he buys it: People do change their minds. But she cannot form the intention to intend to leave him if he buys it unless he buys it. We cannot intend to go to the movies if it rains unless it rains—what would we be intending to do? This would just be a disguised form of bluffing to go to the movies if it rains.

Therefore, the moral thing to do, by parity of reasoning, might be to intend nuclear retaliation. Anything less is likely to produce greater evil.[52] However, embedding a nuclear strike in the conditional intention may not change the morality of the strike. Anthony Kenny pointed out that "a case where intending to do X if A is legitimate must be a case in which actually doing X in circumstances A is legitimate. But if X is some action which is not allowed, whatever the circumstances, then an intention to do X is no more legitimate for being a conditional one."[53] If the strike is never permissible, then it is not permissible even in retaliation or as the consequence of a deterrent intention.

In reply to Kenny a proponent of conditional intention will deny that, in our case, X is forbidden whatever the circumstances. Countercity warfare is morally forbidden, he will say, except as a consequence of a conditional deterrent intention.

In the discussion above ("Launching the Strike"), I concluded that countercity warfare is immoral. If the proponent of conditional intention is right, I must modify that conclusion: Countercity warfare is immoral except as a consequence of a rational deterrent intention aimed at preventing another immoral act—one even more immoral or more probable. If so, an act immoral in itself can be morally right if the alternative is even more immoral. To prevent a greater evil, something otherwise evil might be morally acceptable.

Perhaps this is true, and perhaps it is not. I stand, however, by my earlier analysis (Chapter 4, "A Final Consideration"). I am asking at this point whether murder can ever be morally justified: The discussion could have run the same way if I had been discussing killing the enemy's firstborn sons as a consequence of a deterrent intention, rather than attacking their cities. Perhaps it is justifiable to commit one murder to avert two; perhaps it is justifiable to intend murder in order to prevent it. But shooting civilians in cold blood is not a legitimate act of war. War is a contest between combatants.

There is no contradiction in holding that though in some rare circumstances it might be morally justifiable to shoot civilians, it is not a morally justifiable act of war—not a legitimate act of war at all. There are circumstances under which it might be morally justifiable to execute a man the courts have acquitted, but this is not a right someone could claim as a policeman. Soldiers are forbidden from engaging in certain acts, even to prevent greater evils. These restrictions establish the distinction between military art and unbridled destructiveness; their violation is incompatible with the office.

Threatening to Launch

Even without a real intention to wage nuclear war, one might threaten to do so. The threat would be a bluff, but if the other side did not suspect that, the bluff would be as effective a deterrent as the actual intention would be. And so the government could have a policy of deterrence even if it had no intention of using nuclear weapons. Thus the policy of deterrence may be defensible even if the attack it threatens is not. According to Robert W. Tucker:

> What is the alternative to deterrence, with its threat to do evil? Surely it makes a difference for moral judgment if one assesses the prospects for deterrence breaking down as something close to infinitesimal and the debilitating effects of the deterrent threat as no more than marginal. In this case we are left with the argument that an act which would be unjust to commit ought never to be threatened, however remote the contingency that the act will even be committed and whatever the consequences . . . if the threat is abandoned.[54]

Against this some philosophers have argued that it is immoral to threaten to do that which is immoral. Others counter that it can be moral to threaten immoral acts: To save his life, one might threaten a child with a spanking unless he jumps from a burning building. Even if it would be immoral to punish him for being afraid to jump, the threat might be morally justified to save his life.[55]

I am not sure why it should be thought immoral to threaten to do something immoral if one has no intention of carrying out the threat, though I can see that it may be corrupting. But with this question we arrive at the end of our inquiry because the threat is a political act, not a military one.

We saw in Chapter 4 that belligerent air forces adopted area attacks in response to the defender's ability to cause heavy losses among planes attempting precision attacks. This, I argued, was—subject to proportionality—within the bounds of morality. (The normally astute Elizabeth Anscombe once wrote that the area attacks of World War II did not differ morally from "massacres out of hand." But the aerial equivalent of a "massacre out of hand" would be bombing one's own prisoner of war camps, not attacking defended enemy cities.) The atomic bomb, introduced after these area attacks had become the norm, was used at Hiroshima and Nagasaki in the same role that conventional high explosive and incendiary bombs had by then been performing; the difference was that now a single plane could perform the area attack that hitherto had required hundreds of planes.

In Chapter 5 we saw that the line between terrorist acts and legitimate military operations can be retained only if military commanders refrain from adopting attacks on civilian population as a means to victory. In World War II this was, in general, understood: Only, for example, after the failure of Hansell's precision bombing campaign against Japan did the United States switch to area attacks.

Throughout most of World War II precision bombing was, from a military point of view, the wisest use of the attacker's air resources. The interests of prudence and morality coincided.

The development of the atomic bomb changed that. It became easier and cheaper to destroy a city than to destroy the aircraft factory within it. It is to this day cheaper for the United States to maintain a nuclear deterrent than to maintain a large ground presence in Europe. Given the power of nuclear weapons, and given the air warfare experience of World War II as the environment for their introduction, it was natural to incorporate them as anticity weapons.

But the rise of the guided missile, the development of smaller nuclear weapons and more powerful nonnuclear bombs, and increases in missile and guided bomb accuracy have deprived the nuclear area attack of its moral justification. (Area attacks were never morally justifiable as attacks of choice.)

And in a war against another nuclear power, or a nation with a nuclear-armed protector, the retaliatory destructive ability deprives the nuclear area attack of its military justification. Once again the interests of prudence and morality coincide.

This does not mean that war is obsolete. The dilemma of post–World War II strategic military thinking was captured in the maxim that U.S. strategic nuclear weapons will have failed their purpose if they ever have to be used. The obverse of this dilemma is the problem of how to make the world safe for conventional warfare. Korea, Vietnam, the Falklands, and Afghanistan have shown the way: The U.S. military future lies in the past, whose values, submerged for several decades, rise again to the surface.

Suggestions for Further Reading

The Wizards of Armaggedon by Fred Kaplan (Simon & Schuster, New York, 1983) is an excellent and well-written account of the history of U.S. nuclear strategy. The morality of nuclear war and deterrence has a large literature. The best monograph critical of deterrence is Anthony Kenny's *The Logic of Deterrence* (University of Chicago Press, Chicago, 1985). Kenny's views could be balanced by Paul Ramsey, *War and the Christian Conscience* (Duke University Press, Durham, 1961), Gregory S. Kavka, "Some Paradoxes of Deterrence," in *The Journal of Philosophy* 75 (June 1978): 285–302, reprinted in *War, Morality, and the Military Profession,* ed. Malham Wakin (Westview Press, Boulder, Colo., 1981, and 2d ed., 1986), and William H. Shaw, "Nuclear Deterrence and Deontology," *Ethics* 94 (January 1984): 248–260. The entire April 1985 issue of *Ethics* (vol. 95, no. 3) is devoted to articles criticizing and defending nuclear deterrence.

Notes

Notes to Chapter 1

1. W. D. Ross, *The Right and the Good* (Oxford University Press, Oxford, 1930), p. 41.

2. Philippe Contamine, *War in the Middle Ages,* tr. Michael Jones (Basil Blackwell, Oxford, 1986), p. 291.

3. G. M. Young, *Victorian England: Portrait of an Age,* 2d ed. (Oxford University Press, New York, 1964), p. 17.

4. *Macmillan's Magazine* v 31 (Macmillan, Cambridge, 1875), p. 416.

5. As a consequence, the exploding bullet never came into general use.

6. *Frazer's Magazine,* n.s., vol. 11 (Longman's, Green, London, 1875): p. 188.

7. *Macmillan's Magazine,* p. 411.

8. The University of Tennessee library's computer, when I asked it for the minutes of the conference, could locate only two copies. The one interlibrary loan sent to me arrived unbound, in a folder. As I opened it, pages crumbled at the edges. Words disappeared, breaking into tiny fragments and falling to the floor as dust. I had been sent an original, not a photocopy. The minutes were not valuable.

9. Winston S. Churchill, *The World Crisis,* vol. 1 (Scribner's, New York, 1923), p. 199.

10. "'Eight nations, seventeen countries, twenty parliamentary groups' sighed one Austro-Hungarian statesman." See Edmond Taylor, *The Fall of the Dynasties* (Doubleday, Garden City, N.Y., 1963), p. 72.

11. Telford Taylor, *Nuremberg and Vietnam: An American Tragedy* (Bantam, N.Y., 1971), p. 41.

12. Ibid., p. 20.

13. H.L.A. Hart, *Law, Libery, and Morality* (Vintage, New York, 1963), p. 3.

14. Richard Wasserstrom, "The Laws of War," *The Monist* 56, n. 1 (1972), reprinted in *War, Morality, and the Military Profession,* ed. Malham M. Wakin (Westview Press, Boulder, Colo., 1981).

15. Wasserstrom himself is a professor of philosophy and law.

16. Keith Suter, *An International Law of Guerrilla Warfare* (St. Martin's Press, New York, 1984), p. 183.

17. The Fourth Hague Convention governs land warfare. When I speak of "the Hague conventions" I am generally referring to the Fourth Convention.

When I refer to other Hague conventions, as I do in Chapter 4, I will mention them by name.

18. Sir George Clark, *The Seventeenth Century,* 2d ed. (Oxford University Press, New York, 1961), p. 124.

19. Gerhard von Glahn, *Law Among Nations,* 2d ed. (Collier-Macmillan, London, 1970), p. 63.

20. Lauterpacht heavily revised the classic text of Oppenheim. The resulting book is sometimes referred to as Oppenheim, sometimes as Lauterpacht, but never by its title. The full reference is to Sir Hersch Lauterpacht, ed., *Lassa Oppenheim's International Law: A Treatise,* 7th ed., vol. 2 (Longmans, Green, London, 1952).

21. Von Glahn, *Law Among Nations,* p. 544.

22. Lauterpacht, *Lassa Oppenheim's International Law,* pp. 234–235.

23. Von Glahn, *Law Among Nations,* p. 545. See also Morris Greenspan, *The Modern Law of Land Warfare* (University of California Press, Berkeley, 1959), pp. 4–6

24. H.L.A. Hart, *The Concept of Law* (Oxford University Press, Oxford, 1961), pp. 223–224.

25. The qualifier "generally" is here because of considerations I take up in Chapter 5.

26. J. L. Brierly, *The Law of Nations,* ed. Sir Humphrey Waldock (Oxford University Press, Oxford, 1963), p. 139.

27. For a fuller account of Lauterpacht's view see Hersch Lauterpacht, *Recognition in International Law* (Cambridge University Press, Cambridge, 1947), Chapters 4–5.

28. William Edward Hall, *A Treatise on International Law,* 8th ed., ed. A. Pearce Higgins (Oxford University Press, Oxford, 1924), pp. 17, 20.

29. Brierly, *The Law of Nations,* p. 137.

30. *Mighell vs. The Sultan of Jahore,* Court of Appeal, Queen's Bench Division, 1 Q.B. 149 (1894).

31. Von Glahn, *Law Among Nations,* p. 65.

32. Hall, *A Treatise on International Law,* p. 21.

33. Brierly, *The Law of Nations,* p. 144.

34. "International Law," in Hart, *The Concept of Law,* pp. 208–231.

Notes to Chapter 2

1. Philippe Contamine, *War in the Middle Ages,* tr. Michael Jones (Basil Blackwell, Oxford, 1986), p. 260.

2. Ibid., p. 264.

3. Morris Greenspan, *The Modern Law of Land Warfare* (University of California Press, Berkeley, 1959), pp. 440–442, 462, 490–493.

4. Ibid., pp. 479–480, quoting 40 *American Journal of International Law,* p. 438. Application of General Yamashita, 66 Supreme Court (Reporter) 340–347, 1946.

5. Michael Walzer, *Just and Unjust Wars* (Basic Books, New York, 1977), p. 320, quoting from A. Frank Reel, *The Case of General Yamashita* (University of Chicago Press, Chicago, 1949), p. 280.

6. Whether a particular officer is liable in this way depends on whether he has the power to stop them. Akira Muto, Yamashita's chief of staff in the Philippines, was held liable for atrocities there but not for crimes committed by General Iwane Matsui's troops in China in 1938 when Muto was a staff officer, but not chief of staff.

7. Walzer, *Just and Unjust Wars,* pp. 154–155. The journalist is Reginald Thompson, quoted from his 1951 book, *Cry Korea.*

8. See, e.g., Walzer, *Just and Unjust Wars,* p. 188.

9. Ibid., pp. 318–319.

10. Donald Wells, "How Much Can the 'Just War' Justify," in *War, Morality, and the Military Profession,* ed. Malham M. Wakin (Westview Press, Boulder, Colo., 1981), p. 269.

11. Robert L. Phillips, *War and Justice* (University of Oklahoma Press, Norman, 1984), pp. 9–10. I am not sure how successful this campaign could have been, given the fact that the Byzantine cataphract was a horse archer or given the English longbow. Contamine noted (*War in the Middle Ages,* pp. 71, 274), that the prohibition was not an overwhelming success and that it may have been directed against mercenary archers rather than their weapons. According to Frederick H. Russell, *The Just War in the Middle Ages* (Cambridge University Press, Cambridge, 1975), p. 156, the nobility may have objected to archers because the archers were not nobles.

12. James Dunnigan, *How to Make War,* rev. ed. (Quill, New York, 1983), p. 18.

13. Shelford Bidwell, *Modern Warfare: A Study of Men, Weapons, and Theories* (Allen Lane, London, 1973), p. 133.

14. John Ellis, *The Sharp End: The Fighting Man in World War II* (Scribner's, New York, 1980), p. 160.

15. Dunnigan, *How to Make War,* p. 70.

16. Ellis, *The Sharp End,* pp. 173–174, who is also the source of the British battle-wound casualty figures cited.

17. Ibid., p. 164.

18. Ibid., pp. 164–165.

19. See, e.g., Gerald Dworkin, "Nuclear Intentions," *Ethics* 95 (April 1985), p. 446: "Under the traditional just-war criteria the use of weapons which cannot be used in a manner so as to discriminate between combatants and noncombatants is forbidden." In "War, Nuclear War, and Nuclear Deterrence," in the same issue of *Ethics,* Richard Wasserstrom said that the "intentional or knowing killing" of innocents is immoral (p. 431).

20. *Actes de la Conférence de Bruxelles de 1874 sur le Projet d'une Convention Internationale Concernant la Guerre* (A. Witttersheim, Paris, 1874), p. 41.

21. Roderick Ogley, ed., in *The Theory and Practice of Neutrality in the Twentieth Century* (Barnes & Noble, New York, 1970), p. 74.

22. John Westlake, *International Law—Part II: War* (Cambridge University Press, Cambridge, 1913), p. 128, quoted in Geoffrey Best, *Humanity in Warfare* (Columbia University Press, New York, 1980), pp. 175–176.

23. Sir Hersh Lauterpacht, *Lassa Oppenheim's International Law: A Treatise,* 7th ed., vol. 2 (Longmans, Green, London, 1952), p. 135, where the subject is retorsion.

24. Quoted by Walzer, *Just and Unjust Wars,* p. 210.

25. *Report of the International Committee of the Red Cross on its Activities in the Second World War,* vol. 1, n. 1, p. 520, quoted in Frits Kalshoven, *Belligerent Reprisals* (A. W. Sijthoff, Leyden, 1971), pp. 194–195.

26. And the nature of the fighting indicated that "the armistice had in fact ceased to exist"—Kalshoven, *Belligerent Reprisals,* p. 197. By August "the FFI had assumed the character of a regular army and it behaved accordingly. Thus, many of its actions (such as: occupation of territory, fighting full-scale battles with the German armed forces, conquest of localities, et cetera) presented the characteristics of regular warfare."

27. At the time of World War II Germany and France were parties to the 1929 convention (of the major belligerent powers, the USSR and Japan were not).

28. Walzer, discussing the Annecy case, expressed surprise that the offended side did not just claim to have executed enemy prisoners—without actually carrying out the threat. The reason for this is that if one did it, and the other side discovered the truth, no threat one subsequently made would be credible.

29. See Richard Falk, in Peter D. Trooboff, ed., *Law and Responsibility in Warfare* (University of North Carolina Press, Chapel Hill, 1975), p. 40; Nicholas Fotion and G. Elfstrom, *Military Ethics* (Routledge & Kegan Paul, London, 1986), p. 116; Walzer, *Just and Unjust Wars,* pp. 129–133, 144–147.

30. Chaplain Major John Brinsfield, U.S. Army, has pointed out to me that Cicero, in *De Officiis,* may have. See Walter Miller, tr. *Cicero: De Officiis* (Harvard University Press, Cambridge, 1961), p. 37.

31. Paragraph (c), by specifying "or having no longer means of defense," includes those who surrender only because they have run out of ammunition or because their weapons become otherwise unusable.

32. Keith Suter, *An International Law of Guerrilla Warfare* (St. Martin's Press, New York, 1984), p. 10.

33. Lord McNair and A. D. Watts, *The Legal Effects of War* (Cambridge University Press, Cambridge, 1966), pp. 7–8.

34. Cited by Jeffrey Golden, "Force and International Law," in *The Use of Force in International Relations,* ed. F.S. Northedge (Faber & Faber, London, 1974), pp. 197–198.

35. Lauterpacht, *Lassa Oppenheim's International Law,* pp. 596–598.

36. See "The Moral Context: Protection of Citizens Abroad" in Chapter 3.

37. *Report of the Special Committee On the Question of Defining Aggression* (United Nations General Assembly Official Records: Twenty-Ninth Session, Supplement 19 [A/9619], New York, 1974), p. 11. See Chapter 3 for further discussion of this report.

38. Lauterpacht, *Lassa Oppenheim's International Law,* pp. 202–206.

Notes to Chapter 3

1. Lawrence S. Wittner, *Rebels Against War* (Columbia University Press, New York, 1969), p. 115. Bates-Batcheller was addressing the 1942 national convention of the Daughters of the American Revolution.

2. Less than .33 percent of Americans registering for the draft in World War II declared themselves conscientious objectors. See Charles Chatfield, *For Peace and Justice: Pacifism in America, 1914–1941* (University of Tennessee Press, Knoxville, 1971), pp. 259–260.

3. Donald W. Engels, *Alexander the Great and the Logistics of the Macedonian Army* (University of California Press, Berkeley, 1978), pp. 19–20; the account of ancient logistics given in Chapter 3 is largely from this book.

4. S.L.A. Marshall, *World War I* (American Heritage, New York, 1985), p. 43.

5. John Keegan and Richard Holmes, *Soldiers: A History of Men in Battle* (Viking, New York, 1986), p. 235.

6. Ibid.

7. Marshall, *World War I,* p. 47.

8. Ibid., p. 50.

9. My accounts of these battles are based on Marshall, *World War I.*

10. Ibid., p. 257.

11. Paul Fussell, *The Great War and Modern Memory* (Oxford University Press, Oxford, 1975), p. 46, quoting Louis Simpson.

12. However, because of better medical facilities, losses due to disease were sharply down. Disease brought Union Civil War casualties from 110,000 battle deaths to a 335,000 total; the corresponding World War I figures are 7.5 million and 10 million. Some Civil War brigades took 10 percent casualties from disease before their first action.

13. *1921 Encyclopedia Americana,* vol. 28: 334.

14. Chatfield, *For Peace and Justice,* pp. 259–260.

15. A. J. Muste, quoted in Wittner, *Rebels Against War,* p. 18.

16. Ibid.

17. Ibid., p. 15.

18. Ibid., p. 24.

19. Ibid., p. 37.

20. Jan Narveson, in "Pacifism: A Philosophical Analysis," Ethics 75 (1965): 259–271; reprinted in *War and Morality,* ed. Richard Wasserstrom (Wadsworth, Belmont, Calif., 1970), pp. 63–77, argued that pacifism is logically inconsistent: "If we have any rights at all, we have a right to use force to prevent the deprivation of the thing to which we are said to have a right. But the pacifist, of *all* people, is the one most concerned to insist that we do have some rights, namely, the right not to have violence done to us. . . . In saying that violence is wrong, one is . . . saying that people have a right to its prevention, by force if necessary."

21. Milton S. Katz, *Ban the Bomb: A History of SANE, the Committee for a Sane Nuclear Policy, 1957–1985* (Greenwood Press, New York, 1986), p. 11.

22. Ibid., p. 3.

23. Donald A. Wells, *The War Myth* (Pegasus, New York, 1967), p. 10.

24. Ibid., p. 13.

25. Seventeen years later Wells's views were unchanged: "Nations behave like the most callous vigillantes [sic] toward each other. Leaders in the most respected national posts speak like moral Frankensteins. . . . We know what should and should not be done. We lack the will to do it. . . . But as long as sovereign nations retain the inalienable inhuman right to defend their own ends . . . " See Donald Wells, *War Crimes and Laws of War* (University Press of America, Lanham, Md., 1984), p. 116.

26. Carl Sagan, *Contact* (Simon and Schuster, New York, 1985), pp. 280–281.

27. A microcosmic version of the problems a world government would face is already available to us at the International Court of Justice. A legal writer discussed them under the heading "An Evanescent Mystique": "Some of the prestige which attached to judicial international institutions in the pre-1914 and inter-war periods, was the result of touching but somewhat naive views on the structure and dynamics of international society. Succesive generations of well-meaning international lawyers considered that the . . . settlement of international disputes on the basis of respect for law constituted a practical short cut to world peace through world law, and drew comfort from the reassuring reflection that any international dispute was potentially a legal dispute. Those who knew better too often refrained from stating the obvious that, if this was so, every legal dispute was also potentially a political dispute. . . . The somewhat erratic character of the [Court's] jurisprudence has sharpened such doubts. . . .

"In this situation, the problem-in-chief for governments is not whether a particular dispute should be treated as legal or political . . . The crucial issue is whether the parties consider it advisable to maintain direct control of the dispute or hand it over to settlement by a body of detached, wise and distinguished, but somewhat unpredictable world Solomons . . . If deeds, and not words, are the test . . . the more vital the dispute is, the less is its chance of being submitted to international adjudication." See Georg Schwarzenberger, *A Manual of International Law,* 4th ed., vol. 1, (Praeger, New York, 1960), pp. 247–248.

28. Michael Howard, *The Causes of War and Other Essays* (Harvard University Press, Cambridge, 1983), p. 22. For a fuller account of why nations go to war, see F. S. Northedge, "The Resort to Arms," in *The Use of Force in International Relations,* ed. Northedge (Faber & Faber, London, 1974), pp. 11–35.

29. Some still do. "In 1928 . . . sixty-two nations signed a pact outlawing war," wrote Theodore Draper recently in *Present History* (Vintage, New York, 1984), p. 4.

30. Sir Hersch Lauterpacht, ed., *Lassa Oppenheim's International Law: A Treatise,* 7th ed., vol. 2 (Longmans, Green, London, 1952), p. 185.

31. Ibid., p. 185.

32. It does not follow that the pact allowed nations the ultimate right to determine whether they are acting in self-defense. Nations were understood to have the right to determine that they are under attack and to defend themselves. But that determination could be subsequently judged by some suitable international authority to have been wrong. Nations have the right to immediate defense and to determine whether they are acting in self-defense, but their determinations may subsequently be overruled. But the pact failed to establish that suitable authority, let alone a means of enforcing its decisions.

33. Gerhard von Glahn, *Law Among Nations,* 2d ed. (Collier-Macmillan, London, 1970) p. 521. (Von Glahn wrote in the third person.)

34. See St. Thomas Aquinas, *Summa Theologiae,* 2a2ae, Questions 40, 64; the U.S. Catholic Bishops, "The Just War and Non-Violence Positions," and James F. Childress, "Just-War Theories," both in *War, Morality, and the Military Profession,* 2d ed., ed. Malham Wakin (Westview Press, Boulder, Colo., 1986), pp. 239–276; Frederick H. Russell, *The Just War in the Middle Ages* (Cambridge University Press, Cambridge, 1975); and James Turner Johnson, *Ideology, Reason, and the Limitation of War: Religious and Secular Concepts, 1200–1740* (Princeton University Press, Princeton, 1975).

35. Critics of just-war theory have not always realized this. Donald Wells, in "How Much Can the 'Just War' Justify, " *Journal of Philosophy* 66 (December 1966), pp. 819–829, reprinted in *War, Morality, and the Military Profession,* ed. Malham Wakin, (Westview Press, Boulder, Colo., 1981), argued that the criteria are individually insufficient to show that a war is just, or at least are difficult to apply without considering the case in which they are all satisfied.

36. St. Thomas Aquinas, *Summa Theologiae,* 2,2b, Q. 40.

37. See Chapter 1.

38. Justinian, *Corpus Juris Civilis: Digest,* 9.2.45.4.

39. K. D. Johnson, "The Morality of Nuclear Deterrence," in *The Nuclear Crisis Reader,* ed. Gwyn Prins (Random House, New York, 1984), p. 148.

40. William Edward Hall, *A Treatise on International Law,* 8th ed., ed. A. Pearce Higgins (Oxford University Press, Oxford, 1924), pp. 81–82.

41. And perhaps Hall was right, for at the same time the League of Nations was trying to develop methods for punishing wrongdoers.

42. This has been criticized, for it is a principle of law that an act is criminal only if law forbids it (*nullum crimen sine lege)* and it is debatable whether in 1939 it was illegal to wage aggressive war. See von Glahn, *Law Among Nations,* p. 521.

43. "A threat of force consists in an express or implied promise . . . of a resort to force conditional on non-acceptance of certain demands . . . If the promise is to resort to force in conditions in which no justification for the use of force exists, the threat itself is illegal." See Ian Brownlie, *International Law and the Use of Force by States* (Oxford University Press, Oxford, 1963), p. 364.

44. International law allows territorial waters to be international waterways. The straits connecting the Black Sea and the Mediterranean, for example, are

Turkish waters, but because other nations line the Black Sea, their access to the Mediterranean is a right in maritime law, the straits are an international waterway. The right of innocent passage allows ships to pass through territorial waters to shorten their voyages.

45. *The Corfu Channel Case: Pleadings, Oral Arguments, Documents,* vol. 1 (International Court of Justice, The Hague, 1949), p. 67.

46. Ibid., p. 72.

47. A British representative later said: "The Albanian Government have chosen to assert that our ships were not engaged at the time upon the exercise of the right of innocent passage mainly, I think, on the ground that they were prepared—and they certainly were—to defend themselves . . . I dare say that my French colleagues may re-echo today their distinguished countryman's words and say to the United Kingdom: 'Cet animal est très méchant, quand on l'attaque, il se défend' [this animal is very vicious—when one attacks it, it defends itself]." See ibid., vol. 3, p. 208.

48. Testimony of its commander, Ibid., vol. 4, p. 22.

49. ibid., vol. 1, p. 27.

50. Ibid., vol. 4, p. 124.

51. J. L. Brierly, *The Law of Nations,* ed. Sir Humphrey Waldock (Oxford University Press, Oxford, 1963), pp. 423–424.

52. Albania did not have a minelaying capacity. The most likely theory was that Yugoslavia had cooperated in placing the mines. The judges ruled that in any case Albania must have known that the waters it watched so closely had been mined—the mines were laid only a few hundred yards offshore—yet failed in its duty to notify the world of the danger. The court awarded damages of over £800,000 to Britain for the loss of life and material damage. As of 1988, Albania still had not paid.

53. Lauterpacht, *Lassa Oppenheim's International Law,* 153–154, 156.

54. Schwarzenberger, *A Manual of International Law,* vol. 1, pp. 174–175, 309.

55. Keith Suter, *An International Law of Guerrilla Warfare* (St. Martin's Press, New York, 1984), p. 10. Going even further, he concluded that it is now illegal to declare war (though apparently not to fight one). He did not cite the grounds for this unusual interpretation.

56. See Yehuda Melzer, *Concepts of Just War* (A. W. Sijthoff, Leyden, 1975), pp. 17–50, for a close discussion of this issue.

57. Brierly, *The Law of Nations,* pp. 417–418, said that the records show that Committee III/4 did not intend "to put outside the law forcible self-defense against unlawful acts of force not amounting to an armed attack."

58. Von Glahn, *Law among Nations,* p. 708; I supplied the italics.

59. *Report of the Special Committee On the Question of Defining Aggression* (United Nations General Assembly Official Records: Twenty-Ninth Session, Supplement 19 [A/9619], New York, 1974), p. 11. General Assembly reports and resolutions, it should be noted, are not binding on UN members—they do not have the force of law.

60. "If we wish to retain the idea that aggression is always morally wrongful, we must reject the attempt to define it as 'initiating war.'" See Nicholas Fotion

and G. Elfstrom, *Military Ethics* (Routledge & Kegan Paul, London, 1986), p. 113.

61. See Chapter 2, "Postscript."

62. *Report of the Special Committee On the Question of Defining Aggression* (United Nations General Assembly Official Records: Ninth Session, Supplement 11 [A/2638], New York, 1954), p. 7.

63. Report of the Special Committee On the Question of Defining Aggression (United Nations General Assembly Official Records: Twenty-Fifth Session, Supplement 19 [A/8019], New York, 1970), p. 31.

64. Ibid., p. 36.

65. Ibid., p. 47.

66. The reports are not known for their precision either: Their wording is a consequence of political maneuvering as often as it is of legal reasoning. A careful reading of Article 51, for example, shows that it (unintentionally) allows only UN member-states the right of self-defense.

67. See H.L.A. Hart's comments in Chapter 1 on the different aims of law and morality.

68. Schwarzenberger, *A Manual of International Law*, p. 171.

69. Michael Walzer, *Just and Unjust Wars* (Basic Books, New York, 1977), pp. 74–85.

70. Paul S. Dull, *A Battle History of the Imperial Japanese Navy, 1941–1945* (Naval Institute Press, Annapolis, 1978), pp. 11–12.

71. Ronald H. Spector, *Eagle Against the Sun* (Random House, New York, 1985), p. 99.

72. *Report of the 1956 Special Committee On the Question of Defining Aggression* (United Nations General Assembly Official Records: Twelfth Session, Supplement 16 [A/3574], New York, 1957), p. 24.

73. Ibid., p. 25.

74. *Report of the Special Committee On the Question of Defining Aggression* (United Nations General Assembly Official Records: Ninth Session, Supplement 11 [A/2638], New York, 1954), p. 7.

75. Ibid., p. 81.

76. Ibid., p. 84.

77. Jeffrey Golden, "Force and International Law," in *The Use of Force in International Relations*, ed. F. S. Northedge (Faber & Faber, London 1974), p. 201.

78. He changed from the view he took in Richard Falk, *Law, Morality, and War in the Contemporary World* (Praeger, New York, 1963), pp. 13–16.

79. An Egyptian UN delegate later denied this had ever happened: *Report of the Special Committee On the Question of Defining Aggression* (United Nations General Assembly Official Records: Twenty-Third Session, Agenda Item 86 [a/7185/rev.1], New York, 1968), p. 18.

80. *Report of the Special Committee On the Question of Defining Aggression* (United Nations General Assembly Official Records: Twenty-Fifth Session, Supplement 19 [A/8019], New York, 1970), p. 34. Hostile intent can be seen or suspected where there is none. A power unfriendly to its neighbor and

conducting military maneuvers or training exercises on its own border might be threatening even if no threat is intended. It is therefore wise for states to discuss such maneuvers with those who might be suspicious and to show some sensitivity to their concerns. It is wiser still to be very careful with large maneuvers and to realize that the other side will find them threatening no matter what one says.

81. Von Glahn, *Law Among Nations,* p. 168.

82. The protection of foreign nationals falls under the heading of self-help. I discussed it separately because I want here to consider cases in which wars have traditionally been justified to enforce international rights even if there is no threat to life and limb.

83. Robert W. Tucker, "Morality and Deterrence," *Ethics* 95 (1985), p. 463.

84. Reprisals in this context should not be confused with the *jus in bello* right of reprisal.

85. Falk, *Law, Morality, and War,* p. 15.

86. Ibid., p. 90.

87. The U.S. intervention in Grenada may be another case in point.

88. Hall, *A Treatise on International Law,* p. 342.

89. I supplied the italics.

90. The tribunal's charter went beyond the traditional boundaries of the law of war in a second way. It said that these acts were criminal, not just during the war, but even before, if they were in preparation for the war. Even the milder "persecutions on political, racial or religious grounds," if committed in connection with or in execution of crimes that fell within the tribunal's jurisdiction, were declared to be crimes against humanity, whether or not they violated the laws of the country in which they took place. That such acts might be legal under German law did not deprive these acts of their criminality.

91. Michael Walzer, "The Moral Standing of States," *Philosophy and Public Affairs* (Spring 1980): p. 212.

92. Walzer, *Just and Unjust Wars,* p. 88.

93. See the articles in *Philosophy and Public Affairs* (Summer 1980) by Charles Beitz, David Luban, and Gerald Doppelt, responding to Walzer's article in the Spring 1980 issue, replying to their previous criticism. Quotation is from p. 396.

94. Walzer, "The Moral Standing of States," p. 213.

95. Walzer, *Just and Unjust Wars,* p. 90.

96. Ibid.

97. Ibid., p. 93.

98. Ibid.

99. See Telford Taylor, *Munich: The Price of Peace* (Random House, New York, 1979).

100. Suter, *An International Law of Guerrilla Warfare,* pp. 149–150.

Notes to Chapter 4

1. Cited in Winston S. Churchill, *The World Crisis,* vol. 2 (Scribner's, New York, 1923), p. 490.

2. Tony Carty, "The Origins of the Doctrine of Deterrence and the Legal Status of Nuclear Weapons," in *Ethics and Defence: Power and Responsibility in the Nuclear Age*, ed. Howard Davis (Basil Blackwell, Oxford, 1986), p. 126.

3. Ibid., p. 106.

4. Lee Kennett, *A History of Strategic Bombing* (Scribner's, New York, 1982), p. 24. My account of strategic air warfare before World War II is largely based on this work.

5. Ibid., p. 7.

6. M. J. Armitage and R. A. Mason, *Air Power in the Nuclear Age,* 2d ed. (University of Illinois Press, Urbana, 1985), p. 2.

7. Ibid., pp. 4–5, for this and the two preceding quotations.

8. John Terraine, *A Time for Courage: The Royal Air Force in the European War, 1939–1945* (Macmillan, New York, 1985), p. 10.

9. Martin Middlebrook, *The Nuremberg Raid* (William Morrow, New York 1974), p. 3.

10. Kennett, *A History of Strategic Bombing,* p. 78.

11. Sir Charles Webster and Noble Frankland, *Preparation: The Strategic Air Offensive Against Germany,* vol. 1 (Her Majesty's Stationery Office, London, 1961), pp. 193–196.

12. Ibid., p. 196.

13. Ibid., p. 136.

14. Ibid., pp. 138–139.

15. Ibid., p. 212.

16. Terraine, *A Time for Courage,* p. 126.

17. Ibid., p. 127.

18. Ibid., p. 123.

19. Ibid., p. 147.

20. Quoted in ibid., p. 288.

21. I assume that this was the reasoning behind Portal's reservations given in Terraine, ibid., pp. 703–704; in fact, though the long-range P-51 Mustang would weigh 50 percent more than the Spitfire, advances in design would give it superior, rather than inferior, performance.

22. Ibid., pp. 206–213.

23. Ibid., p. 214.

24. Leonard Mosley, *The Battle of Britain* (Time-Life, Alexandria, Va., 1977), p. 118. The view seems to have originated with George H. Quester, *Deterrence Before Hiroshima* (John Wiley, New York, 1966), p. 118. It was adopted by Barrie Paskins and Michael Dockrill in *The Ethics of War* (University of Minnesota Press, Minneapolis, 1979), and Carty, "The Origins of the Doctrine of Deterrence."

25. Kennett, *A History of Strategic Bombing,* pp. 96–101. One of the reasons the figures were misleading was the behavior of the Spaniards. "John Langdon-Davies, who witnessed the attacks on Barcelona early in 1938, felt that the excitable nature and incorrigible curiosity of the Spaniards would be their undoing: 'They would not take shelter. They preferred instead to blacken every balcony so as to get a good view of the bursting shrapnel'" (ibid., p. 97).

Another source of error was the assumption that casualties would increase numerically with tonnage, but "If a single one-ton bomb killed or wounded fifty Londoners, then a thousand such bombs would not necessarily kill or wound fifty thousand" (ibid., p. 100). The same mistake has been sometimes made by people who write about nuclear weapons: A ten kiloton bomb has ten times the explosive power of a one kiloton bomb, but it will not do ten times the damage. A good deal of its power is spent as overkill near the point of impact.

26. Ibid., p. 109.

27. Roger Parkinson, *Summer, 1940: The Battle of Britain* (David McKay, New York, 1977), pp. 155. 159.

28. Sir Charles Webster and Noble Frankland, *Endeavor: The Strategic Air Offensive Against Germany,* vol. 2 (Her Majesty's Stationery Office, London, 1961), p. 23.

29. Terraine, *A Time for Courage,* p. 267. (Terraine took the Pierse quotation from Webster and Frankland, p. 156.)

30. Kennett, *A History of Strategic Bombing,* p. 129.

31. Quoted in Terraine, *A Time for Courage,* p. 293.

32. Kennett, *A History of Strategic Bombing,* p. 49.

33. Arthur Ferguson, in *Europe—Touch to Pointblank: The Army Air Forces in World War Two,* vol. 2, ed. Wesley Frank Craven and James Lea Cate (University of Chicago Press, Chicago, 1949), p. 325.

34. Ibid., p. 330.

35. Including Lt. John Winant, the son of the U.S. ambassador to Britain. See Roger A. Freeman, *The Mighty Eighth War Diary* (Jane's Publishing Co., London, 1981), p. 125.

36. Terraine, *A Time for Courage,* p. 651, quoting L. F. Ellis, *Victory in the West,* vol. 1 (Her Majesty's Stationery Office, London, 1968), p. 132.

37. John E. Fagg, "The Climax of Strategic Operations," in *Europe—Argument to V-E Day: The Army Air Forces in World War II,* vol 3, ed. Wesley Frank Craven and James Lea Cate (University of Chicago Press, Chicago, 1951), p. 727.

38. Kennett, *A History of Strategic Bombing,* p. 91.

39. *Target Germany: The Army Air Force's Official Story of the VIII Bomber Command's First Year Over Europe* (Simon and Schuster, New York, 1943), p. 19.

40. Elizabeth Anscombe, "War and Murder," in *War and Morality,* ed. Richard Wasserstrom (Wadsworth, Belmont, Calif., 1970), p. 50.

41. Ronald Schaffer, *Wings of Judgment* (Oxford University Press, Oxford, 1985), p. 185.

42. Fagg, "The Climax of Strategic Operations," p. 721.

43. This attitude toward directives was not confined to the Americans: Anthony Verrier, *The Bomber Offensive* (Macmillan, London, 1968), p. 160, said, "it will occasion no surprise . . . that Harris paid as little attention to this directive [Pointblank] as to its predecessor [the Casablanca Directive]."

44. William B. Ziff, *The Coming Battle of Germany* (Duell, Sloan and Pearce, New York, 1942), p. 161.

45. J. M. Spaight, *Air Power and War Rights,* 3d ed. (Longmans, Green, London, 1947), p. 273. The quotation is from Hector Hawton, *Night Bombing* (1944), p. 73.

46. Spaight, *Air Power and War Rights,* p. 271, quoting from his 1943 book, *Volcano Island.*

47. A. Pearce Higgins, *The Hague Peace Conference and Other International Conferences Concerning the Laws and Usages of War* (Cambridge University Press, Cambridge, 1909), pp. 347–348.

48. Ibid., pp. 352–353. See n. 68 infra.

49. Sir Hersch Lauterpacht, *Lassa Oppenheim's International Law,* 7th ed., vol. 2 (Longmans, Green, & Co., London, 1952), p. 511.

50. Ibid., p. 512; Morris Greenspan, *The Modern Law of Land Warfare* (University of California Press, Berkeley, 1959), p. 333.

51. Greenspan, *The Modern Law,* p. 333.

52. Higgins, *The Hague Peace Conferences,* pp. 354–355. I supplied the italics.

53. D. W. Watt, "Restraints on War in the Air Before 1945, " in *Restraints on War* ed. Michael Howard (Oxford University Press, Oxford, 1979), p. 62.

54. Higgins, *The Hague Peace Conferences,* p. 354.

55. Ibid.

56. John Westlake, *Traité de Droit International,* tr. A. de Lapradelle (Oxford University Press, Oxford, 1924), p. 580. (I had access to the French translation of this well thought out work, but not the English original.) The translation is my own, as are the italics.

57. Higgins, *The Hague Peace Conferences,* p. 356.

58. Richard Falk, *Law and Responsibility in Warfare,* ed. Peter D. Trooboff (University of North Carolina Press, Chapel Hill, 1975), p. 40.

59. The term *parliamentaire* refers to the representative of one side who approaches the other side and bears a white flag.

60. John Finnis, Joseph M. Boyle, Jr., and Gemain Grisez, *Nuclear Deterrence, Morality and Realism* (Oxford University Press, Oxford, 1987), p. 265.

61. John Ellis, *The Sharp End: The Fighting Man in World War II* (Scribner's, New York, 1980), p. 162.

62. Ronald H. Spector, *Eagle Against the Sun* (Random House, New York, 1985), p. 543.

63. Proponents of sea power have denied that this was so. They have claimed that the naval blockade alone would have forced Japan to surrender. But commanders could not rely on this hope, and in summer 1945 the United States was preparing to invade Japan. Moreover, if the naval blockade had led to a Japanese surrender, that would most likely have been as a consequence of widespread starvation in Japan, with perhaps even more civilian deaths than the bombing caused.

64. William Edward Hall, *A Treatise on International Law,* 8th ed. A. Pearce Higgins (Oxford University Press, Oxford, 1924), pp. 643–644.

65. Cited by Myres S. McDougal and Florentino P. Feliciano, *Law and Minimum World Public Order: The Legal Regulation of International Coercion* (Yale University Press, New Haven, 1961), p. 604.

66. Hall, *A Treatise on International Law,* p. 645.

67. Moses Maimonides, *The Code of Maimonides—Book Fourteen: The Book of Judges,* tr. Abraham M. Herschman (Yale University Press, New Haven, 1963), p. 217.

68. Hall, *A Treatise on International Law,* pp. 515–516. Hall mentioned that some British naval officers thought such bombardments were legitimate military operations, and even that in 1878 the Russian government had plans for using its Vladivostok fleet against Australia's undefended ports! The article he mentioned appeared in *Revue des deux mondes* 50 (1882).

69. Ibid., pp. 646–647.

70. See, e.g., George I. Mavrodes, "Conventions and the Morality of War," *Philosophy and Public Affairs* 4 (1975): 117–131.

71. For an extensive argument for this point of view see Finnis, Boyle, and Grisez, *Nuclear Deterrence.*

72. In Michael Walzer, *Just and Unjust Wars* (Basic Books, New York, 1977), and in "World War II: Why Was This War Different?" in *War and Moral Responsibility,* ed. Marshall Cohen, Thomas Nagel, and Thomas Scanlon (Princeton University Press, Princeton, 1974), pp. 85–103.

73. Spector, *Eagle Against the Sun,* p. 559.

74. Anscombe, "War and Murder," p. 51.

75. Judith Jarvis Thompson, "The Trolley Problem," *Rights, Restitution, and Risk: Essays in Moral Theory* (Harvard University Press, Cambridge, 1986), pp. 94–116.

Notes to Chapter 5

1. James R. McDonough, *Platoon Leader* (Presidio Press, Novato, Calif., 1985), pp. 109–111.

2. Ibid., pp. 41–43.

3. "Flags had become a means of disciplining and controlling the soldiery—the commissioned ranks of ensign and cornet of horse in later European armies stemmed from the authority which their bearers inevitably acquired" See Malcolm Vale, *War and Chivalry* (University of Georgia Press, Athens, 1981), pp. 147–149.

4. Quoted in John Ellis, *Armies in Revolution* (Oxford University Press, New York, 1974), p. 222.

5. Ibid., p. 150.

6. Geoffrey Best, *Humanity in Warfare* (Columbia University Press, New York, 1980), p. 197.

7. Ibid., p. 198.

8. Walter Laqueur, *Guerrilla: A Historical and Critical Study* (Little, Brown, Boston, 1976), p. 88.

9. Ibid., p. 92.

10. Ibid., p. 219.

11. Bruce Palmer, *The 25-Year War: America's Role in Vietnam* (Simon & Schuster, New York, 1984), p. 42.

12. John S. D. Eisenhower, *The Bitter Woods* (Ace Pub., New York, 1969), pp. 149–153, quoted a legal opinion according to which the German operation was in accordance with the law of war.

13. Morris Greenspan, *The Modern Law of Land Warfare* (University of California Press, Berkeley 1959), p. 59.

14. The requirement of visibility at a distance has never been interpreted to mean that in wartime soldiers can never wear civilian clothes—that a soldier on leave, for example, must remain in uniform. It is meant for combat zones, where the requirement of visibility at a distance functions to identify a hostile soldier when he becomes visible—not when he chooses to reveal his belligerent status.

15. Best, *Humanity in Warfare,* p. 198.

16. Article 23 (f).

17. It is limited in other ways as well. It is illegal, for example, to use false distress signals (e.g., Mayday calls) to lure the enemy into a trap.

18. John Westlake, *Traité de Droit International,* tr. A. de Lapradelle (Oxford University Press, Oxford, 1924), p. 454.

19. Guy Hartcup, *Camouflage: A History of Concealment and Deception in War* (Scribner's, New York, 1980), pp. 11–13.

20. Major-General J.F.C. Fuller, *The Conduct of War* (1962), p. 140.

21. Michael Walzer, *Just and Unjust Wars* (Basic Books, New York, 1977), pp. 182–183.

22. Myres S. McDougal and Florentino P. Feliciano, *Law and Minimum World Public Order* (Yale University Press, New Haven, 1961), pp. 558–559. Keith Suter, *An International Law of Guerrilla War* (St. Martin's Press, New York, 1984), p. 166, quoted this passage in support of the guerrilla's right to dress as a civilian, but McDougal and Feliciano were discussing commandos who remove their deceptive outfits before combat. Their claim (p. 557) was that such commandos should be distinguished from partisans and guerrillas.

23. Walzer, *Just and Unjust Wars,* p. 182.

24. The law of war recognizes that unlawful belligerents are not necessarily criminal and that their acts need not be dishonorable. It recognizes this in granting military spies a special status. A uniformed soldier, spying behind enemy lines, is a lawful belligerent and is entitled to be treated as a normal prisoner of war if he is captured. Spying in uniform is a legitimate extension of reconnaissance. A soldier, however, who hides his affiliation by wearing civilian clothes or an enemy uniform (the sort of thing we typically think of when we think of spying) and then penetrates enemy lines to gather information is not a lawful belligerent and is not covered by the protections of the Hague or Geneva conventions. He is liable to be shot if he is captured. In going out of uniform he forfeits his lawful status. Yet his mission is an honorable one, and he is not a war criminal. This creates a legal difference. Suppose he makes it safely back to his own lines, gets back into uniform, and is then captured by the enemy. He must be treated as any other prisoner of war. He

is unlawful only if caught in an unlawful act. Whereas had his acts been war crimes, he would remain punishable for them. In this case the law itself recognizes that what is unlawful need not be criminal. This applies only to spies gathering information. A spy who kills someone would violate Article 23 (b), which forbids killing or wounding by treachery—an act that is itself a war crime.

25. The *law* is normally taken to be fully binding on both sides. Once we claim that its provisions are not binding on one side on the grounds of inequity, we will have to allow the same case for the other side. If guerrillas are allowed to dress as civilians because otherwise they have no hope of victory, government troops will have to be allowed compensations. Must they, in order to make the struggle more equal, obey the law of war, while the other side ignores it? Should we think of those laws as a handicap imposed on the advantaged side? If ignoring the dress code puts the guerrillas at an advantage and makes it impossible for regular troops to defeat them, should we then, to redress the balance, allow the regular troops to ignore some other law?

The laws of war are based on the assumption that both sides will abide by them. Any dispensation we grant to guerrillas on this score creates an inequity for uniformed soldiers. If the latter fight by the book they are now the ones who are disadvantaged. The laws of war have become a burden to them as long as they fight according to rules that assume the foe is identifiable. Should they still abide by those rules? Should they fight in Vietnam as though it were France in 1944? The guerrilla, able to use ruses unavailable to the government troops, has at least the tactical advantage.

What will the regulars take in compensation? Perhaps they will torture those they suspect are guerrillas, as the normal means of identifying hostiles is denied to them. Perhaps they will execute suspected guerrillas. They will certainly be more likely to shoot people in civilian clothes. They will certainly find some way of trying to compensate—if only because they want to live. And would we say that this is permissible, on the grounds that otherwise they have no hope of victory? See Walzer, *Just and Unjust Wars,* pp. 214–215.

26. Before 1949 it could be argued that in enemy-occupied territory irregulars were mere bandits.

27. See, e.g., Barrie Paskins and Michael Dockrell, *The Ethics of War* (University of Minnesota Press, Minneapolis, 1979), pp. 86–91.

28. Vladimir Dedijer, "The Yugoslav Partisans," in *Guerrilla Strategies: An Historical Anthology from the Long March to Afghanistan,* ed. Gérard Chaliand (University of California Press, Berkeley, 1982), p. 69.

29. Peter D. Trooboff, ed., *Law and Responsibility in Warfare* (University of North Carolina Press, Chapel Hill, 1975), p. 41.

30. Nicholas Fotion and G. Elfstrom, *Military Ethics* (Routledge & Kegan Paul, London, 1986), p. 213.

31. McDougal and Feliciano, *Law and Minimum World Public Order,* p. 549.

32. Ibid., p. 550.

33. Robert L. Phillips, *War and Justice* (University of Oklahoma Press, Norman, 1984), p. 99.

34. Walzer, *Just and Unjust Wars,* p. 182.

35. That puts these cases outside the province of this book, and I will not atempt to address them adequately. My own view, though, is that insurgents and assassins are sometimes morally justified in using the sort of treachery involved here. It may even be true that there have been government agents so evil that it would be immoral not to kill them by treachery if the opportunity arose. But such cases are extremely rare, and the temper of our times is inclined to excess on this score. Every inequity or offense is not an excuse for the most extreme response.

36. Guerrilla attempts to hold terrain, as the French partisans did at Vercors, are frequently disasters—see, e.g., Laqueur, *Guerrilla,* p. 229. But then attempts by regular troops to hold terrain, as the French did at Dien Bien Phu, are also frequently disasters.

37. Katherine Chorley, *Armies and the Art of Revolution* (Beacon Press, Boston, 1973), p. 17.

38. Ibid., p. 5.

39. Phillips, *War and Justice,* p. 99.

40. *Time,* April 1970, p. 32; cited by Phillips in ibid., pp. 86–87.

41. William V. O'Brien, *The Conduct of Just and Limited War* (Praeger, New York, 1981), 178.

Notes to Chapter 6

1. Bernard Brodie, ed., *The Absolute Weapon: Atomic Power and the World Order* (Harcourt, Brace, New York, 1946), p. 21.

2. Quoted in Martin J. Sherwin, *A World Destroyed* (Random House, New York, 1977), p. 27.

3. Fred Kaplan, *The Wizards of Armageddon* (Simon & Schuster, New York, 1983), p. 10.

4. "Impact of the Atomic bomb," in Eugene M. Emme, *The Impact of Air Power* (D. Van Nostrand, Princeton, 1959).

5. Brodie, *The Absolute Weapon,* p. 76.

6. Ibid., p. 74.

7. Kaplan, *The Wizards of Armageddon,* p. 39.

8. In any case, they needed a large army to garrison the empire they acquired in Eastern Europe.

9. Brodie, *The Absolute Weapon,* pp. 46–47.

10. Kaplan, *The Wizards of Armageddon,* p. 47.

11. That is, equivalent in explosive force to that many tons of TNT.

12. Kaplan, *The Wizards of Armageddon,* pp. 77–80.

13. Quoted in John Finnis, Joseph M. Boyle, Jr., and Germain Grisez, *Nuclear Deterrence, Morality and Realism* (Oxford University Press, Oxford, 1987), p. 12.

14. Kaplan, *The Wizards of Armageddon,* pp. 202–219.

15. Ibid., p. 218.

16. Ibid., p. 207. Counterforce targeting was not accepted without opposition. According to Kaplan in ibid., p. 212, when the RAND Corporation's Joseph Loftus discussed counterforce with General Jim Walsh, intelligence chief for the Strategic Air Command, Walsh screamed,"'Goddammit, Loftus, there's only one way to attack the Russians, and that's to hit them hard with everything we have and'—pounding on a large bible he kept on an end table—'knock their balls off.'"

17. Lawrence Freedman, *The Evolution of Nuclear Strategy* (Macmillan, London, 1981), p. 43.

18. Kaplan, *The Wizards of Armageddon,* p. 284.

19. Freedman, *The Evolution of Nuclear Strategy,* pp. 231–232.

20. Gregg Herken, *Counsels of War* (Knopf, New York, 1985), p. 170.

21. Ibid., pp. 161, 168–169.

22. Kaplan, *The Wizards of Armageddon,* p. 316; Herken, *Counsels of War,* p. 169.

23. Kaplan, *The Wizards of Armageddon,* p. 319; my italics.

24. Finnis, Boyle, and Grisez, *Nuclear Deterrence,* pp. 18–19.

25. George H. Quester, *Deterrence before Hiroshima* (John Wiley, New York, 1966), p. 64.

26. Finnis, Boyle, and Grisez, *Nuclear Deterrence,* p. 19.

27. Von Hippel, Frank N., Barbara G. Levi, Theodore A. Postol, and William H. Daugherty, "Civilian Casualties from Counterforce Attacks," *Scientific American* 259 (September 1988): 41.

28. Kaplan, *The Wizards of Armageddon,* p. 371. The dilemma is as real for critics outside the defense and foreign policy establishments as it is for those inside. A book advocating the reduction of U.S. military forces and resolutely opposing counterforce targeting as making nuclear war "easier" decried the fact that superpower arsenals are able to destroy the adversary's civilian centers many times over and yet announced that "the holding of mutual hostages . . . is still the best policy devised, crazy as it is!" See Boston Study Group, *Winding Down: The Price of Defense* (W. H. Freeman, San Francisco, 1982), pp. 87, 100.

29. Lee Kennett, *A History of Strategic Bombing* (Scribner's, New York, 1982), p. 162.

30. James Dunnigan, *How to Make War,* rev. ed. (Quill, New York, 1983), p. 298.

31. Though each MX carries ten warheads. The CEP (circular error of probability) is a circle within which 50 percent of the warheads aimed at the circle's center would land.

32. Some writers have argued that nuclear weapons are inherently illegal. But the legal case is unconvincing. The 1907 Fourth Hague Convention and the 1925 Geneva protocol forbid the use of poison, and some people have argued that radiation poisoning falls under this ban. But there are nuclear weapons that minimize radiation poisoning (neutron bombs), and in any case it is not clear that these prohibitions apply to poisoning as a side effect of the use of a blast weapon. The 1868 Declaration of St. Petersburg asserts that

it is contrary to the laws of humanity to employ weapons "which uselessly aggravate the sufferings of disabled men or render their death inevitable." Some writers have concluded that because of the great pain produced by burns, any weapon that achieves all or a large part of its destructiveness through fire—e.g., napalm, incendiary, and nuclear weapons—is therefore contrary to the declaration. But this argument, too, is inconclusive. If one can disable the enemy without uselessly aggravating his suffering, it is contrary to the St. Petersburg declaration not to do so. But the typical use of a flamethrower is not to cause gratuitous suffering but to attack enemy shielded from line-of-sight weapons by fortifications. The criterion for whether a weapon inflicts unnecessary suffering "has normally been whether [it] inflicts suffering disproportionate to the military advantage to be gained by its use . . . . 'The legality of hand grenades, flamethrowers, napalm and incendiary bombs . . . ' notes Schwarzenberger, 'is a vivid reminder that suffering caused by weapons with sufficiently large destructive potentialities is not "unnecessary" in the meaning of this rule.' Since nuclear weapons are notoriously potent and destructive, their use would seem unaffected by the prohibition of 'unnecessary suffering.'" See Guenter Lewy, "Superior Orders, Nuclear Warfare, and the Dictates of Conscience," *The American Political Science Review* 55 (1961); reprinted in *War and Morality,* ed. Richard Wasserstrom (Wadsworth, Belmont, Calif., 1970), p. 127.

33. Robert W. Tucker, *The Law of War and Neutrality at Sea—International Law Studies,* vol. 44 (U.S. Naval War College, Washington, D.C., 1957), p. 72.

34. See Chapter 4, "Legitimate Targets."

35. See Chapter 4, "The 1923 Hague Draft Rules."

36. Aristotle, *The Nichomachean Ethics,* III, 1113b 26–35.

37. See John J. Englehardt, "The Implications of Sub-Kiloton Nuclear Torpedoes," *U.S. Naval Institute Proceedings* 113 (August 1987): 102–104.

38. See, e.g., Finnis, Boyle and Grisez, *Nuclear Deterrence,* pp. 13–27, where the authors, on the grounds that massive retaliation is the ultimate threat, treated it as the cornerstone of U.S. nuclear policy. Massive retaliation remains the final threat, but with all the rest of the U.S. nuclear policy designed to avoid it, and with the money going into smaller and more accurate weapons, it is misleading to think of it as the cornerstone of the policy. One might as well say that war with the Soviet Union is the cornerstone of U.S. foreign policy.

39. Richard Wasserstrom, "War, Nuclear War, and Nuclear Deterrence," *Ethics* 95 (April 1985): 431.

40. This is in rough agreement with Jeff McMahan, "Deterrence and Deontology," *Ethics* 95 (April 1985): 518.

41. In Chapter 4, I had in mind under the danger the defense creates for attacking personnel: We cannot expect men under fire and at risk to exercise the care they should show if they were in little or no danger. But the danger need not be to personnel; it might be to material or equipment. A ship might be a serious blow. To prevent loss or damage to the ship, the attacker can be justified in exercising less care to avoid civilian casualties than would be

proper if the ship were not in danger—assuming, of course, that the point of the attack is to attack a valid target in the first place.

42. *Precision attack* and *surgical strike* are hopeful terms. Precision attacks can cause heavy civilian casualties, as in the Pointblank attacks on French railroad yards around the time of the D day landings. Area attacks can cause few or no civilian casualties: In World War II there were RAF Bomber Command attacks on Berlin in which bomber aircrew losses exceeded casualties on the ground. Precision attacks under adverse circumstances overlap area attacks under fortuitous circumstances: There is a point at which those on the ground could not distinguish the two or might mistake the one for the other. We want a justification of those collateral casualties based on the value of the target, regardless of whether the attack is labeled an area attack or a precision attack. Some vital and legitimate targets were located in urban residential areas, and some were camouflaged to blend in with the surrounding urban areas. Attacks on those targets would in any case have amounted to area attacks, so whether these targets were attacked day or night, in clear or overcast weather, the results would have been approximately the same. But we cannot justify choosing the attack that will produce greater civilian casualties for the same properly military gain.

43. At any rate, in the situation I am imagining, the military targets could be destroyed by precision attacks over a longer period of time or by area attacks in a shorter period. What must be weighed, then, is not the military value of the targets' destruction against the deaths of innocents but the military value of the *quicker* destruction of those targets— not their destruction in or by itself—against those deaths. By this standard, some of World War II's area bombing would not be justified. We could not, for example, justify the area attacks against Japan on the grounds that they ended the war in six months if precision attacks could have ended the war in nine (using the 66 percent rule from the northern European theater), with perhaps 200,000 fewer civilian deaths.

44. If those casualties were 50,000—there are no real figures.

45. Quoted in Robert W. Tucker, *The Just War* (Johns Hopkins University Press, Baltimore, 1960), p. 66.

46. Anthony Kenny, *The Logic of Deterrence* (University of Chicago Press, Chicago, 1985), p. 48.

47. Gregory Kavka, "Some Paradoxes of Deterrence," *Journal of Philosophy* 75 (June 1978): 285–302.

48. Charles Krauthammer, "On Nuclear Morality," *Commentary* (October 1983); reprinted in *War, Morality, and the Military Profession,* 2d ed., ed. Malham Wakins (Westview Press, Boulder, Colo., 1986), p. 503.

49. David Gauthier, "Deterrence, Maximization, and Rationality," *Ethics* 94 (1984): 474–496.

50. Ibid., p. 486.

51. Gerald Dworkin, "Nuclear Intentions," *Ethics* 95 (April 1985): 456, 459.

52. "By parity of reasoning" on the (controversial) grounds that what holds for "is rational" might hold for "is morally permissible."

53. Anthony Kenny, *The Logic of Deterrence,* p. 48.

54. Robert W. Tucker, "Morality and Deterrence," *Ethics* 95 (April 1985): 478.

55. See William H. Shaw, "Nuclear Deterrence and Deontology," *Ethics* 94 (January 1984): 252:253.

Bibliography

The following bibliography makes no attempt to be comprehensive. It is, with a few exceptions, limited to works cited in this book.

Anscombe, Elizabeth, "War and Murder," in *Nuclear Weapons: A Catholic Response,* ed. Walter Stein (Sheed & Ward, New York, 1961); reprinted in Wasserstrom (1970).

Armitage, M. J., and R. A. Mason, *Air Power in the Nuclear Age,* 2d ed. (University of Illinois Press, Urbana, 1985).

Bailey, Sydney D., *Prohibitions and Restraints in War* (Oxford University Press, London, 1972).

Bainton, Roland H., *Christian Attitudes toward War and Peace* (Abingdon Press, New York, 1960).

Beitz, Charles R., "Nonintervention and Community Integrity," *Philosophy and Public Affairs* 9 (Summer 1980): 385–391.

Bennett, John C., ed., *Nuclear Weapons and the Conflict of Conscience* (Scribners, New York, 1962).

Best, Geoffrey, *Humanity in Warfare* (Columbia University Press, New York, 1980).

Blix, Hans, "Area Bombardment: Rules and Reasons," *British Yearbook of International Law* 49 (1978): 31–69.

Boston Study Group, *Winding Down: The Price of Defense* (W. H. Freeman, San Francisco, 1982).

Bradley, Omar, *A Soldier's Story* (Rand McNally, New York, 1951).

Bradley, Omar, and Clay Blair, *A General's Life* (Simon & Schuster, New York, 1983).

Brandt, Richard B., "Utilitarianism and the Laws of War," *Philosophy and Public Affairs* 4 (1975); reprinted in Wakin (1981).

Brierly, J. L., *The Law of Nations,* ed. Sir Humphrey Waldock (Oxford University Press, Oxford, 1963).

Brodie, Bernard, ed., *The Absolute Weapon: Atomic Power and the World Order* (Harcourt, Brace, New York, 1946).

Brownlie, Ian, *International Law and the Use of Force by States* (Oxford University Press, Oxford, 1963).

Bull, Hedley, ed. *Intervention in World Politics* (Oxford University Press, Oxford, 1984).

Calvocoressi, Peter, and Guy Wint, *Total War: Causes and Courses of the Second World War* (Penguin, New York, 1972).

Chaliand, Gérard, ed., *Guerrilla Strategies: An Historical Anthology from the Long March to Afghanistan* (University of Cal. Press, Berkeley, 1982).

Chatfield, Charles, *For Peace and Justice: Pacifism in America, 1914–1941* (University of Tennessee Press, Knoxville, 1971).

Chorley, Katherine, *Armies and the Art of Revolution* (Beacon, Boston, 1973).

Churchill, Winston S., *The World Crisis,* vol. 1 (Scribner's, New York, 1923).

Clark, Sir George, *The Seventeenth Century,* 2d ed. (Oxford University Press, New York, 1961).

Cohen, Marshall, Thomas Nagel, and Thomas Scanlon, eds. *War and Moral Responsibility* (Princeton University Press, Princeton, 1974).

Contamine, Philippe, *War in the Middle Ages,* tr. Michael Jones (Basil Blackwell, Oxford, 1986).

Craven, Wesley Frank, and James Lea Cate, eds., *The Army Air Forces in World War Two,* vol. 2, *Europe—Torch to Pointblank* (1949); vol. 3, *Europe—Argument to V-E Day* (1951); vol. 5, *The Pacific—Matterhorn to Nagasaki* (1953) (University of Chicago Press, Chicago).

Davis, Howard, ed., *Ethics and Defence: Power and Responsibility in the Nuclear Age* (Basil Blackwell, Oxford, 1986).

Department of the Army, *The Law of Land Warfare* (U.S. Government Printing Office, Washington, D.C., 1956).

Doppelt, Gerald, "Statism without Foundations," *Philosophy and Public Affairs* 9 (Summer 1980): 398–403.

Draper, Theodore, *Present History* (Vintage, New York, 1984).

Dull, Paul S., *A Battle History of the Imperial Japanese Navy, 1941–1945* (Naval Institute Press, Annapolis, 1978).

Dunnigan, James, *How to Make War,* rev. ed. (Quill, New York, 1983).

Dworkin, Gerald, "Nuclear Intentions," *Ethics* 95 (1985): 445–460.

Eisenhower, John S.D., *The Bitter Woods* (Ace Publishing, New York, 1969).

Ellis, John, *Armies in Revolution* (Oxford University Press, New York, 1974).

______, *The Sharp End: The Fighting Man in World War II* (Scribner's, New York, 1980).

Emme, Eugene M., *The Impact of Air Power* (D. Van Nostrand, Princeton, 1959).

Engels, Donald W., *Alexander the Great and the Logistics of the Macedonian Army* (University of California Press, Berkeley, 1978).

Englehardt, John J., "The Implications of Sub-Kiloton Nuclear Torpedoes," *U.S. Naval Institute Proceedings* 113 (August 1987): 102–104.

Falk, Richard A., *Law, Morality, and War in the Contemporary World* (Praeger, New York, 1963).

Finnis, John, Joseph M. Boyle, Jr., and Germain Grisez, *Nuclear Deterrence, Morality and Realism* (Oxford University Press, Oxford, 1987).

Ford, Father John C., "The Morality of Obliteration Bombing," *Theological Studies* 5 (1944); reprinted in Wasserstrom (1970).

Fotion, Nicholas, and G. Elfstrom, *Military Ethics* (Routledge & Kegan Paul, London, 1986).

Freedman, Lawrence, *The Evolution of Nuclear Strategy* (Macmillan, London, 1981).

Freeman, Roger A., *The Mighty Eighth* (Doubleday, Garden City, N.Y., 1970).

———, *The Mighty Eighth War Diary* (Jane's Publishing Co., London, 1981).

Fuller, Major-General J.F.C., *The Conduct of War* (1962).

Fussell, Paul, *The Great War and Modern Memory* (Oxford University Press, Oxford, 1975).

Gauthier, David, "Deterrence, Maximization, and Rationality," *Ethics* 94 (1984): 474–496.

Golden, Jeffrey, "Force and International Law," in Northedge, ed., *The Use of Force in International Relations,* pp. 194–219.

Greenspan, Morris, *The Modern Law of Land Warfare* (University of California Press, Berkeley, 1959).

Hall, William Edward, *A Treatise on International Law,* 8th ed., ed. A. Pearce Higgins (Oxford University Press, Oxford, 1924).

Hart, H.L.A., *The Concept of Law* (Oxford University Press, 1961).

———, *Law, Liberty, and Morality* (Vintage, New York, 1963).

Hartcup, Guy, *Camouflage: A History of Concealment and Deception in War* (Scribner's, New York, 1980).

Hartigan, R. S., "Noncombatant Immunity: Reflections on Its Origins and Present Status," *Review of Politics* 29 (1967).

———, "Saint Augustine on War and Killing: The Problem of the Innocent," *Journal of the History of Ideas* 27 (1966).

Heilbrunn, Otto, *Warfare in the Enemy's Rear* (Praeger, New York, 1963).

Herken, Gregg, *Counsels of War* (Knopf, New York, 1985).

Higgins, A. Pearce, *The Hague Peace Conferences and Other International Conferences Concerning the Laws and Usages of War: Texts of Conventions with Commentaries* (Cambridge University Press, Cambridge, 1909).

Howard, Michael, *The Causes of War and Other Essays* (Harvard University Press, Cambridge, 1983).

Howard, Michael, ed., *Restraints on War* (Oxford University Press, Oxford, 1979).

Johnson, James Turner, *Ideology, Reason, and the Limitation of War: Religious and Secular Concepts, 1200–1740* (Princeton University Press, Princeton, 1975).

Johnson, Vice Air Marshal J. E., *The Story of Air Fighting* (Bantam, New York, 1986).

Kahn, Herman, *Thinking about the Unthinkable in the 1980's* (Simon & Schuster, New York, 1984).

Kalshoven, Frits, *Belligerent Reprisals* (A. W. Sijthoff, Leyden, 1971).

Kaplan, Fred, *The Wizards of Armageddon* (Simon & Schuster, New York, 1983).

Katz, Milton S., *Ban the Bomb: A History of SANE, the Committee for a Sane Nuclear Policy, 1957–1985* (Greenwood Press, New York, 1986).

Kavka, Gregory S., "Some Paradoxes of Deterrence," in *Journal of Philosophy* 75 (June 1978): 285–302, reprinted in Wakin (1981 and 2d ed., 1986).

Keegan, John, *Six Armies in Normandy* (Viking, New York, 1982).

Keegan, John, and Richard Holmes, *Soldiers: A History of Men in Battle* (Viking, New York, 1986).

Kennan, George F., *The Nuclear Delusion: Soviet-American Relations in the Atomic Age* (Pantheon, New York, 1976).

Kennett, Lee, *A History of Strategic Bombing* (Scribner's, New York, 1982).

Kenny, Anthony, *The Logic of Deterrence* (University of Chicago Press, Chicago, 1985).

Lackey, Douglas P., "Missiles and Morals: A Utilitarian Look at Nuclear Deterrence," *Philosophy and Public Affairs* 11 (1982): 189–231.

Laqueur, Walter, *Guerrilla: A Historical and Critical Study* (Little, Brown, Boston, 1976).

Lauterpacht, Sir Hersch, *Lassa Oppenheim's International Law: A Treatise,* 7th ed., vol. 2 (Longmans, Green, London, 1952).

______, *Recognition in International Law* (Cambridge University Press, Cambridge, 1947).

Leed, Eric J., *No Man's Land: Combat and Identity in World War I* (Cambridge University Press, Cambridge, 1981).

Luban, David, "The Romance of the Nation-State," *Philosophy and Public Affairs* 9 (Summer 1980): 392–397.

McDonough, James R., *Platoon Leader* (Presidio Press, Novato, Calif., 1985).

McDougal, Myres S., and Florentino P. Feliciano, *Law and Minimum World Public Order: The Legal Regulation of International Coercion* (Yale University Press, New Haven, 1961).

McMahan, Jeff, "Deterrence and Deontology," *Ethics* 95 (1985): 517–536.

McNair, Lord, and A. D. Watts, *The Legal Effects of War* (Cambridge University Press, Cambridge, 1966).

Maimonides, Moses, *The Code of Maimonides—Book Fourteen: The Book of Judges,* tr. Abraham M. Herschman (Yale University Press, New Haven, 1963).

Marshall, S.L.A., *World War I* (American Heritage, New York, 1985).

Mavrodes, George I., "Conventions and the Morality of War," *Philosophy and Public Affairs* 4 (1975): 117–131.

Melzer, Yehuda, *Concepts of Just War* (A. W. Sijthoff, Leyden, 1975).

Middlebrook, Martin, *The Battle of Hamburg* (Scribner's, New York, 1981).

______, *The Nuremberg Raid* (William Morrow, New York, 1974).

______, *The Schweinfurt-Regensburg Mission* (Scribner's, New York, 1983).

Middlebrook, Martin, and Chris Everitt, *The Bomber Command War Diaries: An Operational Reference Book, 1939–1945* (Viking, Harmondsworth, U.K., 1985).

Miller, Richard I., ed., *The Law of War* (D. C. Heath, London, 1975).

Millett, Allan R., and Peter Maslowski, *For the Common Defense: A Military History of the United States of America* (Free Press, New York, 1984).

Morrison, Wilbur H., *Point of No Return: The Story of the Twentieth Air Force* (Times Books, New York, 1979).

Mosley, Leonard, *The Battle of Britain* (Time-Life, Alexandria, Va., 1977).

Murphy, Jeffrie G., "The Killing of the Innocent," *Monist* 57 (1983): 527–536; reprinted in Wakin, 1st ed. (1981).

Nagel, Thomas, "War and Massacre," *Philosophy and Public Affairs* 1 (1972); reprinted in Wakin, 1st ed. (1981).

Nagle, William J., *Morality and Modern Warfare* (Helicon, Baltimore, 1960).

Narveson, Jan, "Pacifism: A Philosophical Analysis," *Ethics* 75 (1965): 259–271; reprinted in Wasserstrom (1970).

Northedge, F. S., "The Resort to Arms," in Northedge, ed., *The Use of Force in International Relations,* pp. 11–35.

Northedge, F. S., ed., *The Use of Force in International Relations* (Faber & Faber, London, 1974).

O'Brien, William V., *The Conduct of Just and Limited War* (Praeger, New York, 1981).

Overy, R. J., *The Air War: 1939–1945* (Stein and Day, New York, 1980).

Palmer, Bruce, *The 25-Year War: America's Military Role in Vietnam* (Simon & Schuster, New York, 1984).

Parkinson, Roger, *Summer, 1940: The Battle of Britain* (David McKay, New York, 1977).

Paskins, Barrie, and Michael Dockrill, *The Ethics of War* (University of Minn. Press, Minneapolis, 1979).

Phillips, Robert L., *War and Justice* (University of Oklahoma Press, Norman, 1984).

Pompe, C. A., *Aggressive War: An International Crime* (Martinus Nijhoff, The Hague, 1953).

Prins, Gwyn, ed., *The Nuclear Crisis Reader* (Random House, New York, 1984).

Quester, George H., *Deterrence before Hiroshima* (John Wiley, New York, 1966).

Ramsey, Paul, *The Just War: Force and Political Responsibility* (Scribner's, New York, 1968).

———, *War and the Christian Conscience* (Duke University Press, Durham, 1961).

Report of the 1956 Special Committee On the Question of Defining Aggression (United Nations General Assembly Official Records: Twelfth Session, Supplement 16 [A/3574], New York, 1957).

Report of the Special Committee On the Question of Defining Aggression (United Nations General Assembly Official Records: Ninth Session, Supplement 11 [A/2638], New York, 1954).

Report of the Special Committee On the Question of Defining Aggression (United Nations General Assembly Official Records: Twenty-Third Session, Agenda Item 86 [a/7185/rev.1], New York, 1968).

Report of the Special Committee On the Question of Defining Aggression (United Nations General Assembly Official Records: Twenty-Fourth Session, Supplement 20 [A/7620], New York, 1969).

Report of the Special Committee On the Question of Defining Aggression (United Nations General Assembly Official Records: Twenty-Fifth Session, Supplement 19 [A/8019], New York, 1970).

Report of the Special Committee On the Question of Defining Aggression (United Nations General Assembly Official Records: Twenty-Sixth Session, Supplement 19 [A/8419], New York, 1971).

Report of the Special Committee On the Question of Defining Aggression (United Nations General Assembly Official Records: Twenty-Seventh Session, Supplement 19 [A/8719], New York, 1972).

Report of the Special Committee On the Question of Defining Aggression (United Nations General Assembly Official Records: Twenty-Eighth Session, Supplement 19 [A/9019], New York, 1973).

Report of the Special Committee On the Question of Defining Aggression (United Nations General Assembly Official Records: Twenty-Ninth Session, Supplement 19 [A/9619], New York, 1974).

Roberts, Adam, and Richard Guelff, eds., *Documents on the Laws of War* (Oxford University Press, Oxford, 1982).

Russell, Frederick H., *The Just War in the Middle Ages* (Cambridge University Press, Cambridge, 1975).

Saward, Dudley, *Bomber Harris* (Doubleday, Garden City, N.Y., 1985).

Schaffer, Ronald, *Wings of Judgment* (Oxford University Press, Oxford, 1985).

Schiff, Ze'ev, and Ehud Ya'ari, *Israel's Lebanon War* (Simon & Schuster, New York, 1984).

Schwarzenberger, Georg, *A Manual of International Law,* 4th ed., vol. 1 (Praeger, New York, 1960).

Shaw, William H., "Nuclear Deterrence and Deontology," *Ethics* 94 (January 1984): 248–260.

Shawcross, William, *The Quality of Mercy: Cambodia, Holocaust, and Modern Conscience* (Simon & Schuster, New York, 1984).

______, *Sideshow: Kissinger, Nixon, and the Destruction of Cambodia* (Simon & Schuster, New York, 1977).

Sherwin, Martin J., *A World Destroyed: The Atomic Bomb and the Grand Alliance* (Random House, New York, 1977).

Spaight, J. M., *Air Power and War Rights,* 3d ed. (Longmans, Green, London, 1947).

Spector, Ronald H., *Advice and Support: The Early Years of the U.S. Army Involvement in Vietnam—1941–1960* (Free Press, New York, 1985).

______, *Eagle Against the Sun* (Random House, New York, 1985).

Speer, Albert, *Spandau: the Secret Diaries* (Pocket Books, New York, 1977).

Stanton, Shelby L., *The Rise and Fall of an American Army: U.S. Ground Forces in Vietnam, 1965–1973* (Presidio Press, Novato, Calif., 1985).

Summers, Harry G., *On Strategy: The Vietnam War in Context* (U.S. Army War College, Carlisle Barracks, Pa., 1981).

Suter, Keith, *An International Law of Guerrilla Warfare* (St. Martin's Press, New York, 1984).

Target Germany: The Army Air Forces' Official Story of the VIII Bomber Command's First Year Over Europe (Simon and Schuster, New York, 1943).

Taylor, Edmond, *The Fall of the Dynasties* (Doubleday, Garden City, N.Y., 1963).

Taylor, Telford, *Nuremberg and Vietnam: An American Tragedy* (Bantam, New York, 1971).

Terraine, John, *A Time for Courage: The Royal Air Force in the European War, 1939–1945* (Macmillan, New York, 1985).

Thompson, Judith Jarvis, "The Trolley Problem," *Rights, Restitution, and Risk: Essays in Moral Theory* (Harvard University Press, Cambridge, 1986), pp. 94–116.

Trooboff, Peter D., ed., *Law and Responsibility in Warfare* (University of North Carolina Press, Chapel Hill, 1975).

Tucker, Robert W., *The Just War* (Johns Hopkins University Press, Baltimore, 1960).

______, *The Law of War and Neutrality at Sea—International Law Studies,* vol. 44 (U.S. Naval War College, Washington, D.C., 1957).

______, "Morality and Deterrence," *Ethics* 95 (1985): 461–478.

______, *The Nuclear Debate* (Holmes & Meier, New York, 1985).

Vale, Malcolm, *War and Chivalry* (University of Ga. Press, Athens, 1981).

Verrier, Anthony, *The Bomber Offensive* (Macmillan, London, 1968).

Von Glahn, Gerhard, *Law Among Nations,* 2d ed. (Collier-Macmillan, London, 1970).

Von Hippel, Frank N., Barbara G. Levi, Theodore A. Postol, and William H. Daugherty, "Civilian Casualties from Counterforce Attacks," *Scientific American* 259 (September 1988): 36–42.

Wakin, Malham, ed., *War, Morality, and the Military Profession* (Westview Press, Boulder, Colo., 1981, 2d ed., 1986).

Walzer, Michael, *Just and Unjust Wars* (Basic Books, New York, 1977).

______, "The Moral Standing of States: A Response to Four Critics," *Philosophy and Public Affairs* 9 (Spring 1980): 209–229.

Wasserstrom, Richard, "The Laws of War," *The Monist* 56 (1972), reprinted in Wakin, 1st ed. (1981).

______, "On the Morality of War: A Preliminary Inquiry," in Wasserstrom (1970).

Wasserstrom, Richard, ed., *War and Morality* (Wadsworth, Belmont, Calif., 1970).

Webster, Sir Charles, and Noble Frankland, *Preparation: The Strategic Air Offensive Against Germany,* vol. 1, and *Endeavor: The Strategic Air Offensive Against Germany,* vol. 2 (Her Majesty's Stationery Office, London, 1961).

Wells, Donald, *War Crimes and Laws of War* (University Press of America, Lanham, Md., 1984).

______, *The War Myth* (Pegasus, New York, 1967).

Westlake, John, *Traité de Droit International,* tr. A. de Lapradelle (Oxford University Press, Oxford, 1924).

Wittner, Lawrence S., *Rebels Against War* (Columbia University Press, New York, 1969).

Young, G. M., *Victorian England: Portrait of an Age,* 2d ed. (Oxford University Press, New York, 1964).

Ziff, William B., *The Coming Battle of Germany* (Duell, Sloan and Pearce, New York, 1942).

Index